ROYAL HISTORICAL SOCIETY

STUDIES IN HISTORY

New Series

T0366450

LONDON ZOO AND THE VICTORIANS
1828–1859

PAST & PRESENT
a journal of historical studies

LONDON ZOO
AND THE VICTORIANS
1828–1859

Takashi Ito

THE ROYAL HISTORICAL SOCIETY
THE BOYDELL PRESS

First published 2014
Paperback edition 2020

A Royal Historical Society publication
Published by The Boydell Press
an imprint of Boydell & Brewer Ltd
PO Box 9, Woodbridge, Suffolk IP12 3DF, UK
and of Boydell & Brewer Inc.
668 Mt Hope Avenue, Rochester, NY 14620–2731, USA
website: www.boydellandbrewer.com

ISBN 978–0–86193–321–1 hardback
ISBN 978–0–86193–351–8 paperback

ISSN 0269–2244

A CIP catalogue record for this book is available
from the British Library

The publisher has no responsibility for the continued existence or accuracy of
URLs for external or third-party internet websites referred to in this book,
and does not guarantee that any content on such websites is,
or will remain, accurate or appropriate

This publication is printed on acid-free paper

Contents

List of Figures

The author and publisher acknowledge with thanks the following for permission to reproduce material in their collections: the Museum of London for the cover illustration; the City of London, London Metropolitan Archives, for figures 1, 18 and 19; The National Archives, Kew, for figure 3; the Zoological Society of London, for figures 4, 6, 7, 15, 17, 20, 21 and 22; the Wellcome Library, London, for figures 8, 9, 23 and 25; the Syndics of Cambridge University Library for figures 10 and 11; the Delegates of the Bodleian Library, Oxford, for figures 12 and 14; and the City of Westminster Archives Centre for figure 16.

List of Tables

Acknowledgements

London Zoo and the Victorians has taken many years to mature. First and foremost I wish to thank Penelope J. Corfield for her constructive criticism and cheery optimism, which guided me through the tedious round of writing and rewriting. Without her support this project would have been simply impossible. I am also grateful to David Gilbert, Catherine Hall, Marius Kwint, Amanda Vickery and Alex Windscheffel for their helpful comments and suggestions. I am further indebted to many individuals who shared my interests in the zoo's history and discussed the subject at seminars, conferences and on any number of other occasions. At the Royal Historical Society Arthur Burns offered time and expertise to read and comment on my work and Christine Linehan gave the final draft a much-needed polish. I should not forget to mention my friends and colleagues whose advice and assistance has been indispensable: Junko Akamatsu, Pieter Francois, Harumi Goto, Hannah Greig, Uriel Heyd, Akiko Inagati, Emi Konishi, Xabier Lamikiz and Akiko Shimbo. I alone am responsible for any shortcomings that may remain.

Most of the research upon which this book is based was carried out in the library of the Zoological Society of London. I wish to acknowledge Michael Palmer for hunting down uncountable numbers of manuscripts, and the Council of the Zoological Society for giving me permission to reproduce the society's earliest materials. I am also grateful to the staff of the Bodleian Library, the British Library, the British Museum (Department of Prints and Drawings), the Buckinghamshire Record Office, Cambridge University Library, the Derbyshire Record Office, the Herefordshire Record Office, the National Archives, the Natural History Museum, the University of Durham Archive, the London Metropolitan Archives, the National Portrait Gallery Archive, the Royal Institution, the Wellcome Library and Westminster City Archives. Financial support has been provided at various stages of researching and writing. The Tokyo Club Scholarship funded my doctoral studies at Royal Holloway, University of London, while the JSPS Research Fellowship at the University of Tokyo afforded me the time and resources for revising the book. Further research was funded by JSPS KAKENHI grant numbers 2577270 and 23820061. Kanazawa Gakuin University provided me with a pleasant working environment in which to complete this project.

Special thanks go to Toshio Kusamitsu, Takao Matsumura and Akihito Suzuki, who sent me off to the United Kingdom on a voyage of historical exploration, and to Kazuhiko Kondo for his wise words of advice on my work in recent years. Ayako Sakurai has always been an invaluable companion on this long journey and has enlightened me over German sources. All the way through she has shown me the virtue of patience and uncompromising intellectual honesty. For the same period or even longer my parents and brother have given me unfailing support in this and all my other endeavours. In acknowledgement of their affection and tolerance, without which I could not have entered academia, this book is dedicated to my family.

Takashi Ito
Kanazawa
September 2013

Abbreviations

BL   British Library, London
Bodl. Lib. Bodleian Library, Oxford
    JJC   John Johnson Collection
CCD   F. Burkhardt and others (eds), *Correspondence of Charles Darwin*,
            Cambridge 1985–2012
LMA   London Metropolitan Archives
NPGA   National Portrait Gallery Archive, London
PP   Parliamentary Papers
RI   Royal Institution, London
SDUK   Society for the Diffusion of Useful Knowledge
TNA   The National Archives, Kew
ZSL   Zoological Society of London
    MC   Minutes of Council
    MM   Minutes of Meetings
    OG   Occurrences at the Garden

BJHS   *British Journal of the History of Science*
EcHR   *Economic History Review*
EHR   *English Historical Review*
HJ   *Historical Journal*
HWJ   *History Workshop Journal*
JBNH   *Journal for the Bibliography of Natural History*
JECS   *Journal for Eighteenth-Century Studies*
MM   *Mariners Mirror*
P&P   *Past and Present*
VS   *Victorian Studies*

The publication of this book has been assisted by a generous grant
from the late Miss Isobel Thornley's Bequest
to the University of London.

Introduction: The Zoo in History

The path beyond the entrance gate to London's Zoological Gardens led to a long promenade lined with ornamental shrubs. At the far end bears were exhibited in a deep square pit, as depicted by George Scharf in one of his *Six views of the Zoological Gardens* (*see* cover illustration). Here a gentleman holds out a long stick with a bun stuck on the end, while the bear has climbed up a stout wooden pole. The spectators expect the bear to reach out and grab the bun. Contemporary commentators often described animal behaviour in analogy with human nature. In 1829 Toby the Russian black bear, who often had proffered food snatched away from him by two polar bears, was compared in one guidebook to 'good-natured men who are mastered by those of rough natures'.[1] This was a prime example of public interaction with nature presented as spectacle – a scene that sets the stage for this book on the London Zoo, which debates cultural politics, public science and the meaning of the animal world in nineteenth-century Britain. The scene at the bear pit spotlights the multifaceted nature of the zoo.

Although the development of zoos in nineteenth-century Europe and America has recently attracted scholarly attention, it is still necessary to clarify why the subject is important. A number of zoos today are challenged by those who criticise the caging of animals and are denounced as an institutional impediment to the protection of animal welfare. In the light of contemporary ethics, zoos may now seem to be little more than the vestiges of earlier times when humans were less respectful towards animals.[2] When seen from within the society in which they first developed, however, this critique is inappropriate. As argued by Bob Mullan and Garry Marvin in their *Zoo culture* (1987), zoos are essentially anthropocentric institutions that pursue a human strategy to consecrate both an ideal and a practical relationship with the animal world.[3] In the light of this interpretation, the flourishing of zoos in the nineteenth century suggests that irreversible changes in human attitudes towards animals occurred during this period, which deserves thorough investigation in its own right. Moreover, general histories of London and Victorian society are incomplete without a few remarks on the London

[1] Anon., *A picturesque guide to the Regent's Park with accurate descriptions of the Colosseum, the Diorama, and the Zoological Gardens*, London 1829, 44–5.

[2] S. Bostock, *Zoos and animal rights: ethics of keeping animal*, London 1993; D. Jamieson, 'Against zoos', in P. Singer (ed.), *In defense of animals*, Oxford 1985, 108–17; B. G. Norton and others (eds), *Ethics on the ark: zoos, animal welfare, and wildlife conservation*, Washington, DC 1995.

[3] B. Mullan and G. Marvin, *Zoo culture*, London 1987.

Zoo, not least because it was an integral part of the landscape of Britain's metropolis.[4] Yet this does not fully explain why the subject is important. Why, therefore, does the nineteenth-century London Zoo matter?

Another glimpse at Scharf's lithograph might bring to mind a more conventional and contrasting form of animal attraction. As the social history of popular culture has demonstrated, the baiting of a range of animals from bears and bulls to badgers had long been an integral part of popular entertainment, not finally banned until the Police Magistrate, Metropolis Act of 1833 and then by the Cruelty to Animals Act of 1835.[5] Baiting was increasingly perceived as abusive and inhumane treatment of animals, whereas the nascent London Zoo exhibited what was accepted as a respectable form of human-animal interaction. The zoo's success was symbolised by the mounting popularity of the bear pit, examples of which appeared in zoos across Europe and America. Yet it had a time limit. The London Zoo's bear pit was demolished at the beginning of the twentieth century. Should it be revived today, those responsible would probably be accused of disregarding the nutritional requirements of the animals and pandering to the spectators' complacency. Clearly, popular attitudes towards the bear pit – as to the bearbaiting which preceded it – have been transformed. This not only highlights the London Zoo as an active locus of human-animal interaction, but also suggests the ways in which such interactions changed dramatically in the course of the nineteenth century.

The zoo drew boundaries not only between humans and animals, but also between different types of animals. It is often claimed that modern zoos represent the entire animal universe, but in fact they have never exhibited examples of every living species.[6] While the nineteenth-century London Zoo valued animals of exotic rarity and physical appeal such as elephants, lions, tigers, giraffes, hippopotami, anteaters, apes and monkeys, it disregarded domestic animals and worked actively at exterminating vermin within its own space. The zoo's site was surrounded by hare-proof fences, and a rat-catcher was employed: he was paid a halfpenny for every rat taken in his traps.[7] As far as the animals displayed in the zoo were concerned, the quality of their treatment varied according to their exhibitional cost and value.

---

[4] See, for example, R. Porter, London: a social history, London 1994, 351–2; A. N. Wilson, The Victorians, London 2002, 93–4.

[5] E. Fudge, Perceiving animals: humans and beast in early modern English culture, Urbana 2002; E. Griffin, England's revelry: a history of popular sports and pastimes, 1660–1830, Oxford 2005; R. W. Malcomson, Popular recreations in English society, 1700–1850, Cambridge 1973; B. Harrison, 'Animals and the state in nineteenth-century England', EHR lxxxviii (1973), 786–820.

[6] K. Anderson, 'Culture and nature at the Adelaide Zoo: at the frontiers of "human" geography', Transactions of the Institute of British Geography xx (1995), 275–94; G. Mitman, 'When nature is the zoo: vision and power in the art of science of natural history', Osiris 2nd ser. xi (1996), 117–43.

[7] N. A. Vigors to Alexander Milne, 3 Mar. 1831, and Milne to Vigors, 5 May 1831,

Giraffes were the best example: great energy was expended in the acquisition of animals of extreme rarity and exotic charm, but monkeys, which were very popular too, were poorly cared for as they could be replaced cheaply every spring. Although the zoo had its own system of classifying animals, this was not designed to provide a comprehensive picture of the animal world. The zoo's regime was influenced by a number of factors: the discovery of new species; the development of zoological science; the supply system of captive animals; and financial conditions.

Furthermore, the human spectators without whom the zoo would have lost its rationale were also socially divided. Initially the zoo was open only to subscribers to its governing body, the Zoological Society of London, and their friends and families. Under this policy, the zoo was frequented by members of polite society and became a destination for middle-class families. To prevent the admission of the working classes, the society issued admission tickets which allowed only their holders and companions to enter the zoo. Somehow, however, the society lost control of their distribution. Forged tickets were also circulated, so that the excluded could get into the zoo. As a result, the zoo's visitor profile reflects contemporary society, divided along lines of class, but with all its fluidity and flexibility.

The politics of classification, inclusion and exclusion, thus operated in and around the London Zoo. The zoo can be analysed not only as a reflection of important themes in nineteenth-century Britain, but also as a venue where such themes were played out and where society was urged to confront them. Recent investigations of the genealogy of European and American zoos have confirmed their significant presence on the historical landscape; in particular, the nineteenth-century background to their dramatic growth has been illustrated in case studies such as Nigel Rothfels's *Savages and beasts* (2002), a study of the Hamburg Tierpark Hagenbeck.[8] This book aims to contribute to that debate, but it goes further, contemplating how the historical study of zoos could deepen understanding of the contexts within which the zoos operated and which shaped them. This approach challenges the methodological deficiencies of those zoo histories that tend to borrow

---

Zoological Garden papers, TNA, WORK 16/726; ZSL, FAA, MC, iii, fo. 426; v, fos 100–1; W. B. Boulton, *The amusements of old London*, London 1901, i. 37.

[8] N. Rothfels, *Savages and beasts: the birth of the modern zoo*, Baltimore 2002; R. J. Hoage and W. A. Deiss (eds), *New worlds, new animals: from menagerie to zoological park in the nineteenth century*, Baltimore 1996; V. N. Kisling, Jr (ed.), *Zoo and aquarium history: ancient animal collections to zoological gardens*, Boca Raton 2001; E. Baratay and E. Hardouin-Fugier, *Zoo: a history of zoological gardens in the West*, London 2002; D. C. Mehos, *Science and culture for members only: the Amsterdam Zoo artists in the nineteenth century*, Amsterdam 2006; S. Åkerberg, *Knowledge and pleasure at Regent's Park: the gardens of the Zoological Society of London during the nineteenth century*, Umeå 2001; E. Hanson, *Animal attractions: nature on display in American zoos*, Princeton 2002; A. Sakurai, *Science and societies in Frankfurt am Main*, London 2013, ch. iii.

explanatory ideas uncritically from the field of social and cultural history.[9] The pitfalls of adopting analytical concepts are apparent, for instance, in a current narrative of the birth of modern zoos, which explains that the formation of bourgeois society was such a widespread phenomenon in nineteenth-century Europe and that zoos provided a cultural platform for this social group as it developed and consolidated itself.[10] This view defines zoos as a static reflection of bourgeois society, and leaves out important questions, such as how the communal experience of the zoo influenced contemporary awareness of social structure and mobility.

A more revealing testimony is the hegemonic presence of 'empire' as a referential frame. How zoos are analysed within this framework varies, but as far as the London Zoo is concerned the key argument can be summarised: the zoo mirrored British perceptions of the hierarchical social and natural world by underlining (although sometimes undermining) the binary opposition between the coloniser and the colonised, between those humans who craved mastery over nature and those animals who were subject to it. This argument is hermeneutically elaborated but is not firmly documented. If the zoo carried any ideological messages it is necessary to clarify who designed the zoo to do so, how far it was successful, and how such messages were perceived by individual visitors. Asking these questions necessitates examining whether 'empire' remains a valid frame of reference.

The main purpose of this book is not merely to sketch a historical portrait of the London Zoo by adopting explanatory frames such as class and empire. It is rather to explore how the London Zoo used such concepts in the process of establishing its public rationale and thriving in a changing social environment. For this purpose the focus will be upon three distinct yet interrelated themes, which reflect issues from the Victorian era that are still much discussed by historians.

Cultural politics

One of the referential frames within which the historical study of zoos has been placed is the development of urban leisure in nineteenth-century Europe and America. British historians of leisure, who pioneered this field, have examined how economic changes generated by the Industrial Revolution influenced urban popular culture, although also strengthening one

---

[9] This and other problems of cultural history are more generally discussed in P. Mandler, 'The problem with cultural history', *Cultural and Social History* i (2004), 94–117.

[10] L. Davidoff and C. Hall, *Family fortunes: men and women of the English middle class, 1780–1850*, London 1987; J. Kocka and A. Mitchell (eds), *Bourgeois society in nineteenth-century Europe*, Oxford 1993.

particular feature that generally narrows the scope of the study.[11] This is that the communal experience of recreational activities reinforced boundaries between the social groups – boundaries that are often too roughly categorised by 'class'. It is also assumed that social exclusivity exhibited such remarkable consolidation that different classes scarcely encountered each other while at leisure.[12] Hugh Cunningham has argued that 'Within the wide middle-class boundary, lines to demarcate status were carefully drawn, and the upper and lower middle classes would never meet in leisure.'[13] This commentary is not entirely wrong in highlighting the overall trend of leisure culture in nineteenth-century Britain and, not surprisingly, it has influenced the historiography of the London Zoo. Sofia Åkerberg has ascribed the zoo's successful growth in the mid-nineteenth century to 'rational recreation' – the social movement which, according to historians of leisure, exemplified the prevailing norms and values of the rising middle classes.[14] Nigel Roth-fels has also noted that 'this [the London Zoo] was a place designed by the bourgeoisie for its own education and amusement'; this, he considers was the essential characteristic of nineteenth-century zoos.[15]

Nevertheless, any class-based discussion fails to take into account the heterogeneous nature of the zoo's clientele. Initially the London Zoo was not open to all, but in reality it was accessible, legitimately or illegitimately, to a range of social groups, from landed gentlemen to urban professionals, and from middle-class country residents to working-class city dwellers. Moreover, many foreign sightseers visited the zoo, and some of them wrote down their impressions, which were published, in the English, in the form of edited correspondence and diaries. Cunningham has suggested that encounters between different classes through leisure activities were only spasmodic, with the sole exception being the 1851 Great Exhibition.[16] Yet the London Zoo functioned quite differently. It has offered entertainment neither infrequently nor intermittently, but continuously, in Regent's Park, from 1828 up to the present day. It has opened regularly throughout the year, and in its busy season, the summer months, has counted thousands of spectators every week; by the end of the year attendance figures have reached the hundreds

---

[11] For an overview of the history of leisure see H. Cunningham, 'Leisure and culture', in F. M. L. Thompson (ed.), *The Cambridge social history of Britain*, III: *1750–1950*, Cambridge 1990, 279–339. A more recent survey is provided by E. Griffin, 'Popular culture in industrialising England', *HJ* xlv (2002), 619–35.

[12] P. Bailey, *Leisure and class in Victorian England: rational recreation and the contest for control*, London 1978.

[13] Cunningham, 'Leisure and culture', 298.

[14] Åkerberg, *Knowledge and pleasure*, 107–10.

[15] Rothfels, *Savages and beasts*, 34. See also his 'How the caged bird sings: animals and entertainment', in K. Kate (ed.), *A cultural history of animals*, V: *In the age of empire*, Oxford 2007, 96

[16] Cunningham, 'Leisure and culture', 318–19.

of thousands. It was in a society, especially in the metropolis, where class boundaries themselves became relatively fluid and flexible.

It is indisputable that 'class' had came to be used as a common socio-economic category by the 1850s,[17] and that some commercial entertainments flourished by attracting specific social groups: music halls were successful enterprises which drew their audience mainly from among the working and lower-middle classes.[18] Yet the heterogeneous mix that could be found at the London Zoo needs to be placed within a general picture of nineteenth-century leisure habits. As it certainly pioneered a large-scale leisure activity that equally attracted a myriad of people from different walks of life, its large capacity and popularity, which should not be dismissed merely as an exception, raises a question: how did the London Zoo establish itself in the rapidly changing metropolitan environment?

The London Zoo was not the first institution in the city to display animals. The Tower Menagerie and Edward Cross's short-lived Menagerie at Exeter Exchange (popularly known as Exeter Change) had provided popular attractions before the zoo opened in April 1828.[19] In terms of attendance figures, the London Zoo competed with the British Museum, the National Gallery and the Surrey Zoological Gardens (a successful zoo in South London, which was established by Edward Cross after his Exeter Menagerie was demolished during urban regeneration). As Richard Altick's *Shows of London* has eloquently illustrated, a growing number of London residents and visitors came to share opportunities to visit museums, galleries, menageries, parks, theatres and so forth.[20] The London leisure market was a highly selective one within which the London Zoo had to compete. Its success was not necessarily secure from the start; rather it was doubtful since the construction of an open-air menagerie was a completely new social phenomenon, particularly unwelcome to those living nearby and having concerns about the proposed site. The zoo's difficult situation may be compared to the circuses discussed by Marius Kwint. As he has demonstrated, the establishment of the circus as a legitimate leisure genre in the late Georgian era entailed subtle negotiations with the regulatory authority, the public and rival theatre

[17] G. Crossick, 'From gentlemen to the residuum: language of social description in Victorian Britain', in P. J. Corfield (ed.), *Language, history and class*, Oxford 1991, 150–78; D. Cannadine, *Class in Britain*, New Haven 1998; Davidoff and Hall, *Family fortunes*.

[18] D. Kift, *The Victorian music hall: culture, class and conflict*, Cambridge 1996; D. Hoher, 'The composition of music hall audiences, 1850–1900', in P. Bailey (ed.), *Music hall: the business of pleasure*, Milton Keynes 1986, 73–92. See also Cunningham, 'Leisure and culture', 311.

[19] E. T. Bennett, *Tower Menagerie*, London 1829; D. Hahn, *The Tower Menagerie: being the amazing true story of the royal collection of wild and ferocious beasts*, London 2003; H. Ritvo, *The animal estate: the English and other creatures in the Victorian age*, Cambridge, MA 1987, 207–9.

[20] R. D. Altick, *The shows of London*, Cambridge, MA 1978.

proprietors.[21] This was also the case with the London Zoo: like the circus proprietors, the Zoological Society had to negotiate with government officials, neighbours and the public at large. In competition with other forms of urban entertainment, the zoo borrowed some cultural habits from them, and excluded others, in order to enhance its attractiveness. An analysis of the negotiations between these different elements suggests how the zoo managed to create its own niche.

As the zoo secured its institutional status and became enormously popular, its impact on the cultural life of the public grew. The zoo was considered to provide an acceptable form of entertainment for different social groups, but the reasons for visiting it varied greatly: to know more about the classification of animals; to witness the greatness of divine creation; to enjoy instructive amusements. Such might be the apparent motives for visiting the zoo, but behind them was a subtle and almost unlimited diversity. The reasons for visiting the zoo and watching the animals there may seem elusive, but surviving sources do help. We learn, for example, that one gentleman found his children delighted to hear that he would take them to the zoo as a birthday gift; that the children experienced both excitement and novelty, travelling, for the first time, in an omnibus; that the father found a pleasurable symmetry between strolling in the city and rambling in the zoo. These details suggest how a visit to the zoo was part of the cycle of family life and how it meshed with the various cultural activities available in the metropolis.

The London Zoo was not alone in offering cultural experience to a wider audience. The British Museum gradually facilitated public access to its ever-expanding collection from the 1820s onwards. The National Gallery, initially founded at Pall Mall in 1824, was transferred to a grand new mansion in Trafalgar Square in 1838; its visitor numbers increased markedly.[22] There was also a growing number of relatively smaller institutions including the Tower of London, the Gallery of Practical Science, the Museum of Practical Geology and the Royal Naval Hospital at Greenwich, which opened its art gallery even on Sundays. For those who resided outside London, the chance to gain access to art galleries and scientific collections was enhanced by the growth of Literary and Philosophical Societies and of the Mechanics' Institutes.[23] The nationwide development of public institutions raised the ques-

---

[21] M. Kwint, 'The legitimization of the circus in late Georgian England', *P&P* clxxiv (2002), 72–115, and 'The circus and nature in late Georgian England', in R. Koshar (ed.), *Histories of leisure*, Oxford 2002, 45–60. See also B. Assael, *Circus and Victorian society*, Charlottesville 2005.

[22] D. M. Wilson, *The British Museum: a history*, London 2002, 84–6; C. Whitehead, *The public art museum in nineteenth-century Britain: the development of the National Gallery*, Aldershot 2005; J. Conlin, *The nation's mantelpiece: a history of the National Gallery*, London 2006, 57–66.

[23] T. Kelly, *George Birkbeck: pioneer of adult education*, Liverpool 1957; T. Kusamitsu, 'Great Exhibitions before 1851', *HWJ* ix (1981), 70–89.

tion of cultural politics: how was 'culture' to be controlled in the new public domain. As Holger Hoock has demonstrated, the role of the state in relation to the public status of the arts began to be coherently debated by artists, critics and politicians.[24] Coincidently, though in different circumstances, Charles Babbage's claim of 'science in decline' caused serious debates on the relationship between the state, the scientific community and the public, which eventually led to the foundation in 1831 of the British Association for the Advancement of Science.[25] The London Zoo found itself in the middle of the public debate on cultural politics and provided some early lessons for other institutions. The key issue on which it contributed was the monitoring and controlling of public access. During the 1830s and the 1840s, the zoo's admission policy was closely examined by a series of parliamentary committees and influenced the decision of other institutions including the British Museum to extend their opening hours.

Although the zoo was a contested space, at the level of discursive representation it resolved social distinctions into the comprehensive language of the public, which was ever widening but never included the whole public.[26] For contemporary observers this element of the public was an essential part of lived reality. Given the discrepancy between the actual heterogeneity and the imaginary unity of the public, it is worth examining the extent to which this was mediated or sharpened through the social and spatial experience of the London Zoo. Examining these questions helps to advance the historiography of urban leisure and cultural politics in nineteenth-century Britain.

[24] H. Hoock, 'Reforming culture: national art institutions in the age of reform', in R. A. Burns and J. Innes (eds), *Rethinking the age of reform: Britain, 1780–1850*, Cambridge 2003, 254–70, and *The king's artists: the Royal Academy of Arts and the politics of British culture, 1760–1840*, Oxford 2003. See also P. Barlow and C. Trodd (eds), *Governing cultures: art institutions in Victorian London*, Aldershot 2000; C. Duncan, 'From the princely gallery to the public art museum: the Louvre Museum and the National Gallery, London', in C. Duncan (ed.), *Civilising rituals: inside public art museums*, London 1995, 21–47; and L. Colley, *Britons: forging the nation, 1707–1837*, New Haven 1992, 175.

[25] J. Morrell and A. Thackray, *Gentlemen of science: early years of the British Association for the Advancement of Science*, Oxford 1981; R. M. MacLeod, 'Whigs and savants: reflections on the reform movement in the Royal Society, 1830–48', in I. Inkster and J. Morrell (eds.), *Metropolis and province: science in British culture, 1780–1850*, London 1983, 55–90; L. P. Williams, 'The Royal Society and the foundation of the British Association for the Advancement of Science', *Notes and Records of the Royal Society of London* xvi (1961), 221–33.

[26] For historiographical debates on Habermas's theory of 'the public sphere' see H. Mah, 'Phantasies of the public sphere: rethinking of the Habermas of historians', *Journal of Modern History* lxxii (2000), 153–82; C. Calhoun (ed.), *Habermas and the public sphere*, Cambridge, MA 1992; and E. Hellmuth (ed.), *The transformation of political culture: England and Germany in the late eighteenth century*, London 1990.

Public science

The comprehensive image of the public that was demonstrated in the zoo appeared in tandem with that of the emerging scientific community. Since the zoo was managed by the Zoological Society of London, it acted to some extent as a mediator between, on the one hand, the zoological community, which aimed to legitimise its activities in society, and on the other the wider public, many members of which realised that they were helping to support this community by paying for admission to the London Zoo. The zoo's role is therefore relevant to the historiography of public science, which investigates how the very categories of 'science' and its 'public' were historically constructed.[27]

The study of public science has demonstrated that practitioners of the natural sciences were often required to construct an audience that accepted the legitimacy of what they were doing.[28] At first glance, the London Zoo seems to fit this role: the zoo provided a platform where expert zoologists could establish the credibility of their scientific activities and obtain recognition that they would benefit the public. Yet there is one thing that needs to be borne in mind. There was no clear-cut boundary between the creators, distributors and consumers of scientific knowledge in early nineteenth-century Britain.[29] A number of scientific societies that were founded then were not governed by the principles of vocational discipline and hierarchy. Amongst them the most remarkable was the Zoological Society, which had the largest membership, the majority of whom were, however, not expert zoologists but aristocratic patrons or merely zoo-lovers. The Zoological Society could not therefore be termed a professional community in the modern sense. From a modern perspective, the scientific community and the public are two different entities, but in the nineteenth century the language that separated them was only just beginning to evolve.

The ambiguous status of the Zoological Society was one indicator of the complex nature and reception of early Victorian science, which has came to be recognised by scholars over the last few decades. Until then the historiography of science had been dominated by tales of discoveries and theories that have allegedly established the autonomy of science and have framed

---

[27] S. Shapin, 'Science and its public', in R. C. Olby and others (eds), *Companion to the history of modern science*, London 1990, 990–1007.

[28] L. Stewart, *The rise of public science: rhetoric, technology and natural philosophy in Newtonian Britain, 1660–1750*, Cambridge 1992; J. Golinski, *Science as public culture: chemistry and Enlightenment in Britain, 1760–1820*, Cambridge 1992; R. Yeo, *Defining science: William Whewell, natural knowledge and public debate in early Victorian Britain*, Cambridge 1993; S. Schaffer and S. Shapin, *Leviathan and the air pump: Hobbes, Boyle and the experimental life*, Princeton 1985.

[29] A. Secord, 'Botany on a plate: pleasure and the power of pictures in promoting early nineteenth-century scientific knowledge', *Isis* xciii (2002), 28–9, 35.

modern society. Here the lay public was construed as absorbing, simplifying and sometimes even distorting the knowledge communicated by the professional community. This diffusionilist model of science has been challenged by those historians who began to reconstruct the meanings of past ideas and practices, including those which belonged to the realm of so-called popular science. The study of Victorian natural history contributed to the reappraisal of popular science by directing attention beyond the limited circle of experts and expertise.[30] Thus the top-down model of popularisation has been replaced by an interactive approach that defines popular science as a contested arena, which contained competing claims to authentic knowledge of nature.[31]

As this suggests, the historiography of popular science has made a breakthrough by exploring how science was woven into the cultural fabric that gave shape and meaning to everyday life. Anne Secord's study of artisan botanists is, for instance, notable for illustrating the cultural meanings of the Linnaean nomenclature for those otherwise unknown enthusiasts who gathered in public houses to discuss their plant collections.[32] James Secord, Aylen Fyfe and Jonathan Topham respectively have discussed the impact of the dramatic growth of the book trade, roughly from the 1830s onwards, and have demonstrated that the increasing number of cheap, rapidly produced publications became the dominant means of spreading public awareness of science.[33] All the same, science was not all about writing and reading: it also involved other activities such as collecting specimens, conducting experiments and attending lectures. When science is defined as the set of these activities, it needs to be undertaken at a specific site. In the early and mid-

[30] D. E. Allen, *The naturalist in Britain: a social history*, London 1976; N. Jardine and E. C. Spary, 'The natures of cultural history', in N. Jardine, J. A. Secord and E. C. Spary (eds), *Cultures of natural history*, Cambridge 1996, 6–7; J. A. Secord, 'Natural history in depth', *Social Studies of Science* xv (1985), 184.

[31] R. Cooter and S. Pumfrey, 'Separate spheres and public places: reflections of the history of science popularization and science in popular culture', *BJHS* xxxii (1994), 237–67; J. R. Topham, 'Rethinking the history of science: popularisation/popular science', in F. Papanelopoulou, A. Nieto-Galan and E. Perdiguero (eds), *Popularising science and technology in the European periphery, 1800–2000*, Aldershot 1988, 1–20.

[32] A. Secord, 'Science in the pub: artisan botanists in early nineteenth-century Lancashire', *BJHS* xxxii (1994), 269–315.

[33] J. R. Topham, 'Science and popular education in the 1830s: the role of the *Bridgewater Treatises*', *BJHS* xxv (1992), 397–430, and 'Beyond the "common context": the production and reading of the *Bridgewater Treatises*', *Isis* lxxxix (1998), 233–4; J. A. Secord, *Victorian sensation: the extraordinary publication, reception and secret authorship of 'Vestiges of the natural history of creation'*, Chicago 2000; A. Fyfe, *Science and salvation: Evangelicals and popular science publishing*, Chicago 2004; S. Sheets-Pyenson, 'War and peace in natural history publishing: the *Naturalist's Library*, 1833–43', *Isis* lxxii (1981), 50–72; G. Cantor and S. Shuttleworth, *Science serialised: representation of the sciences in nineteenth-century periodicals*, Cambridge, MA 2004; L. Henson and others (eds), *Culture and science in the nineteenth-century media*, Aldershot 2004.

nineteenth century, the loci of science varied from natural history museums and galleries to tropical forests.[34] Although many of these places have been examined by historians, zoos still await attention as sites connected with science.

The London Zoo is an ideal subject for attention when investigating the social and cultural meanings of science at a time when its influence in society was coming to be publicly recognised. As the zoo offered various activities that directly or indirectly familiarised the observer with the scientific knowledge of animals, it is important to explore not only how these activities were designed by the zoo but also how they were experienced by individual visitors. Moreover, the study of this particular open-air space has unique benefits. Although recent research on Victorian science has tended to emphasise the role of visual experience in making science appealing and communicable, the activities offered by the zoo testify to the importance of smelling, hearing and touching too. If reading a book on elephants at home was a way of gaining information about the animal, enjoying an elephant ride at the zoo could be another step towards knowledge. It is therefore necessary to consider how interactively the spectators employed their senses not only to enjoy the attractions provided by the zoo, but also to understand the meaning of their experience.

When the cultural implications of the zoo experience are considered, its collective aspect should be noted. Memories of watching and touching animals could be discussed with a family, could be conveyed via correspondence to a distant friend, or could even be shared with an anonymous audience through being published, perhaps as as an article in a magazine. As individual experiences were transmitted through various channels, zoo-inspired motifs sometimes appeared in popular song and stories. In fact, there was a rich fund of commentaries on and illustrations of the attractiveness of the London Zoo, which played a significant role in communicating the zoo experience to a wider public and from generation to generation.[35] As a result, the zoo experience was increasingly perceived as a service commodity, but it is misleading to think of this as the natural outcome of the growth of a mass consumer culture.[36] The zoo negotiated efficiently with the competitive

[34] A. Fyfe and B. Lightman (eds.), *Science in the marketplace: nineteenth-century sites and experiences*, Chicago 2007; D. N. Livingston, *Putting science in its place: geographies of scientific knowledge*, Chicago 2003; C. Smith and J. Agar (eds), *Making space for science: territorial themes in the shaping of knowledge*, Manchester 1998, 2; F. Driver, *Geography militant: cultures of exploration and empire*, Oxford 2001; S. Forgan, 'The architecture of display: museums, universities and objects in nineteenth-century Britain', *BJHS* xxxii (1994), 139–62; D. Outram, 'New spaces in natural history', in Jardine, Secord and Spary, *Cultures of natural history*, 249–65.

[35] See, for example, [A. N. Cecil], *London parks and gardens*, London 1907, 100.

[36] T. Richards, *The commodity culture of Victorian England: advertising and spectacle, 1851–1914*, London 1991.

leisure market to maintain the attractiveness of the services that it provided for the public.

So far a euphoric vision of Victorian science as open and eager to recruit new members rather than dominated by the principle of rigorous discipline and vocational hierarchy, has been highlighted. The comprehensive aspect of Victorian science has been demonstrated in many studies, but it is not the whole picture. In early nineteenth-century Britain there was no clear demarcation between the producer and the consumer of scientific ideas and practices. All the same, changes were taking place: different scientific practices were being categorised, and 'science' was being presented as a body of collective knowledge with its own institutional basis, cognitive content and professional ethics.[37] It is therefore necessary to contemplate how the influence of science in society grew, and with it the division, as commonly found today, between disciplined science and popular spin-off. An early investigation on this subject described the rise of the professional community by tracing the discourse of spokesmen for British science such as Thomas Huxley.[38] As Aileen Fyfe and Bernard Lightman have rightly pointed out, the arguments of such men should not be taken at face value, because they were articulated in order to authenticate disciplinary science, sometimes by defining competing ideas and practices as illegitimate.[39] The views, therefore, of Huxley and other spokesmen for science on the changing status of science in the nineteenth century should not be accepted uncritically.[40] Other types of sources have to be examined to see how science was defined not only by those who promoted it, but also by those who consumed it for their own purposes.

To this end, this book discusses a court case that identified the London Zoo as a witness to the developing separation of 'legitimate' from 'popular' science. In the 1850s a heated debate arose at Queen's Bench on the subject of whether the activities offered by the zoo were purely scientific or combined with other elements, and whether the latter was for the public good. These questions were broadly related to the issue of local taxation and affected those public institutions, including the Zoological Society, that were granted exemption from the parochial rate. At a time when problems with the Poor Law Reform of 1834 remained unsettled, the zoo's case could be linked to

---

[37] J. Pickstone, 'Science in nineteenth-century England: plural configurations and singular politics', in M. Daunton (ed.), *The organisation of knowledge in Victorian Britain*, Oxford 2006, 29–60; R. MacLeod, *Public science and public policy in Victorian England*, Aldershot 1996; L. Daston and P. Galison, *Objectivity*, Cambridge, MA 2007. For general discussions on the professions and professionalisation see P. J. Corfield, *Power and the professions in Britain, 1700–1850*, London 1995.

[38] F. M. Turner, 'Public science in Britain, 1880–1919', *Isis* lxxi (1980), 589–608.

[39] A. Fyfe and B. Lightman, 'Science in the marketplace: an introduction', in Fyfe and Lightman, *Science in the marketplace*, 2.

[40] A. Desmond, *Huxley: from devil's disciple to evolution's high priest*, London 1997.

the debate on how far the government could support scientific institutions without jeopardising the provision of social services. The court was thus required to judge whether the particular form of science that was offered at the London Zoo qualified for tax exemption.

Legal documents are not a typical source for the social historian of science. This is probably related to the point at which this book diverges from mainstream historiography of science. Its primary focus is the social life of people, not the social life of text genres, objects or spaces.[41] The difference can be clarified, for instance, by considering the methodological assumption that knowledge was transmitted by being materialised into books which were then read.[42] According to this argument, individuals remain important, chiefly because without them the meanings of texts would never be deciphered. This book, however, takes the view that individuals were not just vessels through which texts and objects produced meanings, but that they were relatively, if not completely, independent agents who modelled and modified the ways in which they appropriated knowledge. The nineteenth-century London Zoo offered a forum, not just for the making of knowledge, but also for its communication.

Animal history

The third theme of the book is concerned with place of the London Zoo in animal history. The zoo was not alone in making animals visible and influencing popular attitudes towards them. The sight of animals also affected popular images of the metropolis. A stream of horse traffic could be admired in a mood of public celebration of London's 'progress' and 'civilization', while large livestock herds at Smithfield Market amazed sightseers as evidence for the enormous scale of meat consumption in the city.[43] The perception was emerging that animals were being sacrificed to metropolitan luxury and blatant commercialism, and this motivated animal welfare campaigners to crusade against cockfighting, baiting, dogcarts, vivisection and other practices

---

[41] For the difference between these two approaches see P. Burke, *Popular culture in early modern Europe*, rev. repr., Aldershot 1994, pp. xxi–xxii. For the study of 'object biography' see S. J. M. M. Alberti, 'Objects and the museum', *Isis* xcvi (2005), 559–71, and L. Daston (ed.), *Biographies of scientific objects*, Chicago 2000.

[42] R. Chartier, *Cultural history: between practices and representations*, Ithaca 1988, and *The order of books: readers, authors, and libraries in Europe between the fourteenth and eighteenth century*, Cambridge 1994.

[43] B. Adams, *London illustrated, 1604–1851: a survey and index of topographical books and their plates*, London 1983; L. Peltz, 'Aesthecizing the ancestral city: antiquarianism, topography and the representation of London in the long eighteenth century', *Art History* xxii (1999), 472–94; A. Potts, 'Picturing modern metropolis: images of London in the nineteenth century', *HWJ* xxvi (1998), 28–56.

that were deemed wanton cruelty to animals.[44] The increasing presence of animals and its impact on urban culture has been emphasised by the study of 'animal history', or the history of human-animal relationships, which aims to revaluate the complex roles played by animals in human histories.[45]

Theoretically, the application of the term 'animal history' would suggest a reassessment of a human-centred view of history and a discussion of the possibility of recovering the agency of animals in historical narratives.[46] Although it seems impossible to assume the agency of those who had no means of keeping records about themselves, the London Zoo gives a clue for pursuing this agenda, if from a different perspective. When the zoo first appeared, it created the illusion that the animals were well treated and thereby revealed their original nature to the visitors. Some of the animals were even individually identified, like Toby, and were described as individuals who were supposed to have some intelligence and emotion. This, of course, was an anthropocentric illusion: it cannot be said that zoo animals recovered their agency in the zoo. It is none the less true that the illusion was so realistic that many zoo visitors were enchanted with the apparent harmony of human-animal interaction. The difference between representation and reality suggests the importance of distinguishing the three dimensions of the zoo: how it was idealised, how it was actually managed, and how its animals were perceived. Discussing these dimensions separately and considering the gaps between each of them suggests that the idea of animal agency needs to be historically situated.

Apart from the idea of animal agency, there were various ideological influences under which the historical experience of the London Zoo was formulated. Among them, empire is held to have provided so predominant a context that one research approach identifies the nineteenth-century London Zoo as a reflection of the British Empire. As Jonathan Burt has argued, however, this assumption dismisses the crucial fact that popular attitudes towards the zoo and its animal displays were often mixed and ambiva-

[44] H. Kean, Animal rights: political and social change in Britain since 1800, London 1998, 39–69; D. Donald, '"Beastly sights": the treatment of animals as a moral theme in representations of London, c. 1820–50', Art History xxii (1999), 514–44.

[45] M. Henninger-Voss (ed.), Animals in human histories, Rochester 2002; L. Kalof and B. Resl (eds), A cultural history of animals, Oxford 2007; D. D. Morse and M. A. Danahay, Victorian animal dreams, Aldershot 2007; P. J. Atkins (ed.), Animal cities: beastly urban histories, Aldershot 2012. Issue 4 of the Journal for Eighteenth-Century Studies xxxiii (2010) is dedicated to the subject of 'representing animals', which testifies to the growing interest in this interdisciplinary field of study.

[46] The idea of 'animal agency' is developed from the study of animal geography: C. Philo, 'Animals, geography and the city: notes on inclusions and exclusions', in J. Wolch and J. Emel (eds), Animal geographies: place, politics, and identity in the nature-culture boundaries, London 1998, 51–71. See also S. E. MacFarland and R. Hediger (eds), Animals and agency: interdisciplinary exploration, Leiden 2009.

lent.[47] Although the zoo could convey ideological messages, they were always subject to different interpretations. The gap suggests that the zoo's place at the junction of animal and imperial history is worthy of further analysis.

First of all, if the 'imperial' context is to be discussed, a definition of 'empire' is required. This has varied over time and its transformation merits study in itself, but there is a conventional explanation: the first British Empire, which began to develop in North America and the West Indies in the seventeenth century, rested on a system of commercial regulation and was characterised by British settlements overseas. When this first empire gave way to the second is open to debate, but one possibility is the period between 1783 and 1860 with British territorial expansion in India and Africa.[48] In 1876 Queen Victoria was crowned Empress of India and the British Empire was 'officially' established. Apart from definitions based on chronology and patterns of expansion, there is also the concept of 'informal empire' – the extensive areas situated outside official 'imperial' territories yet predominantly under Britain's influence – which has been regarded as useful for understanding Britain's hegemonic power from the mid-nineteenth century onwards.[49]

Scholars have also come to perceive the history of Britain and its overseas empire in parallel and to analyse their interactions from various perspectives.[50] Natasha Glaisyer argues that the British Empire, particularly its long eighteenth-century presence, should be conceived as 'a set of networks through which knowledge and ideas were exchanged, trust was negotiated, goods were traded, and people travelled'.[51] The virtue of a networked concept of empire is, as noted by David Lambert and Alan Lester, 'to consider metropole and colony, or colony and colony, within the same analytical frame, and without necessarily privileging either one of these places'. Catherine Hall's *Civilizing subjects*, which has adopted this approach most successfully, links the study of the Baptist missionaries to Jamaica, and of the town of

---

[47] J. Burt, 'Violent health and the moving image: the London Zoo and monkey hill', in Henninger-Voss, *Animals in human histories*, 258–92.

[48] For a full discussion see P. J. Marshall, 'The first British empire', and C. A. Bayly, 'The second British empire', in R. W. Winks (ed.), *The Oxford history of the British Empire*, V: *Historiography*, Oxford 1999, 43–53, 54–72.

[49] J. A. Gallagher and R E. Robinson, 'The imperialism of free trade', *EcHR* vi (1953), 1–15.

[50] A. Lester, *Imperial networks: creating identities in nineteenth-century South Africa and Britain*, London 2001; S. J. Potter (ed.), *Imperial communication: Australia, Britain and the British Empire, c. 1830–50*, London 2005; D. Lambert and A. Lester (eds), *Colonial lives across the British Empire: imperial careering in the long nineteenth century*, Cambridge 2006; C. Hall and S. O. Rose (eds), *At home with the empire*, Cambridge 2006; G. B. Magee and A. S. Thompson, *Empire and globalisation: networks of people, goods and capital in the British world, c. 1850–1914*, Cambridge 2010.

[51] N. Glaisyer, 'Networking: trade and exchange in the eighteenth-century British Empire', *HJ* xlvii (2004), 451.

Birmingham, the 'midland metropolis' and 'a stronghold of missionary and abolitionist activity in the 1830s', and reveals how the mental landscapes of nineteenth-century men and women (or at least of those who are analysed in her book) were structured by the questions of empire, missionary, race and the relationship between the coloniser and the colonised.[52] Similarly, the network model has influenced the historiography of imperial science. It was initially argued that science was a tool of territorial expansion and governance, with colonies presented as mere theatres for European science. Recent research, however, questions this dictum by demonstrating that colonial fields provided the essential experience and information for the development of modern sciences, and has demonstrated that the development of scientific knowledge entailed interplays between different loci in the British Empire.[53]

A key question is whether the networked conception of empire is appropriate for the analysis of the London Zoo. At first glance, the answer might appear to be definitely affirmative. Imperial networks modelled the overseas infrastructure that enabled the London Zoo to thrive in the nineteenth century. The zoo was a hub of communications through which animals were traded, their collectors travelled and zoological knowledge was circulated. The East India Company, which sometimes supported the transportation of animals from South and South-East Asia, is generally considered to exemplify the zoo's association with the empire. This could be even seen in parallel with Kew Gardens, which Richard Drayton has discussed in his *Nature's government* (2005), placing the long history of Kew Gardens in the context of Britain's interaction with the colonial field and identifying the ideologies that fostered the development of botanical science and British expansion. In his view, the interplay between science and empire was 'an ideological symbiosis rather than a mere combination of scientific and imperial means and motives', often intermediated by the 'Christian assumptions about man's place in nature'.[54] If this line of argument is adopted, then the London Zoo becomes another variation of science/empire symbiosis – a notion which has indeed influenced many zoo histories.

This book challenges the concept of 'imperial zoo' for two reasons. Firstly, because it restricts the zoo's geographical context: although animals were obtained through imperial networks, they were also collected from areas

[52] C. Hall, *Civilising subjects: metropole and colony in the English imagination, 1830–67*, London 2002, 12, 20–1.

[53] R. MacLeod (ed.), *Nature and empire: science and the colonial enterprise*, Osiris 2nd ser. xv (2000); M. Harrison, 'Science and the British Empire', *Isis* xcvi (2005), 56–63; K. Raj, *Relocating modern science: circulation and the construction of knowledge in South Asia and Europe, 1650–1900*, Basingstoke 2007.

[54] R. Drayton, 'Science, medicine, and the British Empire', in Winks, *Oxford history of the British Empire*, v. 264–76, and *Nature's government: science, imperial Britain, and the 'improvement' of the world*, New Haven 2000. See also S. Sivasundaram, *Nature and the godly empire: science and Evangelical mission in the Pacific, 1795–1850*, Cambridge 2005.

outside British hegemonic influence. The networks of animal collectors stretched far beyond imperial (either formal or informal) boundaries and were given dynamism by extra-imperial factors. The scope and diversity of animal-collecting activities thus poses a question: can this extra-imperial dynamism be explained in terms of the science/empire symbiosis? In fact, an exclusive focus on the macroscopic relations between 'science' and 'empire' tends to explain everything in terms of Britain's hegemonic power as well as the binary opposition between the coloniser and the colonised. The pitfall of reductionism stems from the assumption that those who appeared to have acted for the British overseas enterprise set 'empire' as a key context that modelled their actions and their relations to the world. This is apparent, for instance, in one study of Joseph Banks's plant collectors, which defines them as 'agents of empire', who 'helped to incorporate new lands and colonies into a British scientific and industrial hegemony'.[55] This kind of metaphorical application of 'imperial science' comes into question when the networks of the London Zoo's collaborators are closely examined. Empire was not the only context within which these individuals perceived and negotiated their roles. The very diversity of their reasons for collecting wild animals, of their attitudes to nature, and of their own personal perceptions of the world – which cannot necessarily be reduced to the British Empire – requires a complex language of explanation that differs from the notion of imperial zoo.

Secondly, in general terms the historical narrative of the London Zoo has been stereotyped. It has been argued that the zoo owed its successful development to British imperial expansion, and in return contributed to the creation of a mass imperial identity. Harriet Ritvo has argued that the zoo represented a British imperial vision of the world – a vision that integrated the ordering of chaotic nature with Britain's conquest of its overseas empire.[56] Robert Jones has elaborated upon this view, defining the zoo as 'a primary vehicle for the British empire's model of self-display', and has emphasised that among the many ideologies that were created around and within the zoo, the most important was 'the idea of the zoological garden as a showcase for British imperial endeavour'.[57] To dub the zoo 'a showcase' also chimes with recent literature on Victorian exhibition culture, which has assumed that the empire was visualised and experienced through a variety

[55] D. Mackay, 'Agents of empire: the Banksian collectors and evaluation of new land', in D. P. Miller (ed.), *Visions of empire: voyages, botany and representations of nature*, Cambridge 1996, 54.
[56] H. Ritvo, 'The order of nature: constructing the collection of Victorian zoos', in Hoage and Deiss, *New worlds, new animals*, 50, and *Animal estate*, 205–43.
[57] R. W. Jones, "The sight of creatures strange to our climate": London Zoo and the consumption of the exotic', *Journal of Victorian Culture* ii (1997), 1–26. See also D. Donald, *Picturing animals in Britain*, New Haven 2007, 159–97, and P. Blanchard and others (eds), *Human zoos: science and spectacle in the age of colonial empires*, Liverpool 2008.

17

of public displays ranging from museums and galleries to shopping areas.[58] The validity of this assumption should be examined before speculating that the imperial elements could be decoded from the zoo and its animal display.

Certainly, the influence of the British Empire was undeniable, but this does not necessarily mean that the zoo's exhibition policy was designed exclusively for the purpose of spreading an imperial ideology. The extent to which the geographical context was translated into animal display should be examined, and the day-to-day responses of the zoo visitors should be taken as an indicator of whatever messages they received. Although the scattered evidence of letters and diaries, recording visits to the zoo, has not yet been fully investigated, the digitalisation of archive catalogues and the development of bibliographical databases have recently enabled searches to be carried out on a rich variety of personal documents. By exploring these sources, in addition to other types of materials, this book emphasises that the significance of the zoo, especially prior to the 1870s, was so variously defined that the zoo's animal displays could not be deciphered using any single code of ideological symbolism. The London Zoo thus developed through the nineteenth century in a context of hermeneutic flexibility,

This book is structured semi-chronologically, while interweaving its three main themes. A variety of visual sources are also used. As the London Zoo was a popular attraction, a large number of prints were produced by artists and for illustrated weeklies such as the *Illustrated London News* and *Punch*, many of which have been collected in the scrapbooks held in the Zoological Society's archive. A selection of these illustrates the main features of the zoo during its first decades, and their careful examination helps to explore how the zoo was idealised and perceived. Some of them were drawn in a realistic manner, but there were also satirical prints that often anthropomorphised the zoo animals. They are altogether useful for analysing how the zoo presented its animals as a subject for public consumption.

Chapter 1 explores the earliest development of the London Zoo from when building work started in 1826 to the formulation of its management policy around 1835. When the Zoological Society began work in Regent's Park, it faced public scepticism as well as opposition from government officials and neighbours. The society's records and the official documents deposited at the National Archives reveal how the zoo tackled these problems and came to be recognised as an essential cultural amenity of the metropolis. The key to success was that it departed from previous forms of animal spectacle by inventing a harmonious image of human-animal interactions. The other

---

[58] S. Qureshi, *Peoples on parade: exhibitions, empire and anthropology in nineteenth-century Britain*, Chicago 2011; J. A. Auerbach and P. H. Hoffenburg (eds), *Britain, the empire and the world at the Great Exhibition of 1851*, Aldershot 2008; F. Driver and D. Gilbert (eds), *Imperial cities: landscape, display and identity*, Manchester 1999, 1–17; J. Schneer, *London 1900: the imperial metropolis*, New Haven 1999.

important element attached to the zoo's exhibition policy was the scientific identity of the Zoological Society. The influence of science was less noticeable than the picturesque landscape that surrounded the zoo, but it becomes evident when compared to the exhibition policy of the rival Surrey Zoological Gardens.

Once over the difficult early years, the Zoological Society sought to organise an exhibition that would symbolise the rise of British zoology, especially in rivalry with the French *Muséum national d'histoire naturelle*. The society eagerly sought to collect giraffes, whose existence had been doubted until the late eighteenth century. Although it was difficult to capture this unusually tall animal and to transport it alive to London, the Zoological Society persisted and finally obtained four giraffes and exhibited them in the mood of public celebration of 1836. By taking this particular example, chapter 2 discusses how the Zoological Society negotiated with naval and commercial networks to collect animals from abroad, and considers its implications for the analysis of animal display in the zoo.

By the time of the giraffe exhibition, the London Zoo had experienced an unexpectedly large influx of visitors. Partly because of the zoo's tremendous popularity, and partly because of the problematic operation of its admission procedure, the zoo attracted a far wider range of people than its proprietor had initially conceived. This problem was not entirely confined to the zoo's management, but was related more broadly to the question of how 'culture' should be controlled in the new public domain of museums, galleries and art institutions. Chapter 3 focuses on this issue during the period from 1828 to 1847 when the zoo was open, officially, only to a restricted public. The diversity of the zoo audience in terms of social status, gender, age and nationality is identified by using both statistical data and observations made by contemporary visitors. This highlights the zoo as a point of reference for the ongoing debates on the reform of art galleries and scientific institutions, and its contribution to the growing demand for the direct transmission of culture to a wider public.

The Zoological Society finally resolved to abandon its exclusive admission policy and opened the zoo to the general public in 1847. The timing of this crucial decision was opportune, as the leisure market was to be galvanised by the Great Exhibition of 1851. As a result, the London Zoo regained its popularity, but its commercial success began to undermine the assumption that the Zoological Society was a voluntary association. To explore the transformation of the zoo and the society, chapter 4 examines two contrasting periods in the zoo's history: from 1837 to 1847, the decade of downward spiral in popularity and hence income; and from 1847 to 1859, a period of restructuring and rehabilitation. It also focuses on a series of debates which arose, first within the society and eventually in the law courts, concerning how the society's public rationale should be justified. As the zoo became more and more an amusement park, the society's commercial role in running it undermined its institutional identity. These debates none the less testified to a growing public awareness that the dual objects of the Zoological Society – promotion of 'legitimate' science and the provision of 'rational recreation' – were efficiently integrated by the London Zoo.

The presence of science was certainly less marked at the zoo as it gained commercial success, but this did not necessarily mean that the Zoological Society abandoned the pursuit of scientific enterprise. In fact, the society launched a large-scale project of collecting a variety of game birds from the Himalayas in 1856. The ultimate goal of the project was to 'acclimatise' these exotic birds in the Scottish Highlands, and then to establish the London Zoo as the centre of a science of 'acclimatisation' that would be based upon intensive collecting and an extensive breeding programme. Chapter 5 examines the cultural backgrounds against which a science of 'acclimatisation' was imported from France and was translated as the means of establishing a 'zoological empire' under the control of the Zoological Society. Although the project foundered, the concept of acclimatisation did survive among gentleman breeders and continued to involve specialist zoologists. The trajectory of acclimatisation thus epitomised the zoo's ambivalent claim to science.

The three themes of the book are drawn together in the conclusion, which reconsiders the flourishing of the nineteenth-century London Zoo, as represented by the throngs of people around the bear pit. Public enthusiasm, depicted in Scharf's lithograph, suggests that the growth of the zoo signified a successful blend of science and entertainment, and that this was based on more than mere passive spectatorship. The zoo evoked and received various reactions from the public and changed accordingly: thus it became a prime locus of human-animal interactions.

1

The Site of Animal Spectacle

'Like too many of our modern associations and companies, this is extremely sonorous on paper; but alas for the execution of the design – is it not altogether visionary? Yet we understand it is patronised by some very influential men; and no one could be sorry to see the experiment tried.'[1]

The London Zoo is in the same place today as it was nearly two centuries ago. On a current map of Greater London, it occupies a tiny triangle, sandwiched between the spacious grounds of Regent's Park and Primrose Hill, and seems to fit naturally into its surroundings. This was not the case, however, when plans for a zoo began to be made in the late 1820s. For its contemporaries the construction of the zoo was a new social experience. London had already played host to animal spectacles such as the Exeter Exchange Menagerie, the Tower of London Menagerie and Smithfield Market, but the scale envisaged for the new zoo's collection as well as the space in which it was exhibited was incomparable. The London Zoo was innovatory in topographical terms too. It was well away from the crowded areas of the city and was surrounded by the picturesque landscape of Regent's Park. However, judging from the scale and location of the zoo, its construction appeared to be a speculative rather than promising venture.

In the course of becoming established in Regent's Park, the London Zoo's sponsors entered into a series of negotiations with those who had conflicting interests, both in the construction site and in the surrounding area. The establishment of Britain's first zoo (and of those ideals that are characteristic of the modern zoo) was the result of complex interactions between different agents, ideas and localities. An analysis of this process sheds light on the transition from 'menageries' to 'zoological gardens', an issue of great importance for the study of human-animal relationships. At first glance, the London Zoo might appear to be so distinct from its surroundings that its framing of human-animal relationships was specific and limited, but the zoo was none the less integral to the topographical transformation of London and played a significant part in its development. The social experience of the zoo reveals its meanings in the light of analogy and comparison with other sites of human-animal interactions in the city, and becomes even more explicit when the locality of the London Zoo is properly identified in the context of metropolitan topography.

---

[1]   *Literary Gazette*, 7 May 1825, 296.

The zoo in the city

In March 1825 Sir Thomas Stanford Raffles, the former governor of Singapore, drafted the first prospectus for the Zoological Society of London. During his long stay in south-east Asia, Raffles had become interested in natural history, and upon his return to England he sought to establish a national institution for the study of zoology that could rival the French *Muséum national d'histoire naturelle*.[2] In the prospectus he appealed at great length to a wide range of interests, such as the advancement of zoological science, the application of such research to industry and manufacture, the provision of instructive amusement and the diffusion of natural theology.[3] Raffles was optimistic that more than a hundred subscribers would be ready to join.

The proposition did indeed appeal to Nicholas Aylard Vigors and his colleagues in the Zoological Club of the Linnean Society. Although the club had begun as a subgroup of the Linnean Society, it provided enthusiastic zoologists with a semi-autonomous scholarly forum and published their discussions in the *Zoological Journal* (1824–34). However, the club's position within the Linnean Society was insecure, as it had rejected the Linnaean nomenclature and instead advocated a 'quinary' system. William Sharp Macleay, entomologist and civil servant, who had invented this new system in the late 1810s, asserted that it constituted a comprehensive system of classification: species, orders and families were divided into sets of five bounded by a circle. It became popular among metropolitan zoologists, who discussed the possibility of replacing the Linnaean with their new 'English' nomenclature. They followed Vigors in joining the Zoological Society and establishing their own institutional premises.[4]

In the meantime, Humphry Davy, as president of the Royal Society, swiftly intervened in the constitution of the Zoological Society. Since his appointment in 1820, Davy had faced increasing demands for the reform of scientific societies by men of scholarly merit and reputation. In his view, however, collaboration with the landed elite was vital if the public status of science and government support were to be secured. This had been the strategy taken by his more powerful predecessor, Joseph Banks, who had for a long time dominated the scientific community by taking advantage of political

---

[2] S. Raffles, *Memoir of the life and public services of Sir Thomas Stamford Raffles*, new edn, London 1835, ii. 361–2, 366–73; J. S. Bastin, 'Sir Stamford Raffles and the study of natural history in Penang, Singapore and Indonesia', *Journal of the Malaysian Branch of the Royal Asiatic Society* lxiii (1991), 1–25; Ritvo, *Animal estate*, 205–6.

[3] 'Prospectus of a society for introducing and domesticating new breeds or varieties of animals, such as quadrupeds, birds, or fishes, likely to be useful in common life; and for forming a general collection in zoology', 1 Mar. 1825, Zoological Gardens papers, WORK 16/722.

[4] A. Desmond, 'The making of institutional zoology in London, 1822–36', *BJHS* xxiii (1985), 133–85.

patronage and personal connections with the landed gentry.[5] Although Davy could not aspire to Banks's pre-eminences, he actively involved himself in the foundation of the Zoological Society in order to to maintain his influence in the emerging field. When asked for support by Raffles, Davy helped to recruit, but took a different approach. This was reflected in the revised prospectus of the Zoological Society circulated in March 1826.[6] Unlike the first, it comprised several short paragraphs, which proclaimed that the object of the society was the display and domestication of wild animals and the provision of successfully bred specimens for the subscribers. It omitted references to 'a philosophy of Zoology', with its associations with the quinarian system of taxonomy. Davy was interested in recruiting members from those landed gentlemen who preferred to collect exotic animals rather than discuss scholarly nomenclature.

The Zoological Society of London was founded in April 1826 with Raffles as president and Vigors as secretary. The treasurer was Joseph Sabine, secretary of the Horticultural Society, which had awarded him a gold medal for reordering the society's financial structures and entrusted him with the management of its botanical gardens.[7] His professional experience as Inspector of Assessed Tax (promoted to Inspector-General in 1830) also counted, but, more important, his presence balanced the influence of Vigors and his allies in their advocacy of taxonomic zoology. Sabine was to be responsible for the programme of experimental breeding, which aimed to supply exotic animals to aristocratic sponsors. Furthermore, Davy sat on the society's council and acted to preserve close relations with polite society. When Raffles suddenly died of a brain tumour in July 1826, Davy argued that aristocratic patronage was essential for the further development of the infant society. When Henry Petty-Fitzmaurice, 3rd marquis of Lansdowne, the living epitome of Grand Whiggery, took over the presidency, Davy was relieved, writing to Thomas Andrew Knight, president of the Horticultural Society, that 'this gives it [the Zoological Society] a chance of existence, for both his influence & talent are likely to be useful to a nascent So[ciety]'.[8]

The membership of the council hinted at potential tensions between specialist zoologists and gentlemen breeders. As its main goals the society

---

[5]   D. P. Miller, 'Between hostile camps: Sir Humphry Davy's presidency of the Royal Society of London, 1820–7', *BJHS* xvi (1983), 1–47.

[6]   Prospectus of the Zoological Society of London [Mar. 1826], Bodleian Library, Oxford, JJC, London Play Places 8 (65); J. Bastin, 'The first prospectus of the Zoological Society of London: new light on the society's origin', *JBNH* v (1970), 369–88.

[7]   H. R. Fletcher, *The story of the Royal Horticultural Society, 1804–1968*, London 1969, 113.

[8]   Davy to T. A. Knight, 10 Dec. 1826, Humphry Davy papers, Royal Institution, London, HD/26/D/2m. For Lansdowne's position and influence in high politics see P. Mandler, *Aristocratic government in the age of reform: Whigs and Liberals, 1830–52*, Oxford 1990, 101–3.

itemised the establishment of a zoological garden, the construction of a zoological museum, the promotion of experimental breeding, the organisation of scientific meetings, and the publication of specialist journals. Different members of council had different priorities. Advocates of taxonomic zoology craved the expansion of the museum collection and sought to take control of scientific meetings, whereas gentleman menagerists simply wanted to build up their collections of exotic animals. The zoological garden could provide a common focus since the collection of living animals could contribute both to scientific research and to breeding projects. At least, for the first few years, the two groups cooperated rather than competed.

In March 1826, Raffles and George Eden, 1st earl of Auckland, a political *protégé* of the marquis of Lansdowne and vice-president of the Zoological Society,[9] submitted an application to construct a menagerie in Regent's Park to the Commissioners of Woods and Forests,[10] who managed the Crown estates under the supervision of the Treasury. The society asked for a piece of ground in the middle of the Inner Circle (*see* Figure 1 [A]), but this was rejected. Since the nursery there supplied trees and shrubs for the park, the commissioners judged that it should not be imperilled by what seemed to be an experimental project.[11] As the project for the menagerie seemed about to flounder, Davy intervened, asking Robert Peel to arrange a meeting with John Arbuthnot, the first Commissioner of Woods and Forests. Their meeting ended successfully, as Davy optimistically wrote to Peel that 'I confidently hope [I] have smoothed all difficulties in the way of allotment of ground in the Regent's Park to our Society.'[12] In July 1826 the commissioners agreed to let an area of five acres forming a triangular plot in a remote corner (*see* Figure 1 [B]) for a limited tenancy of twenty-one years.[13]

The society's choice of Regent's Park was reasonable. In the mid-eighteenth century the area around Marylebone had been a semi-rural playground for fashionable society; farms supplied hay and dairy produce for London.[14] In the aftermath of the Napoleonic Wars, the area was transformed into a picturesque garden known as Regent's Park and began to be integrated into

9 Mandler, *Aristocratic government*, 126.

10 The official name was the Commissioners of Woods, Forests and Land Revenues until 1832 when it was changed to the Commissioners of Woods, Forests, Land Revenues, Works and Public Buildings.

11 Later the ground became the Royal Botanic Garden: G. Meynell, 'The Royal Botanic Society's garden, Regent's Park', *London Journal* xi (1980), 135.

12 Davy to Robert Peel, 10 Mar. 1826, Home Office papers, TNA, HO 44/16, fo. 21.

13 Commissioners of Woods and Forests to George Eden, 1st earl of Auckland, 23 Mar. 1826, and Treasury to Commissioners, 23 Mar., 27 July 1826, Zoological Gardens papers, WORK 16/722; ZSL, MC, i, fo. 19.

14 W. W. Wroth and A. E. Wroth, *The London pleasure gardens of the eighteenth century*, London 1896, 93–110; E. Mckeller, 'Peripheral visions: alternative aspect and rural presences in mid-eighteenth century London', *Art History* xxii 1999, 495–513.

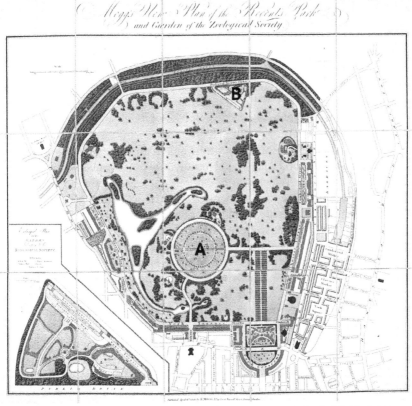

Figure 1. Location of the Zoological Gardens in Regent's Park, LMA, Main Print Collection, p5390098.

Key
A= Jenkin's nursery; proposed site of the zoo
B = Agreed zoo site

the expanding residential areas of the metropolis.[15] By the 1820s the basic layout of the park had been completed together with the building of villas within it, and terraces around it, but there was still room for other facilities. Regent's Park was connected with the West End via the newly-built Regent Street and Portland Place. Since it was hoped that the zoo would be easily

---

[15] For the early history of Regent's Park see J. Summerson, *John Nash: architect to King George IV*, London 1935; T. Davis, *John Nash: the Prince Regent's architect*, Newton Abbot 1973; J. M. Crook, 'Metropolitan improvements: John Nash and the picturesque', in C. Fox (ed.), *London: world city, 1800–40*, New Haven 1992, 77–96; and J. Anderson, 'Marylebone Park and the New Street: a study of the development of Regent's Park and the buildings of Regent Street, London, in the first quarter of the nineteenth century', unpubl. PhD diss. London 1998.

accessible to prospective patrons in polite society, the proposed location must have appeared very attractive.

The construction of the zoo, however, did not go smoothly. Davy had a stroke after the meeting with Arbuthnot and in January 1828 left for the continent where he spent the rest of his life. A few months before departure, he had written again to Thomas Knight with a brief note on the progress of the construction work.[16] It implies that Davy was kept informed about the zoo, but he could no longer assert his political influence. The three leading members of the society, Vigors, Sabine and Auckland, took his place and worked on the practical arrangements for building the zoo along the line that Raffles and Davy had initially drawn. However they came up against the Treasury's reluctance to honour the agreement made by Davy and Arbuthnot. The Treasury recognised that the Regent's Park estates were a luxurious residential quarter and intended to maximise land revenue by enhancing its picturesque scenery. It was therefore concerned that the zoo's facilities – sheds, huts and stables – would intrude on the grand vistas of the park and impair property values. The presence of carnivores could also cause anxiety among the tenants in the neighbouring properties. The *Literary Gazette* spoke, ironically, for the Treasury: 'though we do not know how the inhabitants of the Regent's Park will like the lions, leopard and linxes [sic] so near their neighbourhood'.[17]

The Treasury certainly doubted that tenants in and around the park, who were of considerable social status, would approve of the project. In winter 1826 it directed the Commissioners of Woods and Forests to clarify the covenant which prevented tenants in the park from erecting any buildings other than villas.[18] Despite receiving the obvious warning, the Zoological Society continued in its building work, expecting, over-optimistically, that the commissioners' approval would follow shortly. In October 1828 John Maberly MP, who owned St John's Lodge, denounced the commissioners for failing to observe the covenant and threatened to sue the society for 'the actual violation of the rights of Individuals'.[19] As a result, the society had to abandon building work on its winter repository, which meant that many animals were lost in the following cold months. No substantial work could be undertaken until Maberly left St John's Lodge, which he did in 1829 due to the failure of his own business.[20]

[16] Davy to [Knight], 17 Jan. 1826, Davy papers, HD/26/D/2p.

[17] *Literary Gazette*, 6 May 1826, 282.

[18] 'Case', 29 Nov. 1826; William Green to Milne, 2 Jan. 1827; Auckland to Commissioners of Woods and Forests, 20 Jan. 1827, Zoological Gardens papers, WORK 16/723.

[19] John Maberly to Milne and Joseph Sabine, 13 Oct. 1828, ibid., WORK 16/724.

[20] Thorne, R. G. (ed.), *The history of parliament: the House of Commons, 1790–1820*, London 1986, iv. 483–5; E. C. Samuel, *The villas in Regent's Park and their residents*, London 1959, 26.

Subsequently, the Zoological Society faced an even stronger opponent, John Nash, who had enjoyed the favour of George IV and had by then become the official architect to the Commissioners of Woods and Forests. His critical contribution to the redevelopment of Regency London is well known, but he did not confine himself to the neo-classical transformation of urban architecture. Nash acted as a property developer, being a lessee of eighteen and a nominator to sixty-seven of the 1,236 plots on the crown estates around the park.[21] He suggested to the Treasury that he should be allowed to erect more villas in the park. He considered that the strip of land situated between the Outer Circle and Regent's Canal would suffice for his scheme, but that land had been effectively occupied by the Zoological Society in anticipation of the conclusion of a legal agreement.[22] While Nash's estimation of the rental value of his proposed villas was £1,050–£1,260 *per annum*, the rent paid by the society was to be £480 *per annum*.[23]

Nash considered that the society's occupancy of the crown lands threatened his plans and he tried to stop the lease going ahead. In May 1830 he was instructed to examine a draft lease prepared for the society, but told the Commissioners of Woods and Forests that a comprehensive long-term agreement could not be concluded without affecting the development of the crown estates.[24] In August 1830 he was directed to revise the lessee's covenants so that the value of the crown estates would be maintained, but again he demurred, demanding that the society should provide fuller information on its plans.[25] Nash continued to create obstacles to the Zoological Society securing its rights in Regent's Park until October 1830, when he was suspended from office, due to an explosion of public criticism of his extravagance in the construction of Buckingham Palace.[26]

While difficult negotiations with government officials and neighbouring tenants continued, the Zoological Society consolidated its *raison d'être*. When Raffles drafted the society's first prospectus, he had already stated that the proposed zoological garden would differ from ancient Roman circuses, with their vulgar displays of gladiatorial combat and contests between ferocious beasts. This, however, was a provisional statement. As the Zoological Society tackled a series of problems arising from the construction of the London Zoo, its ideals crystallised. In its appeal to government officials the society emphasised that the London Zoo would enhance the picturesque beauty of Regent's Park and was at one with the interests of both the tenants

---

[21] Anderson, 'Marylebone Park', 228–9.

[22] The use of this piece of land was approved by the Commissioners of Woods and Forests in August 1829: Office of Woods, Forests and Land Revenues, Minutes, 24 July, 7, 14 Aug. 1829, TNA, CRES 25/33.

[23] John Nash to Milne, 4 Sept.1828, Zoological Gardens papers, WORK 16/724.

[24] Milne to Nash, 25 May 1830, and Nash to Milne, 1 July 1830, ibid. WORK 16/725.

[25] Nash to Milne, 14 Sept. 1830, ibid.

[26] Summerson, *John Nash*, 229–76.

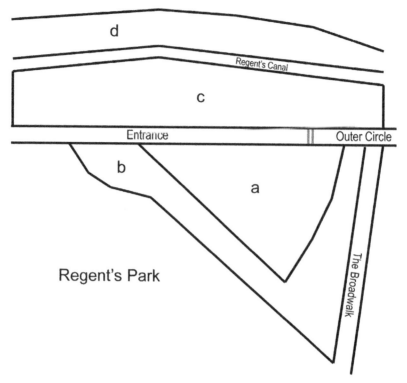

Figure 2. Layout of the London Zoo.

Key
a = original ground of five acres obtained in 1826
b = additional ground of five and half acres obtained in 1831; plots a and b rented at £141 10s.
c = additional ground north of the Outer Circle rented at £468 6s.8d.
d = ground of approximately three acres rented at £74 2s.6d.

and the landlord (the Crown); that its members pursued the advancement of zoological science; that the wide variety of living animals served as an essential research source; and that it was therefore necessary to ensure adequate facilities to keep the animals alive and healthy.[27]

The institutional identity of the Zoological Society was legally confirmed when it received its royal charter in 1829. The society had moved swiftly to this stage, unlike many of the other scientific institutions which were emerging in the early nineteenth century. Since the royal charter clarified the society's status as a public institution, it helped it finally to obtain its

[27] Auckland to Commissioners, 28 May 1827, and 'Memorial to the Lord Commissioners', 1828, Zoological Gardens papers, WORK 16/723, 724.

lease.[28] In the same year, the collections of the Royal Menageries at the Tower of London was transferred to the London Zoo (that at Windsor Great Park had been presented to the society in the previous year).[29] This event signified that the Zoological Society had come to be recognised as the primary institution responsible for keeping and exhibiting animals for public benefit. Until then the society had been just one of the agents competing to gain control of the land in Regents Park, which was, for the time being, let to them for the experimental construction of an alfresco menagerie, and which was in Nash's view to be integrated into his grand scheme of property development in and around Regent's Park. The London Zoo thus emerged from the interactions between competing agents, ideas and localities. How this process was embedded in the zoo's spatial structure needs to be explored further.

First of all, the overall layout of the zoo. It was divided (*see* Figure 2) into the north and the south gardens, which were connected by a tunnel under the Outer Circle towards the east of the site. The south garden consisted of the triangular five-acre plot (a) originally let to the Zoological Society in 1826, to which was added further land (b) to make a total of 10.5 acres. A wide variety of animals (ranging from deer and ducks to monkeys and macaws) were accommodated on the original ground, while strict regulations were imposed on the mode of occupancy of the additional ground. The east border had to be surrounded by a thick plantation, and in the west and south the height of the buildings was regulated to a maximum of 8ft. The society had no other option but to use this land as pasturage. Restrictions were not so strict on the design of the north garden, which occupied a piece of land north of the Outer Circle and south of the Regent's Canal, with a frontage of 1,405ft on the public drive (c). Here the society was permitted to house large herbivores such as elephants and rhinoceros. The winter repository, the construction of which had once been abandoned due to Maberly's opposition, was also erected on this site. In addition the lease of 1831 granted land on the north bank of the Regent's Canal (d) for the purpose of constructing aviaries and enclosures for small animals, although as the ground was clayey, damp and apt to give way, the sort of buildings that could be erected was limited.

Clearly, the zoo's layout had to cope with the irregular shape of the land available to it, as well as its legal obligations. None the less, Decimus Burton, the acclaimed architect of the villas in Regent's Park, who was commissioned by the society to design both the layout and buildings for the zoo, made

---

[28] Milne to Vigors, 21 Oct. 1831, and Vigors to Milne, 22 Oct. 1831, ibid. WORK 16/726.

[29] *The Times*, 23 Nov. 1831, 4; William Fremantle to Auckland, 10 Apr. 1830, and Auckland to Fremantle, 25 Aug. 1830, Fremantle papers, Buckinghamshire Record Office, Aylesbury, D/FR108/10/2, D/FR108/10/4.

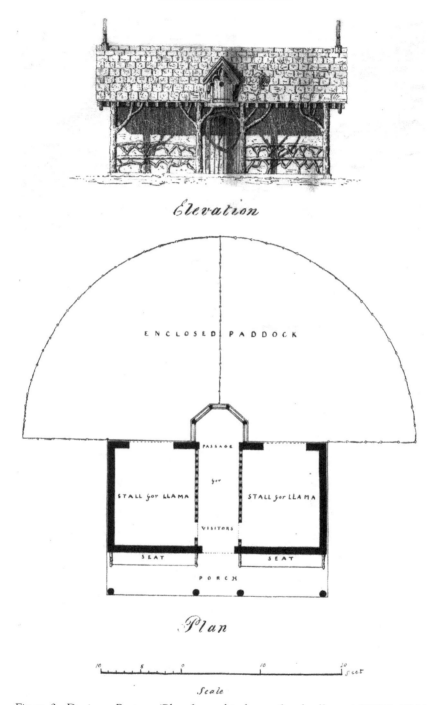

Figure 3. Decimus Burton, 'Plan for gothic house for the llamas' (1828), TNA, WORK 16/724.

the best use of the limited area available.[30] He placed sheds, huts, aviaries and enclosures at regular intervals along winding paths, and made the paths intersect at many points so that visitors could stroll among changing landscapes at their own pace. Burton was not the first architect to apply the principles of English landscape gardening to the design of a menagerie. That of the *Muséum national d'histoire naturelle* in Paris had already adopted what it called *jardin anglais*. Burton's innovation was rather the promenade walk, which started at the entrance gate and ran along the south-west border of the original five-acre plot. As the promenade was raised and later lined with ornamental trees, it blocked the view into the zoo from the outside and prevented the zoo's scenery from intruding on the surrounding landscape. Furthermore, Burton had planned to extend the promenade as an elevated terrace under which would be the carnivore dens with their open-air yards. Despite its elegant design, this extension did not go ahead: others believed that a closed, heated building, rather than exposure to fresh air, was necessary to the health of captive animals.[31]

The promenade therefore stopped at the bear pit, which became the most popular attraction in the zoo.[32] As buns were sold at a nearby stall, spectators could feed the bears as they climbed up the pole to catch the food. When the visitors had had enough fun with the bears, they could look back at a view that highlighted the unique nature of the zoo's landscape. The architectural style varied, from rustic to gothic, and from functional Tuscan to ornamental Corinthian, contrary to the orthodox principles of picturesque landscaping. At the same time, Burton drew together and integrated the spectacle of a range of exotic and unfamiliar animals, while leaving each of them to make their own separate appeal. The design of stables and aviaries aimed to display animals and birds most aesthetically. This policy was exemplified by Burton's llama house, situated in the middle of the south garden, and proclaimed by an 1829 guidebook as 'one of them most beautiful objects in the grounds'.[33] Its design was symmetrical, with a porch and a gable roof (*see* Figure 3), and with decorated seats: a shady retreat where tired strollers could rest. The path from the gate ran between two stalls towards the back of the house, where llamas could be seen in their enclosure. If instead spectators left the building and went round to the enclosure, the llamas could then be seen from a different angle against a picturesque background. When a clock tower was placed on the roof of the llama house in 1831, it became the zoo's land-

[30] Dana Arnold, 'A family affair: Decimus Burton's designs for the Regent's Park villas', in Dana Arnold (ed.), *The Georgian villa*, Stroud 1996, 105–17.

[31] C. Mitchell, *Zoological Society of London: centenary history*, London 1839, 27.

[32] V. N. Kisling, Jr, 'The origin and development of American zoological parks to 1899', in Hoage and Deiss, *New worlds, new animals*, 118.

[33] T. Allen, *A guide to the Zoological Gardens and Museum: with a brief account of the rise and progress of the Zoological Society*, London 1829, 11–12.

Figure 4. James Hakewill, 'View from the emu house', from *Ten views of the Zoological Gardens*, London 1831.

mark building.[34] Llamas were then replaced by camels, which added to the exotic allure. This decision suggests that the society was flexible in its planning, updating the zoo's layout according to the kinds of animals available.

By the time that the lease was concluded in 1831, the principles for landscaping the zoo had been established: a synthesis of exotic spectacle and picturesque scenery. This was articulated visually in James Hamewill's *Ten views of the Zoological Gardens* (1831), which was presumably commissioned by the Zoological Society.[35] As Hakewill was a landscape architect and a topographical painter his images echoed contemporary landscape painting.[36] His 'View from the emu house' (*see* Figure 4) shows two men and one woman observing the emus in the enclosure, which is embellished by a small pond and a variety of exotic plants. Behind them the ornamental fountain appears

[34] *Reports of the council and auditors of the Zoological Society of London*, London 1832, 11. The Clock Tower is the earliest surviving building in the zoo, although it was rebuilt twice: P. Guillery, *The buildings of London Zoo*, London 1993, 26.

[35] Adams, *London illustrated*, 513–14.

[36] He was well known for his *Picturesque tour of Italy*, some of the plates in which were engraved after J. M. W. Tuner's water-colours based on Hakewill's drawings: C. Powell, 'Topography, imagination and travel: Turner's relationship with James Hakewill', *Art History* v (1982), 408–25.

to be towering up into the sky, and in the distance can be seen the llama house, at this date without the clock tower.

The crowds of spectators disappeared in Hakewill's design, although the zoo was often visited by several thousand people in a day. Instead, one third of the canvas is occupied by sky, affording unbroken vistas beyond the actual boundary of the zoo. In other words, the zoo's landscape was freed from its physical limits. To represent the zoo as being 'liberated' from its own spatial boundary has deeper implications here, since it symbolised the zoo's triumph. Hakewill's lithographs demonstrated that rather than being merely absorbed into the surrounding scenery the zoo had appropriated the landscape of Regent's Park to create its unique vision. Indeed, the Zoological Society had by that time ceased to receive severe complaints about the smell and filth of the animals and had instead begun to receive favourable reviews from newspapers and periodicals. This does not mean, however, that the zoo's image, as represented in Hakewill's lithographs, was necessarily shared by the public. It is important to differentiate the three aspects of the zoo: how it was idealised, how it was actually administered and how it was perceived by the public. The disjunction between these three elements is the key to understanding what made the zoo so different from any other site of animal spectacle.

Animals in picturesque landscapes

Shortly after the opening of the London Zoo in March 1828, the *Mirror of Literature* described its animals as appearing to enjoy 'much greater advantage than when shut up in a menagerie' as well as 'the luxury of fresh air, instead of unwholesome respiration in a room or a caravan'.[37] As a growing number of newspapers and periodicals assessed the zoo, this kind of narrative soon became a *cliché*.[38] The setting in Regent's Park contributed to the elaboration of such platitudes. This is exemplified by a fictional travelogue for children, *A month in London: Or some of its wonders described*, which demonstrated how adult mentors should guide children through the cultural attractions on offer in the metropolis. One day, a respectable gentleman took an American tourist with his two children to the London Zoo. Upon entering the grounds, the children were struck by their encounters with the real animals and found them 'accommodated with their peculiar food, lodging and pastime, as nearly as possible'. This impression was in contrast with 'the unhappy beasts within the booths of a country fair', which were

---

[37] *Mirror*, 6 Sept. 1828, 148.
[38] These phrases were, for instance, reiterated in F. Coghlan, *A visit to London: or stranger's guide to every object worthy of attention in the metropolis*, London 1833.

'tormented in a savage tone of expostulation'.[39] Such imagery owed most to the idyllic, spacious surroundings of the zoo, as an anthropomorphic deduction could easily be drawn: the lives of the zoo animals were as happy and comfortable as those of inhabitants in and around the park. Air quality was also an important factor. The American novelist Herman Melville noted a sharp contrast between the outskirts and the centre of the city. On his omnibus journey from Newgate Street through Paddington and Edgware Road to St John's Wood and then round Regent's Park to Primrose Hill, Melville realised that 'Towards Hampstead the open country looked green, & the air was pretty clear; but cityward it was like a view of hell from Abraham's bosom. Clouds of smoke, as though you looked down from Mt. Washington in a mist.'[40]

In essence, 'spacious ground', 'fresh air' and 'cleanliness' are the key words that characterise contemporary commentaries on the London Zoo during its earliest years. At that time, people's sensibility about smell became stronger, as the sanitary reform movement gathered momentum in addressing the poverty and disease that had been aggravated by the metropolitan expansion. Reformers targeted air quality, because until the rise of bacteriology in the late nineteenth century it was believed that disease was caused by 'miasma' or poison in the air exuded from rotting animals, decomposing vegetables, stagnant water and putrefying soil.[41] The fear of smell and the obsession with purified air intensified. According to Edwin Chadwick, a driving force in sanitary reform, 'all smell is, if it be intense, immediate, acute disease'. Hence if one prescription was to eliminate odour, the other was to create a deodorised space in the city.[42] A sharpening awareness of the smell and filth of animals could justify, for example, John Nash's opposition to the unrestricted development of the London Zoo in Regent's Park. When its grounds began to expand, Nash actually denounced the zoo for exuding a 'noisome smell', which endangered those who walked in the park for their health. He wrote to the Commissioners of Woods and Forests that 'the nuisance must

[39] J. Taylor, A month in London: or, some of its modern wonders described, London 1832, 87–91.

[40] E. M. Metcalf (ed.), Journal of a visit to London and the continent by Herman Melville, 1849–50, Cambridge, MA 1948, 32.

[41] C. Hamlin, Public health and social justice in the age of Chadwick: Britain, 1800–1954, Cambridge 1998, 59–60, 110; M. Brown, 'From foetid air to filth: the cultural transformation of British epidemiological thought, ca. 1780–1848', Bulletin of the History of Medicine lxxxii (2008), 515–44.

[42] R. Porter, The greatest benefit to mankind: a medical history of humanity, New York 1998, 10, 259, 411, 428. For further discussion of the history of smell see A. Corbin, The foul and the fragrant: odour and the French social imagination, Leamington Spa 1986; C. Classen, D. Howes and A. Synnott, Aroma: the cultural history of smell, London 1994; M. S. R. Jenner, 'Civilization and deodorization? Smell in early modern English culture', in P. Burke, B. Harrison and P. Slack (eds), Civil histories: essays presented to Sir Keith Thomas, Oxford 2000, 127–44.

increase as the numbers and variety of animals increase and may become such a nuisance as to require legislative authority to abate'.[43]

Nash's prophecy did not come true. Initially Regent's Park had been accessible only to neighbouring tenants, but in 1834 it was opened to the public in order to meet the social demand for fresh air and open space for exercise.[44] The Broad Walk was laid out, providing pedestrian access from the south corner of the park to the zoo. At this stage, the zoo was no longer seen as harmful to the metropolitan population. In fact, as one Chadwickian reformer testified, the sanitary condition of the zoo was judged superior to that of the crowded streets:[45]

> [O]bserve the state of society in that large room which is appointed to every class of animals, where every want is relieved, and every appetite and passion gratified in full view of the whole community. In the filthy and crowded streets in our large towns and cities you see human faces retrograding, sinking down to the level of these brute tribes, and you will find manners appropriate to the degradation.

Since this remark was made for a particular political reason, rather than as a faithful description of the zoo, it is necessary to examine whether it was a view generally held. Surviving records such as letters and diaries, in which visitors noted their personal impressions, suggest that they were quick to appreciate the idealised aspects of the zoo. On 22 May 1830 Anne Chalmers, a seventeen-year-old girl of good family in London, noted in her diary: 'It[London Zoo] is a most delightful spectacle, the animals have so much more liberty than in common menageries.'[46] Many spectators seemed to compare the zoo with circuses, menageries and shows of performing animals in general. Comparisons were especially made with the Royal Menagerie at the Tower of London. Thomas Sopwith, a civil engineer from Newcastle-upon-Tyne, on his first visit to London in March 1830, estimated the zoo to be one of the most interesting places that he saw. By contrast, his subsequent visit to the Tower Menagerie was disappointing: 'as a menagerie the thing was much more confined and insignificant'.[47] A similar opinion was expressed by Charles Knight, who researched the habits of animals at the London Zoo,

43 Nash to Milne, 25 May, 14 Sept. 1830, Zoological Gardens papers, WORK 16/725.

44 H. W. Lawrence, 'The greening of the squares of London: transformation of urban landscape and ideals', *Annals of the Association of American Geographers* lxxxiii (1993), 90–118.

45 This is quoted in Brown, 'From foetid air to filth', 536.

46 *Letter and journals of Anne Chalmers*, ed. A. W. Blackie, London 1923, 111.

47 T. Sopwith, *Reminiscences of first visits to Scotland, London, and the south west of England in the years 1828, 1830, and 1833*, privately published 1847, 76–7; B. W. Richardson (ed.), *Thomas Sopwith*, London 1891, 82. See also Hahn, *Tower Menagerie*, 236.

the Tower Menageries and the travelling menageries at the Bartholomew Fair, and concluded that the zoo provided the best living conditions.[48]

The ways in which spectators interacted with animals was of great importance. Allowing visitors to feed the animals was not the zoo's own invention, but combined with enjoyment of the spaciousness and beauty of the surrounding landscape had an innovative and unique allure. This was evidenced by the attraction of the bear pit, as one German traveller recorded in her autobiography:[49]

> Now we went on to the Zoological Garden[s]; right by the entrance one finds the dwelling of a beautiful bear; friend Petz [bear] was very trusting; he begged constantly for one more present, soon we had wasted so much money at one bread-seller sitting beside [the bear pit] that we were ashamed of ourselves. The park is splendid there. That the number, the beauty and the diversity of the animals are so great, for that vouches the ease, with which England could get everything from its estates.

Many individual visitors seemed to appreciate the zoo's ideals: they rarely knew what was happening behind the scenes. Martin Lichtenstein, another German visitor and the future founder of the Berlin Zoological Garden, was an exceptional observer who gained a chilling insight into the economy of animal collection. In autumn 1832 many monkeys died of pneumonia, but it scarcely mattered as he reported that purchasing new monkeys in the spring would cost much less than heating and looking after them during the winter.[50] If, therefore, the animals looked fresh and sound, as was noted in many personal records, they might be of the same species but not be the same individuals as had been seen in a previous season. Moreover, the zoo's daily journal suggests that the actual physical environment of the zoo was at odds with the spectators' first impressions and, in fact, caused stress and distress to the animals. A few examples from the journal highlight the real conditions under which the animals were kept. On 22 October 1830 a frustrated kangaroo 'killed itself against the fence of the padock [sic]'. A week later another accident was noted: 'Dotterel [was] killed by the Quails.' The 'boa constrictors', which had been delivered 'in very ill health', died the next day. Together with the boars a 'green monkey' arrived only to die within a fortnight.[51] The steady flow of new animals made it difficult to realise that many animals received little care and died without attention being given to them. When an unidentified vulture died on 28 September 1830, the

[48] C. Knight, *Passages of a working life*, London 1864, ii. 149.

[49] M. Belli-Gontard, *Lebens-Erinnerungen*, Frankfurt-am-Main 1872, 262. The author was the wife of a wealthy merchant of Frankfurt-am-Main. She visited the London Zoo during her stay in London from 1836 to 1837.

[50] I. Jahn, 'Zoologische Gärten in Stadtkultur und Wissenschaft im 19 Jahrhundert', *Berichte zur Wissenschaftsgeschichte* xv (1992), 217.

[51] ZSL, QAA, OG, 28, 30 Sept., 1, 22, 29, 30 Oct. 1830.

writer of the journal could not help but note that 'Hawks died (never been named).'[52] Edward Crisp eventually launched a physiological investigation into the diseases of captive animals in the 1850s. His observations continued to hold true even if they were applied to explain the high mortality of the previous period: 'most of the animals in question are living in an artificial state, many of them exposed to a temperature much lower than that which was natural to them; their food, too, generally different from that which they were accustomed to obtain in their native haunts'.[53]

Overall, enthusiasm outweighed criticism in the early years of the zoo. When the zoo was first opened, spectators were apt to let their attention be captured by the zoo's novelty rather than by its smell and filth, principally because the purpose of their visit was to have fun. Although there were critics who advocated improvement in the drainage, and in the ventilation and heating system in the buildings, their claims were not unanimously approved by the Zoological Society. This is partly because the demands for reform arose out of conflicts over the control of science amongst the very different members of the society. Science apparently featured less in the spacious grounds and picturesque scenery of the zoo's spatial structure, but was certainly significant. This has to be seen in the context of the turbulent political climate within the Zoological Society in the late 1820s and 1830s.

Scientific identity

The construction of the zoo was not the only aim of the Zoological Society, although it was given priority by gentleman menagerists and promenaders who wanted to enhance its attractiveness. For specialist zoologists, however, it had to be run in parallel with the establishment of a zoological museum, which would demonstrate the society's serious commitment to science. They therefore urged the society to lease a building at Bruton Street, Piccadilly, in 1826, for this purpose. The museum swiftly expanded with the large number of specimens that the society regularly received from colonial officers and officials. By 1828 it was reported to have already collected 600 mammals, 4,000 birds, 1,000 reptiles and fish, 1,000 testaciea and crustacea, and 30,000 insects.[54]

As the museum gathered its rich anatomical resources, it provided a research forum for specialist zoologists within the Zoological Society, who began to intervene in administrative matters. They formed a majority at the general meetings, which were rarely attended by aristocratic breeders

---

52 ZSL, OG, 28 Sept. 1830.
53 E. Crisp, 'On the causes of death of the animals in the Society's Gardens from 1850 to the present time', *Proceedings of the Zoological Society of London* xxxiii (1860), 175.
54 Desmond, 'Making of institutional zoology, 232

and wealthy promenaders, and demanded funds to expand the museum. The political influence of these individuals was demonstrated when they forced the council to give up the breeding farm in Kingston, Surrey, which had been set up to promote the domestication of ornamental animals and to supply gentleman breeders. Joseph Sabine had charge of this project, but it was soon alleged that he had gained his position through Tory nepotism. It was also discovered that his *protégé*, a paid secretary at the Horticultural Society, had misappropriated its funds. This scandal struck a decisive blow at Sabine's career: he was forced to resign as secretary of the Horticultural Society. A further allegation was that he had defrauded the Zoological Society. Pro-museum specialists alleged that he enjoyed the privilege of private use of a cottage at the Kingston Farm in return for his services to aristocratic clients. Eventually, Sabine had to resign amid a storm of protest at the society's general meeting in April 1830.[55]

The collapse of the Kingston Farm initiative should not be interpreted simply as a triumph for pro-science specialists against gentlemen breeders, for leading council members were still unified, regardless of their differing political positions. They made strenuous attempts to prevent a schism in the society. Although Vigors was a Whig, he stood by the Tory-affiliated Sabine in stating that 'amongst 1,600 members of the society, no second person would be found with so much knowledge, practical skill, and zeal as Mr. Sabine possessed'. In a similar tone, Auckland declared that 'Mr. Sabine was the only person in the society who could pursue this primary object of the institution.' Lansdowne did not intervene, despite his distaste for Toryism, and confirmed the solidarity of the executive members of the council amidst the sectarian wrangling.[56] The council's unity helped the nascent society to survive its first turbulent years.

Ironically, however, these key figures took a back seat as they were required instead to concentrate upon national politics. In 1830 Auckland was appointed President of the Board of Trade in Earl Grey's new reform government, and in the following year Lansdowne resigned as president of the society as his role as 'virtual ambassador from the moderate country gentry to the Whig government' became increasingly important in the coalition government.[57] In 1832 Vigors was elected to the reformed parliament with a seat in Calrow and promptly resigned as secretary, although he remained on the council.

The council of the Zoological Society subsequently split into two hostile camps. One centred upon the new president, Edward Smith-Stanley (13th earl of Derby from 1833), who owned one of the largest private menag-

---

[55] *The Times*, 15 Mar. 1830, 5; *Magazine of Natural History* iii (1830), 292; Desmond, 'The making of institutional zoology', 227–8.

[56] *The Times*, 2 Apr. 1830, 4.

[57] Mandler, *Aristocratic government*, 103.

eries at his principal country seat, Knowsley Hall, Lancashire. Unlike his predecessor, Stanley had an obviously personal interest in the administration of the society. As a devoted collector of exotic animals, Stanley occasionally exchanged animals from his collection with the Zoological Society and was in favour of the breeding programme. Under his presidency, William John Broderip, an Oxford graduate and Tory magistrate, became a significant, particularly once Auckland and Vigors had gone. As a close friend of William Buckland, a distinguished Oxford geologist, Broderip was part of the Oxford circle of gentlemen naturalists. Another important player was Richard Owen, a rising zoologist at the Royal College of Surgeons, who was also a member of the Oxford circle. Although Owen made an attempt to distance himself from party strife by declining Stanley's request to become a vice-president of the Zoological Society, his opponents criticised him as the epitome of 'corruption' and 'nepotism' in the scientific community.[58]

The growth of the Tory coterie on the council was accompanied by the increasing opposition of the anti-establishment group. The flag-bearer was Robert Edmund Grant, professor of comparative anatomy at University College London, who specialised in the study of lower vertebrates and advocated reform of scientific and medical societies.[59] Grant's pro-science stance was supported by Robert Gordon, member of parliament and secretary to the board of council, who represented the interests of the society's chief donor, the East India Company.[60] Pro-science advocates found another influential ally in William Henry Sykes, who joined the council of the Zoological Society in 1833. During his service with the East India Company, Sykes had been engaged in statistical and natural history research and had donated several new species to the Zoological Society, among which *Cercopithecus albogularis* or Sykes's monkey was regarded as the most valuable.[61] After he retired and returned home, Sykes sought to build a new career in the metropolitan scientific community.[62] All these new members were elected to the council in the early 1830s and put their reform plans on the agenda. They

---

[58] ZSL, MC, iv, fos 53, 162; v, fo. 215; S. J. Woolfall, 'History of the 13th earl of Derby's menagerie and aviary at Knowsley Hall, Liverpool (1806–1851)', *Archives of Natural History* xvii (1990), 1–47. See also R. Owen, *The life of Richard Owen*, London 1894, i. 96–7. In 1837 Owen was elected Hunterian Professor of the Royal College of Surgeons.

[59] A. Desmond, *The politics of evolution: morphology, medicine, and reform in radical London*, Chicago 1989.

[60] Gordon entered parliament in 1812 and joined Henry Brougham's circle of young Whigs. He was also known as 'staunch supporter of opposition': Thorne, *House of Commons, 1790–1820*, iv. 37–8.

[61] *Reports of the council and auditors* (1832), 7.

[62] Later, in 1840, Sykes joined the board of directors of the East India Company. He also entered parliament as 'a liberal and unpledged supporter of Lord Palmerston': J. Sykes (ed.), *Biographical notices of Colonel William Henry Sykes, F.R.S., M.P.*, London 1857.

were also supported by Thomas Wakley, publisher of the radical *Lancet*, who tried to represent the 'outdoor' voices of rank-and-file specialists.[63]

The strife culminated at the council ballot in 1835.[64] At the annual meeting of the society, the council's proposal to remove Grant and Gordon was overthrown by a majority of its members. However, Derby, in the chair, declared the result null and void on the ground that there were quite a few members who had not yet paid subscriptions and therefore that their votes were not valid. A second ballot took place at the next meeting which approved the original motion, partly due to Derby's efforts to mobilise Tory-affiliated absentees.[65] Although supporters of Grant and Gordon used public media such as *The Times* to muster anti-council members to the ballot, it failed to prevent them from losing their two powerful representatives on the council.[66]

The political conflicts within the Zoological Society, which began with the rise of the reform lobby and ended up with the triumph of the Tory coterie, certainly affected the management of the London Zoo. Whereas the Tory coterie perceived zoo animals either as breeding stock or garden orna-ment, zoological careerists regarded them as research material and demanded that the society should pay attention to the cost of maintaining the zoo and its animals. As a result, the reforming lobby urged the council to create the new post of medical superintendent with a salary of £100 *per annum*, to which William Youatt, veterinary surgeon and lecturer at University College London, was appointed in May 1833.[67] The council also began to monitor feeding in an attempt to find out the appropriate type and amount of provisions for the zoo animals.[68] An improvement in the heating system was discussed on the recommendation of Joseph Cox, radical lobbyist and a disciple of Robert Grant.[69] Cox furthermore contributed to the setting up of the Health and Treatment of Animals Committee, which took charge of examining the records of diseases and deaths of the zoo animals. It was asked to investigate the recent death of a very rare vicuna, as well as to recommend

[63] S. S. Sprigge, *The life and times of Thomas Wakley*, London 1899; Corfield, *Power and the professions in Britain*, 139, 147.

[64] For further details of the political conflict in the Zoological Society see Desmond, 'The making of institutional zoology', 235–41.

[65] A letter from Derby to William Pepys, an instrument-maker associated with the Royal Institution and the late Humphry Davy, suggests his eagerness to defeat the reforming lobby at the council ballot: Edward Smith-Stanley, 13th earl of Derby, to W. H. Pepys, 23 May 1835, William Hazledine Pepys papers, RI, Pep/B/89.

[66] *The Times*, 29 Apr. 1835, 1. The *Spectator* (2 May 1835, 421) also conveyed the angry voice of one anonymous member, who was furiously indignant to witness 'the unprecedented and indecent behaviour' of the earl of Derby in the chair.

[67] ZSL, MC, iii, fos 138–9.

[68] ZSL, MC. iii, fo. 210.

[69] ZSL, MC, iii, fos 165, 177, 187.

ways of reducing animal mortality by examining 'evidence' from the society's records and personnel.[70]

For the reforming administrators, a scientific approach was to be taken, not only towards animal resources but also the zoo itself. In financial terms, the zoo had to be managed economically and efficiently. In February 1836 an anonymous correspondent to *The Times* castigated the council of the Zoological Society for allowing conditions at the zoo to remain harmful to its animals: the ground remained undrained and the buildings were slight and flimsy: 'many of the animals', wrote this critic, 'were standing deep in mud and water, and their bodies covered with filth'. Judging from the content and tone of this letter, it was written by a supporter of the reforming lobby, who resented the Tory triumph at the council ballot in the previous year. It should not be taken at face value, but William Broderip, vice-president of the society, had none the less to concede in his zoo guide published in the *Quarterly Review* that the loss of animals was 'considerable'.

The reforming administrators sought to extend the principle of efficiency to almost every aspect of zoo management. Sykes proposed erecting turnstiles at the zoo entrance that would mechanically collect admission fees, with the expectation that the society could dispense with the existing gate-keepers. Although automation was not a success, the turnstile at the exit did stop illegitimate admissions.[71] Likewise, Gordon set up the Garden Discipline Committee, which specified working practices among the staff and reported on cases of irregular conduct. Together with other reformers, including Sykes and Vigors, this committee aimed to reduce costs by discharging unsatisfactory employees.[72] Such measures indicate how the scientific identity of the Zoological Society influenced the zoo's management, through their fight against what they perceived as the Tory monopoly of the society's important resources and offices. The significance of scientific motifs becomes more evident in the light of the London Zoo's rivalry with its competitor, which appeared on the other side of the Thames in 1831.

Situated close to the well-established Vauxhall Gardens, the Surrey Zoological Gardens (subsequently the Surrey Zoo) was to all intents and purposes an individual commercial venture, although its official governing body took the form of a voluntary society by obtaining royal and aristocratic patronage.[73] John Edward Gray of the British Museum was also recruited as

---

[70] ZSL, MM, i, fo. 15; MC, iv, fos 135–6, 210.

[71] ZSL, MC, iii, fos 106, 357, 363, 378, 409–10, 423, 435, 442–3; iv, fos 85, 156, 163, 174.

[72] ZSL, MC, iii, fos 458, 462.

[73] Prospectus of the Surrey Zoological Gardens, *c.* 1830, Bodl. Lib., JJC, London Play Places 7 (23)

Figure 5. Surrey Zoological Gardens: Mount Vesuvius and the Bay of Naples (1837)

an honorary member.[74] Its actual proprietor was Edward Cross, owner of by former Exeter Change Menagerie, which had an exhibitional philosophy which was was clearly at odds with that of the London Zoo. He was not as eager to expand the living collection as the Zoological Society, but he saw the animals as an integral part of the spectacle. The Surrey Zoo had a more distinctive spatial structure than the London Zoo. An octagonal conservatory was located on the west side of the ground, and on the east side a large artificial pond that featured a small island. Clearly, the Surrey Zoo was better situated than the London Zoo for hosting spectacular events such as flower shows, firework displays, balloon ascents, promenade concerts and gigantic panoramas (*see* Figure 5).[75] Provision of such attractions enabled the Surrey Zoo to get off the ground more quickly than had the London Zoo.

The increasing popularity of the Surrey Zoo posed a question for the Zoological Society: should it introduce such entertainments or continue to confine itself to the display of animals. The former option would be favoured by those aristocratic breeders and urban promenaders who wanted

[74] Letter addressed to John Edward Gray, n.d. (c. 1831?), John Edward Gray papers, BL, MS Add. 29717, fo. 48; A. Booth, *The stranger's intellectual guide to London for 1839–40*, London 1839, 146.

[75] Anon., *A companion to the Royal Surrey Zoological Gardens*, London 1835; E. B. Chancellor, *The pleasure haunts of London*, London 1925, 489–90. Cross retired in 1844. William Tyler, the new proprietor of the Surrey Zoo, sought to strengthen its musical attractions by introducing orchestral performances. The proprietorship was later obtained by the Surrey Music Hall Company and the zoo was closed in 1877.

to improve the exotic appeal of the zoo, whereas the opposition took the latter view. As the division of opinion hardened, the council took a decisive step towards the establishment of a herbaceous department. In 1834 the annual report of the Zoological Society proudly stated that it had obtained '2447 new or additional kinds of ornamental shrubs and herbs' from botanic gardens at Kew, Oxford, Cambridge, Glasgow, Edinburgh, Manchester and Birmingham. Practical arrangements were made by Joseph Sabine, who had been restored to his administrative position as vice-president of the society. To evade accusations of overspending, the report added that a large part of its acquisitions had been obtained by gift.[76]

Spending on plants increased, as Sabine promoted the purchase of exotic items, but led to criticism from specialist zoologists. In 1836 the Revd Frederick William Hope, president of the Entomological Society, who had been elected onto the council of the Zoological Society in the previous year, observed that expenditure on plants had doubled between 1831 and 1835, amounting to nearly £900 *per annum*. Hope proposed that expenditure should be reduced, since the introduction of rare plants was 'not a legitimate object of the society'. His motion was seconded by Vigors, but it was rejected by the other council members present.[77] Hope again tried to cut spending by suggesting that expenses over £500 should require the approval of a general meeting of the society, but only Vigors supported his motion.[78] The Tory coterie, which had by this time taken control of the council, appointed Sabine as superintendent of the plant department and gave him limited power to use the society's funds and staff.[79]

With the introduction of exotic plants, the council gradually but steadily improved recreational facilities at the zoo. In February 1829 the Zoological Society received an application from the wife of one Samuel Dawes, warehouseman and confectioner of Albany Street, to open a stall in the zoo, but delayed its decision presumably because the selling of confectionery was held to compromise the society's status as a scientific institution.[80] With increasing attendance at the zoo, however, there were flocks of beverage salesmen at the exit, waiting for thirsty visitors to emerge after several

---

[76] *Reports of the council and auditors* (1834), 9.

[77] ZSL, MC, iv, fos 321, 337.

[78] ZSL, MC, iv, fo. 331, 382, 433–4.

[79] ZSL, MC, iv, fos 424, 433; v. 27–8. Sabine, however, died shortly afterwards, in 1837. An obituary acknowledged that 'his interference in the management of the Zoological Society' had led to 'serious dissensions', but had been supported by 'a numerous body of friends', which implies the Tory coterie and its allies within the society: *Gentleman's Magazine* (Apr. 1837), 435–6.

[80] ZSL, MC, i, fos 136, 141–2. Dawes had initially been a warehousemen, but it seems that after he went bankrupt in 1827 his wife ran a confectioner's shop on Albany Street. He became insolvent again in 1830: G. Elwick, *Bankrupt dictionary: from December 1820 to April 1843*, London 1843, 112.

hours without any refreshment. *The picturesque companion to the Regent's Park, Zoological Gardens, Colosseum, and Diorama* (1832) complained that 'a number of pot boys' were hanging around the gate with cans of beer.[81] As a result, the council resumed its discussions by appointing a special committee consisting of Vigors, Sykes and Marshall Hall, physician and ally of the anti-nepotistic Robert Grant. They specified that the potential tenant should be 'the more respectable confectioner', whose products would be of 'a superior description'. Dawes's application was therefore examined again, and the sale of drinks and light refreshments had commenced by the opening of the summer season of 1835.[82] Outdoor sitting areas were arranged, with chairs and benches in front of the monkey cage and the elephant house.

By improving its floral displays and recreational facilities, the London Zoo came to resemble more closely commercial pleasure gardens. Yet it did not cross the Rubicon: unlike its powerful commercial rival, the London Zoo restrained itself from hosting those showy events that were irrelevant to the avowed object of the Zoological Society, viz. the advancement and diffusion of zoological knowledge. In April 1833 some council members proposed that music performance should be held in the evenings (as in the Vauxhall Gardens), but this was an alarming suggestion to other council members and was thrown out at the next meeting: it opponents had rallied its forces to outnumber the proponents. Subsequently, the society's general meeting recommended that the council should make arrangements for concerts 'as an experiment', but the proposition was again vetoed by a majority of seven at the council meeting.[83] The society's reluctance to move into such ventures again came to the fore when balloon ascents became very popular with the public. In 1836 the Vauxhall Gardens contracted with Charles Green, a famous balloonist, to undertake an ascent, and it seemed that other proprietors might be tempted to follow suit. The London Zoo, however, remained unwilling to become involved while Edward Cross invited Green's *Royal Nassau* in 1838, in his foiled attempt to add variety to the entertainments that he provided.[84]

Judging from the council minutes, it seems that there was a fear of associating the zoo with anything that might appear to be a commercial venture. Here the scientific identity of the Zoological Society provided a counter-balance against the profit-oriented management. Reforming administrators

[81] Anon., *A picturesque companion to the Regent's Park, Zoological Gardens, Colosseum, and Diorama*, London 1832, 28.

[82] ZSL, MC, iii, fos 443, 448, 453; iii, fos 46–7, 61, 207, 214–15, 219.

[83] ZSL, MC, iii, fos 201, 383, 435–6; MM, i, fo. 397.

[84] ZSL, MM, i, fo. 314; iv, fo. 210; *Mirror*, 26 May 1838. The ascent from the Surrey Zoo, however, ended in failure, and the balloon was destroyed by the disgruntled crowd: Altick, *Shows of London*, 323 n. 84. See also J. Conlin, 'Vauxhall revisited: the afterlife of a London pleasure garden, 1770–1859', *Journal of British Studies* lxv (2006), 718–43.

defined the zoo primarily as a resource for scientific research and insisted that it be managed economically and efficiently. A series of reforms were accordingly put into effect in the early 1830s, and even after their supporters had lost the initiative to the Tory coterie in 1835, science continued to be a crucial focus for the society. As a result, the London Zoo expanded its recreational facilities, but it did not go as far as its rival, the Surrey Zoo, which demonstrated the antithesis of a science-oriented management. At a time when urban entertainments were becoming increasingly commercialised, the scientific identity of the Zoological Society underscored the management policy of the London Zoo.

The vision of harmony

In the aftermath of the Napoleonic Wars, the government implemented a series of urban regeneration projects, termed 'metropolitan improvements' by contemporary critics. It is true that London had already undergone earlier periods of urban development and that the areas covered by the metropolitan improvements were limited. Yet their impact was immense in certain areas, where new streets were laid out, lined with neo-classical buildings. The Houses of Parliament, the Bank of England, London Bridge, London University and the British Museum were all restructured or newly built and came to represent the political, economic and cultural identity of the nation.[85] Regent's Park was a pivotal locus of urban regeneration during its earlier stage. Although the area within and surrounding the park was restructured as a residential quarter, it also hosted two amusement buildings that offered cutting-edge visual spectacle. One was the Colosseum, designed by Decimus Burton as an octagonal version of the Pantheon. In it was installed a panorama of the metropolis as if viewed from the Cupola of St Paul's Cathedral. There was also an indoor garden with a display of antique statues, ornamental plants and foreign animals.[86] The other was the Diorama, which exhibited landscape painting that appeared to change gradually by means of the skilful use of specifically arranged materials and artificial lights.[87] One of the earliest guides to Regent's Park was entitled a *Picturesque guide to the Regent's Park: with accurate descriptions of the Colosseum, the Diorama, and the Zoological Gardens* (1829), suggesting that Regent's Park had become a fash-

---

[85] B. Bergdoll, *European architecture, 1750–1890*, Oxford 2000, 120–7.

[86] Altick, *Shows of London*, 173–83; Dana Arnold, 'Decimus Burton and the urban picturesque', in Dana Arnold (ed.), *The picturesque in late Georgian England*, London 1995, 51–6.

[87] Altick, *Shows of London*, 163–72.

ionable new attraction, and it indeed featured in contemporary 'silver fork' novels as the north end of the map of Nash's urban regeneration.[88]

Urban regeneration also affected visual representations of the metropolis. The period from the 1820s to the 1850s marked the appearance of a new genre of topographical painting, which was characterised by James Elmes's *Metropolitan improvements* (1827). Whereas previously topographical prints were concerned with the preservation of antiquarian monuments, *Metropolitan improvements* associated the new neoclassical public buildings with the rise of 'Modern Rome'.[89] The book could be read as a virtual tour of London that began with the celebrated Regent's Park and passed through various sites of urban development on its way to St James's Park. The growing popularity of the new topographical paintings suggests that there was a desire to possess a comprehensive view of the city by means of a range of different views of different localities. This was reflected in the common format of publication. Prints appeared serially with short commentaries so that they could eventually be gathered together into a folio volume which would present a complete picture of London.[90]

Architectural grandeur was not the only means of representing urban social life. The sight of animals was also one of the critical elements that formed popular perceptions of London. The exploitation of domestic animals such as cattle, sheep and carriage horses became a pictorial motif for the visual representation of metropolitan luxury and excessive commercialism, while increasing awareness of animals in the city arguably fostered the animal welfare movement. At the same time, however, a different mode of depicting animal life was created, largely by the London Zoo. In contrast with the crowded livestock market and the heavy traffic in the city, the zoo presented an ideal vision of animal life. Most revealing was Leigh Hunt's opening comment for his literary tour of the zoo: 'This sudden exhibition of life, in shapes to which we are unaccustomed, reminds us of the wonderful and ever-renewing vitality of all things. Those animals look as fresh, and strong, and beautiful, as if they were born in a new beginning of the world.'[91]

Although Hunt became sceptical when he observed the actual living condition of the zoo animals, it is obvious that initially he was impressed with their vitality. If this form of expression had a visual counterpart, it was George Scharf's *Six views of the Zoological Gardens* (1835). The first five of

[88] R. Hyde and V. Cumming, 'The prints of Benjamin Read, tailor and printmaker', *Print Quarterly* xlii (2000), 262–84; E. Copeland, 'Crossing Oxford Street: silverfork geopolitics, *Eighteenth-Century Life* xxv (2001), 116–34

[89] Peltz, 'Aesthecizing the ancestral city'.

[90] Adams, *London illustrated*; Potts, 'Picturing the modern metropolis'; C. Arscott, 'The representation of the city in the visual arts', in M. Daunton (ed.), *The Cambridge urban history of Britain*, III: *1840–1950*, Cambridge 2000, 811–32.

[91] J. H. L. Hunt, 'A visit to the Zoological Gardens', *New Monthly Magazine* (Aug. 1836), 479.

the six lithographs depicted popular attractions at the zoo: the aviary, the bear pit, the monkey cage, the clock tower and the elephant house. The last picture, of Tommy the chimpanzee, was added later when his arrival caused a public sensation.[92] These lithographs became the most popular illustrations of the zoo at that time, and are still occasionally reproduced to show what the London Zoo looked like in its early days. Yet they should be interpreted as constructed representations of the zoo, characterised by the representation of harmony in two respects: the social mingling of people from different walks of life, and the interactions between zoo animals and human spectators. An analysis of the social background, business practice and cultural life of this artist helps to explain how harmony between different social classes and with other living beings was visualised and prevailed.

George Scharf was born in Bavaria into a wealthy tradesman's family and studied lithography in Munich.[93] In the aftermath of the Napoleonic Wars, he settled in London and set himself up in scientific and topographical lithography.[94] His earnings largely depended on regular commissions from a number of geologists and zoologists among whom were William Buckland, Richard Owen and Charles Darwin. Scharf was not good at bargaining: on one occasion he regretted 'working too cheap for Darwin', and on another he was advised by Charles Hullmundel, who was in the same business but more profitably, to 'ask a price which may pay you, as they [clients] expect it will come high'.[95] In July 1836 Scharf had to withdraw from the New Water Colour Society, which provided a social point of connection for topographical lithographers, because he could no longer afford the monthly subscription of 5s.

However, although Scharf did not make a fortune, he could afford to provide for his family (two sons, his wife and her sister) and to enrich their cultural life. He often worked more than ten hours a day, but he spent his limited spare time in taking his family to explore the sights and spectacles of London, such as the exhibitions at the Royal Academy and the New Water Colour Society, the British Museum, the Gallery of Practical Science, the Surrey Zoo and, most frequently, the London Zoo. He sometimes attended

---

92 W. Blunt, *The ark in the park: the zoo in the nineteenth century*, London 1976, 38–9.

93 For the history of lithography see M. Twyman, *Lithography, 1800–50: the techniques of drawing on stone in England and France and their application in works of topography*, London 1970.

94 P. Jackson, *George Scharf's London: sketches and watercolours of a changing city, 1820–50*, London 1987; F. S. Schwarzbach, 'George Scharf and early Victorian London', in I. B. Nadel and F. S. Schwarzbach (eds), *Victorian artists and the city: a collection of critical essays*, New York 1980, 93–105.

95 Scharf journal, entries for 21 July 1836 and 30 June 1838, Sir George Johann Scharf papers, National Portrait Gallery Archive, London, NPG7/3/7/2/1/2; Charles Hullmandel to Scharf, 'Thursday 25 Oct.', Scharf papers, NPG7/3/7/2/2/23. The Water Colour Society provided a social point of connection for topographical lithographers, as shown by Twyman, *Lithography*, 171–4.

Figure 6. George Scharf, 'View of the elephant paddock and the wapiti house', from *Six views of the Zoological Gardens*, London 1835.

lectures at the Mechanics' Institute and scientific meetings at the Geological and the Zoological Societies and was fascinated by Richard Owen's lecture on comparative anatomy.[96] His interest in that subject, which was at the frontier of zoological study at that time, was likely to have come from his expectation that scientific knowledge would improve the accuracy of his zoological illustrations. On another occasion he was interested in William Buckland's *Geology and mineralogy considered with reference to natural theology* (1836), one of the earliest examples of a popular science bestseller, written for a non-specialist audience.[97] Certainly, Scharf belonged to those social groups that enjoyed widening access to sites of scientific knowledge and the media through which it was disseminated.

In June 1834 Scharf began working on his zoo illustrations, which took a year to complete. Initially, some prints were purchased individually by his acquaintances and regular clients. At that time Scharf seemed to be desperate for money, because his adolescent sons had not yet found ways to

[96] Scharf journal, entries for 12 Dec. 1836 and 15 Apr. 1837, Scharf papers, NPG7/3/7/2/1/2.
[97] Topham, 'Role of the *Bridgewater Treatises*', 397–430, and 'Beyond the "common context"', 233–62.

earn their own livings.[98] In such circumstances, his personal connection with Richard Owen, who sat on the council of the Zoological Society, counted for a great deal. Presumably with Owen's approval, Scharf obtained the exceptional permission of the society to publish his works and even to sell them at the zoo gate.[99] During the first fortnight, ten prints were sold at the gate; within less than a month, sales had doubled to twenty-two. Scharf confessed in his diary that this was more than he could have expected.[100] He realised that favourable reviews appearing in many journals, especially those printed in the *Morning Advertisers* and the *True Sun,* had dramatically improved sales. He noted that 'such Printsellers as would not take any before' were offering to sell his lithographs.[101] Sales indeed boomed: 646 sets (441 in plain and 205 in colour) were sold in 1836.[102]

Close examination of the lithographs and their production process helps to explain their popularity. 'A view of the Elephant paddock and Wapiti house' (*see* Figure 6) indicates that the angle of the scene was selected to frame all the main features: the wapiti, the rhinoceros, the elephant and the paddock with a pond specifically designed for elephant bathing. In the foreground a gentleman is feeding the elephant. Close by a group is watching the animal grab a bun with his trunk. To the right of the scene, there is another group of spectators sitting on chairs, perhaps observing the feeding of the elephant, or simply indulging in conversation under the trees. The scene thus tells of several stories taking place in different places within and around the Elephant paddock. They are drawn together and brought to life by the girl cutting across the foreground towards the enclosure for a close look at the feeding. Another girl, half turning away from the elephant as though in fright or in awe, also adds to the animation of the scene. Overall, animals, spectators, architectures, plants and ornaments were integrated into a picturesque scene with the emphasis on harmony and animation. This style of composition is shared with the other four lithographs (excluding a portrait of a chimpanzee).

The principles of Scharf's designs become more explicit when compared to Hakewill's *Ten views of the Zoological Gardens* (1831). Notable characteristics of Hakewill's lithograph are unbroken vistas, horizontal depth and limited human presence. His 'View of the Terrace Walk' (*see* Figure 7) constitutes a vista from the beginning of the promenade towards the bear pit. The appearance in the background of a church and neoclassical terraces suggests that the Hakewill is drawing in landscape which lies beyond the

---

[98]   Scharf journal, entries for 4, 18 July 1835, Scharf papers, NPG7/3/7/2/1/1.

[99]   Scharf recorded that one of the council members of the society appeared to have tried to prevent him from selling his lithographs at the zoo gate: ibid. 23 Nov. 1835; ZSL, MC, iv. fos 118, 180, 259.

[100] Scharf journal, entry for 7 July 1835, Scharf papers, NPG7/3/7/2/1/1.

[101] Ibid. 8 Nov. 1835.

[102] Ibid. 2 Feb. 1837.

Figure 7. James Hakewill, 'View of the terrace walk looking towards the bear pit', from *Ten views of the Zoological Gardens*.

zoos boundaries, and hence confirms his background as a landscape painter. By contrast, for Scharf, whose topographical prints portray everyday life and social scenes in the vibrant urban milieu, the most important element was to capture a moment of animation which appeared casually through the interplay between different components of the scene. Indeed, Scharf explained this in his own words, in a draft letter in which he was attempting to challenge the zoo's regulations on the hours for drawing:[103]

> The impulse of the moment, when the artist could catch an animal in an interesting attitude or expression, or see any other time the effect of buildings, groups of figures, trees etc., particularly at sunset, should, I think, no more be halted by restriction, than the naturalist of another sort, the poet or author, should be hindered to describe of what he observes at the moment.

Scharf's emphasis on animation, involving throngs of spectators, was appreciated by the *Spectator*: 'The subjects and the animals are very accurately delineated. The animation of the scene on a fine day, when the gardens are thronged, is also well represented.'[104] While the reviewer regretted that the

---

[103] Draft letter inserted in volume 2 of Scharf journal. His request was, however, rejected by the Zoological Society: Scharf papers, NPG7/3/7/2/1/2.
[104] *Spectator*, 12 Dec. 1837, 187.

overall atmosphere of the zoo was not presented more clearly, he acknowledged that Scharf was one of the few artists capable of sketching 'populous scenes at all tolerably'. On the whole, prints from his *Six views of the Zoological Gardens* were categorised as urban topography, thereby ranking lower than landscape painting in the artistic hierarchy, but they were regarded as a successful examples of the genre.

The brisk sale of Scharf's lithographs not only supported the artist financially but also benefited the zoo. Since his zoo illustrations were acclaimed by art critics, the zoo was offering aesthetically approved pictorial motifs and secured its status as a fashionable urban resort. Since Scharf produced various visual images of London as well as a being a beneficiary of the growing public institutions of art and science, it is likely that his business practice and cultural condition together helped to create a painting style that aestheticised the harmony of human-animal interactions. In this sense, Scharf was not only a key witness but also a critical contributor to the zoo's development as a cultural amenity for the metropolis.

At some point in the early 1830s, Joseph Wilkins, an old-fashioned country resident, recorded his travels to London in a diary, which was later published by the Religious Tract Society. Although it is hard to tell whether the diary is a genuine record, it was certainly edited to explain how best to learn from a visit to London without succumbing to metropolitan vices. One day, Wilkins took his nephew Frank to the Tower Menagerie, but as Frank was disappointed by its limited collection, they went to the London Zoo by taking an omnibus for the first time. The drive gave Frank time to reflect: as the name of the place that they were heading for was unfamiliar to him, he wondered why Londoners called it the 'Zoological Gardens' rather than the 'Wild Beast Gardens', just as they dubbed the carriage that he was on board 'omnibus' rather than just 'coach'.[105] This casual thought would be a natural response for a young visitor, but probably the most important one for the London Zoo.

Obviously, the use of the term 'zoological' signified the scientific orientation of the management of the animal collection. As expressed in the first prospectus of the Zoological Society, the London Zoo had to be distinguished from any previous form of animal exhibitions (such as the Exeter Change Menagerie and the Tower Menagerie). Although science was not an explicit component in the actual structure of the zoo, it was still an essential element that underpinned the society's management of the zoo, especially when compared to the commercial entrepreneurship of such as the Surrey Zoo. By contrast, the term 'gardens' had positive connotations: extensive

---

105 Anon., *Walks in London, or extracts from the journal of Mr. Joseph Wilkins*, London [?1840], 91–4. The year of their visit to London is not recorded, but it was presumably before 1831, when the transportation of the animals from the Tower Menageries to the London Zoo took place (hence Frank's disappointment), and definitely before 1835, when the last animal was removed from the Tower.

grounds, picturesque scenery and fresh air. In a mood of public celebration of 'metropolitan improvements', various newspapers and periodicals disseminated these images, which many spectators seemed to appreciate on their first visit to the zoo.

By the mid-1830s the London Zoo was established as a new urban amenity. Although this was the achievement of the governing body of the Zoological Society of London, problems remained. One was related to the conflict between science and commerce in the management of the zoo; the other was linked to its privileged admission system. As the zoo enjoyed increasing popularity, the admission system could not function effectively and attracted public criticism. The 1835 council election provided the Zoological Society with an opportunity to address these issues on the initiative of the rising Tory coterie. However, priorities shifted: to the acquisition of the new animals that would symbolise the development of the Zoological Society. In tracing this change, the next chapter explores the third theme of the book – the meaning of collecting and displaying animals.

2

Collecting and Displaying

The top celebrity in Paris in 1827 was not a human, but Zaraf the giraffe. For the first time since the sixteenth century a giraffe had been brought to Europe. On 30 June she was welcomed at the *Muséum national d'histoire naturelle* by thousands of Parisians, with great enthusiasm and curiosity. During the summer season, she was such a popular sensation that there was a new fashion boom: 'every fashion turned to *à la giraffe*; and even the ladies wore dresses, and the men carried handkerchiefs, bearing the portrait of the animal'.[1] A similar celebration was repeated nearly a decade later, this time in London, but on an even larger scale. Britain's first public exhibition of giraffes was hosted by the London Zoo and was the most frequently visited attraction of that year. The extraordinary popularity of the giraffes in both Paris and London could be partly explained by the rarity and extraordinary appearance of the animal, but it was also culturally constructed within a specific historical context.

By taking the example of the sensational exhibition of the giraffes, this chapter discusses two interrelated themes concerning the London Zoo. The first centres on the networks of animal collecting that enabled the Zoological Society to obtain its giraffes. The society took the advantage of the interconnected system of communication that operated across the British Empire. This system was not, however, identical to the animal collecting networks which often stretched way beyond the colonial field. This leads to the question of whether it is valid to define the animal-collecting networks within the referential frame of empire. The other theme is the implications of animal display. The zoo has been analysed as a manifestation of British imperial desires, endeavours and anxieties, but whether this approach is best suited to explain the meaning of animal display is worthy of further analysis.

An enigma of natural history

Empire has recently provided a powerful frame of reference for the cultural history of Victorian Britain. While a variety of sites and institutions ranging

---

[1] Knight, *Menageries*, ii. 342; *Le Belle Assemblée*, 1 Sept. 1828, 120. Zaraf is today portrayed as a heroine in documentary novels and children's books which broadly illustrate the history of human-animal relationships. See, for example, M. Allin, *Zaraf: a giraffe's true story, from deep in Africa to the heart of Paris*, London 1998, and L. Hillard, *A giraffe for France*, Sydney 1998.

from museums and galleries to high streets has been analysed within this framework, an interpretation has gained currency that suggests that empire offered a narrative space in which national identity *vis-à-vis* colonial 'otherness' was represented by means of spectacular displays and exhibits.[2] The London Zoo has not escaped analysis in these terms. Harriet Ritvo has suggested that it emerged from a two-fold imperial project: for mastery of the colonies, and for mastery of nature. Likewise, Robert Jones has labelled it 'a showcase for the British imperial endeavour': animals were displayed as a colonial commodity, ready to be 'consumed' by those spectators who purchased the opportunity to enjoy watching them.[3] The London Zoo appeared to perform the same ideological function as colonial exhibitions and ethnological galleries, which together accelerated the commodification of the exotic within an imperial cultural frame. The 'imperial approach', however, has methodological deficiencies. Studies of nineteenth-century spectatorship tend to focus on the late Victorian era when imperial ideologies were brought into scenes of everyday life, but there are few comparable studies of the early nineteenth-century. As a result, the imperial approach can too easily be applied to a period when British imperial culture – as demonstrated in John MacKenzie's *Imperialism and popular culture* (1986) – had yet to reach its height.[4] The situation of the London Zoo in the 1830s can only be correctly understood if it is placed in its appropriate context, and not by viewing it retrospectively, from the heyday of imperial propaganda.

Moreover, in grouping it with other colonial exhibitions, the imperial approach fails to take note of the zoo's unique characteristics. The similarities, rather than differences between various forms of Victorian spectatorship are plainly expressed, for instance, in one article on ethnographical shows:

> Comparable spaces of spectacles such as zoos, botanical gardens, circuses, temporary or permanent exhibitions staged by missionary societies and museums of natural history, all exhibited other races and/or other species and testified to the imperialism of the nineteenth-century nation-state.[5]

A reductionistic attitude to empire has unfavourable side effects. Clearly, it

---

[2] Blanchard and others, *Human zoos*; Qureshi, *Peoples on parade*; P. Hoffenberg, *An empire on display: English, Indian, and Australian exhibitions from the Crystal Palace to the Great War*, Berkeley 2001; Auerbach and Hoffenberg, *Britain, the empire, and the world*; Schneer, *London 1900*; E. Rappaport, 'Art, commerce, or empire? The rebuilding of Regent Street, 1880–1927', *HWJ* viii (2002), 94–117.

[3] Ritvo, *Animal estate*, 205–42, and 'Zoological nomenclature and the empire of Victorian science', in B. Lightman (ed.), *Victorian science in context*, Chicago 1997, 336; Jones, '"The sight of creatures strange to our climate"', 2–5.

[4] J. M. MacKenzie (ed.), *Imperialism and popular culture*, Manchester 1986.

[5] R. Corbey, 'Ethnographic showcases, 1870–1930', *Cultural Anthropology* viii (1993), 338–69.

cannot explain why so many different forms of spectatorship – from museums to music halls – developed in the course of the nineteenth century, and how they differed from each other in shaping, and being shaped by, the cultural life of the people.

Above all, the imperial approach pays little attention to the disjunction between the two different sets of operation that enabled the zoo to function: capturing animals and transporting them alive to the zoo on the one hand, and arranging for them to be displayed to the public on the other. The concept of 'imperial zoo' assumes that the former operation and the latter were smoothly integrated, and that an analysis of animal display reflects (and in some cases responds to) the imperial ideologies that shaped the zoo. It is wrong, however, to interpret 'collecting' and 'displaying' as seamlessly connected: the meanings of the animals could change when they were transferred from the first stage to that of the latter.

To avoid the methodological pitfalls of the concept of 'imperial zoo', it is helpful to consider various questions: why were certain animals particularly valued for exhibition; how were the animal-collecting networks activated to acquire the required animals; how were these animals then displayed in the zoo; and how did spectators understand them. By answering these questions, this chapter aims to present a vantage point from which a full range of agents and places – including those located beyond the reach of the British Empire – could be placed in perspective. Although the giraffe exhibition seems to present just one case study, analysis of it casts light on a significant moment, when hitherto disconnected agents and places were coordinated to form extensive networks. The popularity of the exhibition also produced a rich variety of documents showing how the zoo set the spatial frame within which encounters with the giraffes were given shapes and meanings. These peculiarities help to outline the distinctive aspects of 'collecting' and 'displaying'.

Why was the giraffe so special? Until the late eighteenth century the giraffe had often been thought to be a creature of myth like the unicorn, the griffin and the phoenix.[6] In a natural history print of 1663 by Wenceslaus Hollar (see Figure 8), a giraffe is depicted together with a camel, a flying dragon and other small animals and plants. As this image provides no clear boundary between the real and the imaginary, the giraffe could be perceived in either way. In another print produced a century later by Andrew Bell, co-founder of the Encyclopaedia Britannica (1768–71), the height of the giraffe is clearly exaggerated (see Figure 9), even though this print was made for the English edition of Buffon's Histoire naturelle, générale et particulière (1785), the most comprehensive and authentic natural history book of its time. Obviously, these prints were not drawn from life: they were based on textual references that could be traced back to Pliny's Natural history, in

---

6   B. Laufer, The giraffe in history and art, Chicago 1928; A. I. Dagg and J. B. Foster, The giraffe: its biology, behaviour and ecology, New York 1976, 1–9.

Figure 8. Wenceslaus Hollar, 'A giraffe with a camel and a flying dragon' (1663), from *Animalium, ferarum, & bestiarum, florum, fructuum, muscarum, vermiumque*, London 1674. Wellcome Library, London, no. 24373i.

which the giraffe was named *Camelopardalis* for its singular combination of the camel's figure and the leopard's dappled skin.[7] While the influence of Pliny's description was notable in Bell's print, the idea that the giraffe was a half-fabulous creature remained unchanged.

By the end of the eighteenth century, however, both naturalists and explorers had come to believe that what had been described as the *Camelopardalis* by the Romans did indeed exist. While new information was increasingly gathered from travellers who had observed wild giraffes in the African interior, some material objects thought to be their bones and skins were sent to England too. In 1787 William Paterson, a botanical collector travelling inland from Cape Town, measured the body of a giraffe that his companion had shot down. Its remains were then brought back to England and came into the possession of John Hunter.[8] The accumulation of information tantalised naturalists, because they had no way of testing its veracity. Thomas Maude of Westminster sighed over the lack of reliable information in his *Observations on a subject in natural history* (1792), a small tract dedicated to Joseph Banks: 'Numerous are the icons of this quadruped, but most of them

[7] J. Bostock and H. T. Riley (eds), *The natural history of Pliny*, London 1855, ii. 277.

[8] W. Paterson, *A narrative of four journeys into the country of the Hottentots and Caffraria in the years 1777, 1778, 1779*, London 1789, 126–7; L. C. Rootmaaker, *The zoological exploration of South Africa, 1650–1790*, Rotterdam 1989, 176

Figure 9. Andrew Bell, 'A giraffe in the wild towering above an African tribesman' (1785), from Georges-Louis Leclerc, comte de Buffon, *Natural history, general and particular*, trans. William Smellie, Edinburgh 1785. Wellcome Library, London, no. 39851i.

Figure 10. Thomas Bewick, 'Cameleopard', from *A general history of quadrupeds*, Newcastle-upon-Tyne 1790. Cambridge University Library.

seem to have been made from loose descriptions verbally given by relators, rather than from the object.'[9] An erroneous depiction of the animal could be found in Thomas Bewick's *A general history of quadrupeds* (1790). It is a faithful visual translation of what Pliny had written in his *Natural history* – the mixture of camel's form and leopard's spotted skin (*see* Figure 10) , but it was almost impossible to judge whether the picture was of a real giraffe, because there were only few who had seen the animal with their own eyes. The solution was to bring the animal back alive. Although this seemed a far from easy task, Maude believed that it would not be long before natural history would gain credit for providing accurate knowledge about 'the figure

[9]   T. Maude, *Observations on a subject in natural history*, London 1792, 5. Only twenty-four copies were printed, for distribution to the author's close friends. Two are in the British Library.

FRONTISPIECE.

Encampment among the Great Namaquais.

Figure 11. François de Vaillant, *Travels from the Cape of Good-Hope into the interior parts of Africa*, London 1790, frontispiece. Cambridge University Library.

and economy of this almost secreted curiosity'. For Maude, the giraffe was a symbol of the promised advance of natural history.[10]

There were some grounds for optimism. In the 1780s François Le Vaillant, a French explorer and ornithologist, had organised a series of expeditions into the African interior from the Cape Province and had documented his encounter with wild giraffes.[11]

Published in English in 1790, his two-volume *Travels from the Cape of Good Hope into the interior parts of Africa* became a substantial source of information about this mysterious creature. The first volume has a picture of a giraffe on the front page, suggesting that Le Vaillant himself recognised that the discovery of the giraffe was one of his great achievements. Le Vaillant appears in the right foreground as a dignified, master-explorer, who is directing his two hounds in the chase (*see* Figure 11). In the direction in which the dogs are running, stands the giraffe, motionless and almost afloat, on the border between the two different elements in the picture. In an appendix male and female giraffes are described, with illustrations which emphasise the difference between the sexes and demonstrate that Le Vaillant had carefully examined both.

It was not only the French explorer who demystified this enigma of the natural world. In the 1810s William John Burchell, an English naturalist, travelled in the African interior and published *Travels in the interior of South Africa* (1822–4).[12] Like Le Vaillant, he was eager to observe with his own eyes 'the tallest of all the quadrupeds in the world'. When his party found its footsteps, his expectation grew:[13]

> from the time of the Romans until the middle of the last century, [the giraffe] was so little known to the nations of Europe, as to have been at length considered by most people as a fabulous creature, one not existing on the globe. No person who has read, even the popular books of natural history, could, I think, behold for the first time, the ground over which he is walking, imprinted with the recent footsteps of a *camelopardalis*, without feeling some strange and peculiar interests at the sight.

By the time that he finished his travels, Burchell had collected over 50,000 specimens including the bodies of male and female giraffes, one apiece, which were then donated to the British Museum. Now, with the authentic

---

[10] Ibid. 34.

[11] S. Huigen, *Knowledge and colonialism: eighteenth-century travellers in South Africa*, Leiden 2009, 119–45; M. L Pratt, *Imperial eyes: travel writing and transculturation*, London 1992, 86–7, 93.

[12] M. Gunn and L. E. Codd, *Botanical exploration of South Africa*, Cape Town 1981, 109–10; F. Driver and L. Martins, '"The struggle for luxuriance": William Burchell collects tropical nature', in F. Driver and L. Martins (eds), *Tropical vision in the age of empire*, Chicago 2009, 59–74.

[13] W. J. Burchell, *Travels in the interior of South Africa*, London 1824, ii. 248.

stuffed specimen exhibited in the museum's stair-well, Burchell had established that what had been thought to be a fabulous creature really existed.[14]

Finally, a living giraffe was brought to England in 1827. It was a gift from the Egyptian pasha to George IV, who kept it at Windsor as a pet. Although it was not exhibited to the public, many copies of a picture claiming to be a real sketch of the giraffe were distributed. When supplying one of these pictures, the *Literary Gazette* sought to confirm its authenticity by insisting that the sketch had been drawn from life when the giraffe was first brought ashore.[15] By the late 1820s, therefore, knowledge of the giraffe had circulated beyond a limited circle of naturalists and explorers. There were a number of people who believed in the animal, even though they had hardly had a chance to see it with their own eyes.

For the proprietors of animal shows and zoos, the giraffe should have been an ideal acquisition. Even before the opening of the London Zoo, menageries and shows of performing animals had been familiar to London residents and visitors. While elephants and lions had become commonplace, proprietors sought the unusual and the bizarre, as is suggested by the popularity of freak shows, both human and animal, during this period.[16] A large array of handbills, collected in the John Johnson Collection of the Bodleian Library, give a first-hand glimpse of how they tried to rouse the curiosity of the public. One announced the exhibition in the Strand in 1821 of a monstrous American bison, though with a somewhat dubious description: '[He] weighs nearly two tons and when full grown stands upwards of seven feet high!'[17] Another bill (*see* Figure 12), circulated by Wombwell's travelling menagerie, stressed the novelty of its collection. The snappy copy begins 'Living Wonders! Just Arrived!', emphasising that it was not to be a display of stuffed specimens, but of living animals, newly brought to England. 'The Ravenous Wolf' was said to be 'the only one to be seen in the Kingdom', while an orangutan was roughly translated as the 'Wild Man of the Woods'. Malformed animals were sometimes put on show. At Charing Cross, a 1s. show of 'the Wonderful American Hen with three wings and four legs' took place in 1837.[18] It might be assumed that professional zoologists would denounce such as vulgar curiosity, but in fact they could articulate, if not in public, personal interest in freaks. In January 1844 Michael Faraday wrote to Richard Owen to ask if Owen wished to obtain a 'tripeded' frog from him. The inquiry reminded

14 *Penny Magazine*, 30 June 1832, 124.

15 *Literary Gazette*, 25 Aug. 1827, 553–4; R. Lydekker, 'On old pictures of giraffes and zebras', *Proceedings of the General Meetings of the Zoological Society of London* ii (1904), 339–42.

16 Q. Sadiah, 'Displaying Sara Baartman: the "Hottentot Venus"', *BJHS* lxii (2004), 233–7; T. Neil, 'White wings and six-legged muttons: the freakish animal', in M. Tromp (ed.), *Victorian freaks: the social context of freakery in Britain*, Columbus 2008, 60–75.

17 Bodl. Lib., JJC, Animals on Show 1(20).

18 Ibid. 3 (25).

Living Wonders!

Just Arrived,

To be seen Here,

One of the moſt beautiful Animals in the World,

The Great Male Panther,

Or Hunting Tiger,

The Ravenous Wolf, the only one to be seen in the Kingdom,

The Great Mufflong,

From Mocco--the Lion's Provider--the Racoons--the Catamundays,
the Sleeping Sloth--the Long-Armed Ape, and

Wild Man of the Woods,

The White Faced Ape, from Barbary--the Ring-tailed Monkey, or
Whistler of the Wood--the Orange Marmaset,

The smallest of all the Monkey Tribe--the largest of all Birds in the Air,

The Condor Vulture,

The Black Eagle, from Rusia--the Scarlet Maccaws, from Demirara,
The Horned Owls, from Hudson's Bay--the Love Bird, from Botany Bay,
The large and small Cockatoos, from Botany Bay,
The Grey Necklace Doves, from *Barbary.*
And various other Birds too numerous to mention.

Foreign Birds and Beasts bought, sold, or exchanged,

At Wombwell's Managerie, 207, Piccadilly.

Sutton, Printer, Britannia-street, Gray's Inn Road, London.

Figure 12. An announcement for Wombwell's menagerie. Bodleian Library, Oxford, JJC, Animals on Show 3 (25).

Owen that his father-in-law, William Clift, had once caught a 'quinqueped' frog. In his reply Owen humorously added that 'the unhappy individual [was] fated to pay for his ancestor's profusion … If one frog has five legs another must have three: the proper quantity being allowed'.[19] Owen was indeed one of the keenest observers of the giraffes when they arrived at the London Zoo.

Early nineteenth-century London witnessed a growing and constant demand for the exhibition of animals that were extraordinary in size, physical appearance or personality, yet also real. This set the stage for the giraffe exhibition at the London Zoo.

Beyond the empire

'[B]ut our giraffes – our four giraffes!', a British zoologist crowed when the London Zoo took delivery of four giraffes in May 1836. The exclamation was soon echoed in triumph in the *Mirror*, a pioneer of illustrated weeklies covering topical news of science, art and literature.[20] The exhibition of the four giraffes did indeed cause a sensation, but how joyfully they were welcomed by the British public is hard to imagine without looking back ten years.

When the Egyptian pasha presented the king of England with a giraffe in 1827, he also sent a specimen to France. George IV's giraffe was kept in the Royal Menagerie, then in Windsor Great Park, as the king's favourite pet, but died a few years later as a result of a poor diet and an injury that it had received when captured.[21] By contrast, the French giraffe was displayed in the *Muséum national d'histoire naturelle* and survived. So sharp was the contrast with France that there was even a rumour that the king's giraffe had been destroyed by its corpulent master riding on it for fun. The giraffe remained an object of chagrin and jealousy until the Zoological Society was able to exhibit its own four giraffes in May 1836. Hence the exclamation: 'If we compare the livestock the English collection scarcely equals the French; our feline animals are very inferior; but our giraffes – our four giraffes!'

This gives a deeper insight into the inferiority complex that British zoologists had been suffering *vis-à-vis* France. In the aftermath of the Napoleonic Wars, it was obvious that Britain had achieved supremacy in terms of trade, commerce and military power. In the realm of science, however, British preeminence seemed uncertain; there were even claims that Britain was lagging far behind France. In 1826 the renowed geologist Charles Lyell asked a question of the readership of the *Quarterly Review*:[22]

---

19 *The correspondence of Michael Faraday*, ed. F. A. J. L. James, London 1996, iii. 180.
20 *Mirror*, 3 Dec. 1836, 369.
21 *John Bull*, 5 May 1828.
22 [C. Lyell], 'Scientific institutions', *Quarterly Review* (June 1826), 150.

As England is not only the most affluent of modern nations, but the grand centre of commercial activity and communication between the most distant portions of the globe; as her colonial possessions are more diversified in climate and local character than those of any other European empire, we may naturally ask why her museums do not display a proportional extent and magnificence, and set all foreign rivalry at defiance?

Charles Babbage would be ready to answer this question. In his polemical *Reflections on the decline of science in England and on some of its causes* (1830), he insisted that the backwardness of British science was the result of the poor organisation of scientific institutions and called for reform of the Royal Society.[23] Outside the scientific community, Babbage's 'science in decline' claim seemed to be accepted, as it justified further criticism of the kind of science that did not bring any public good. The author of a review article published in the *Athenaeum* in January 1831 agreed with Babbage, suggesting that a more significant cause of the decline was that men of science did not work to benefit the wider public. With a view to building good relations between the scientific community and the wider public, the reviewer demanded the application of science to commerce, to industry and to recreation.[24]

Such criticism was sound, especially when it was directed towards natural history, especially zoology. Botany and horticulture seemed more advanced than zoology, because Joseph Banks, former President of the Royal Society (1778–1820), had promoted the study and importing of foreign plants and had successfully established Kew Gardens, a landmark of botanical science that boasted a large collection and applied it to the horticultural luxury market and to agriculture.[25] On entomology, Kirby and Spencer published *An introduction to entomology* in 1822–3, which was acclaimed for transforming a conventionally dry subject, concerned with nomenclature and terminology, into entertaining but accurate narratives of the vibrant life of insects.[26] By contrast, zoology lacked a national institution of significance or any outstanding literary work that had caught the public imagination. It was castigated as a subject of complacent idle curiosity, a leisure activity for eccentric gentlemen. When the English translation of Cuvier's *Animal kingdome* appeared in 1828, the *Athenaeum* lamented the lack of an English-language equivalent:[27]

> As to natural history, it is esteemed as little more than an object of idle curiosity to a few, from which no amusement can be derived, and no profit.

[23] For the movement for reform of scientific institutions see Miller, 'Between hostile camps', 1–47.

[24] *Athenaeum*, 8 Jan. 1831, 25.

[25] Miller, 'Between hostile camps', 1–4; Drayton, *Nature's government*, 83–124.

[26] W. Kirby and W. Spencer, *An introduction to entomology: or elements of the natural history of insects*, London 1822–3; *Athenaeum*, 18 June 1828, 533.

[27] *Athenaeum*, 8 Apr. 1828, 341.

It is neither a luxury nor necessary of life, therefore, it is neglected; it is abandoned to the attention of a few gentlemen, whose independent fortune, or distinguished spirits, enable them to pursue knowledge for its own sake: and the profits of it, such as they are, fall to the share of Messrs Cross and Wombwell, *et id genus omne.*

Cross was by then the well-known proprietor of the Exeter Change Menagerie, while Wombwell ran a large travelling menagerie, the most popular attraction at the Bartholomew Fair in London.[28] The commentary made no reference to the London Zoo, which had not yet opened. What was expressed between the lines was that while France boasted the *Muséum national d'histoire naturelle*, where Cuvier was a professor in comparative anatomy, Britain had no equivalent institution.

That Britain was considered to play second fiddle in zoology helps to explain the eagerness of the Zoological Society to collect living giraffes. In order to establish its scientific reputation, the society needed a spectacular event or acquisitions which would bring home the outstanding nature of its animal collection. Giraffes could become that symbol. In fact, prior to the eventual arrival of the four giraffes in 1836, the Zoological Society had made several vain attempts to acquire one. The first, offered for sale in 1831 via a Fellow of the society, died on board ship. In 1833, after another approach, the zoo agreed to purchase a giraffe at the excessive price of £500, but again the animal died while being shipped from the Cape of Good Hope.[29] In the following year, another Fellow, James Burton, arrived at Leghorn [Livorno] in Italy with a giraffe and offered to sell it to the society. Although the society was willing, it feared that Burton would leave the animal at Leghorn for onward transportation rather than bringing it to London himself. Eventually, the society brought the negotiations to an end by insisting that 'a purchase would not be completed till after inspection in England'.[30] Several months later a similar offer reached the society from an agent in Spain, this time a price of £2,000 for a six-year-old giraffe. The society was reluctant to negotiate 'for the purchase at a high price of an animal at a distance from London'.[31]

These attempts suggest that capturing giraffes was possible, but the price extraordinarily high due to their rarity and the difficulty of catching them alive. It also became clear that the most difficult task was to secure their transport to London, which could not be achieved without close collaboration with naval and colonial agents. The intermediary in this was

---

28 *Morning Chronicle*, 8 Sept. 1828.
29 ZSL, MC, iii, fos 226–7, 230–1, 253; H. Scherren, *The Zoological Society of London: a sketch of its foundation and development and the story of its farm, museum, gardens, menageries and library*, London 1905, 61–2.
30 ZSL, MC, iii, fos 317–19, 325–6
31 ZSL, MC, iv, fo. 46; Scherren, *The Zoological Society*, 62.

J. R. Bouchier, an otherwise unknown Collector of Customs at Malta and a corresponding member of the Zoological Society. After the Napoleonic Wars, Britain had taken control of Malta and made use of it to defend her naval interests in the east and central Mediterranean.[32] As Malta had become a thriving naval base, Bouchier was at the heart of the imperial communication network. In 1833, following instructions from the Zoological Society, Bouchier contacted Patrick Campbell, Britain's consul-general in Egypt, who had occasionally donated living animals to the society, and solicited his support in negotiating with certain parties for the capture and shipment of giraffes.[33]

At the end of the year an agreement was reached with George Thibaut, a French trader living in Cairo, who in April 1834 set off with his Nubian attendants. He captured five giraffes in Kurdufan (Kordofan), in the central region of what is now Sudan, but four of them died as a result of the severe winter on their way back to Dongola (Dunqulah) in north Sudan. The second attempt of Thibaut's party led to four giraffes being brought safely to Malta in November 1835, and after a period of quarantine they were disembarked to over-winter on the island, where they could recuperate in the warm Mediterranean climate. Housed in special quarters, they were under the charge of Rear-Admiral Thomas Briggs, Superintendent of the Malta Dockyards. Like Campbell, he had donated a number of animals to the London Zoo and was therefore credited as a collaborator of the Zoological Society.

On 3 May 1836 the four giraffes were shipped from Malta to London, but even before their departure, on 9 January, the success of Thibaut's expedition had been reported in *The Times*.[34] Thibaut had kept a detailed record of his expedition, which was read at a scientific meeting of the Zoological Society. It was then published in the society's *Proceedings* and was later cited in a 6s. guide to the giraffes of the London Zoo.[35] As a result, while still on board ship, the giraffes were the subject of wide interest. So far all seemed to be going well for the society, but its plans were suddenly threatened by Edward Cross, proprietor of the Surrey Zoo who in the spring of 1836 purchased three giraffes, then in Alexandria. He dispatched his right-hand man, J. E. Warwick, to take charge of transporting them to London. (Warwick had once been employed by the Zoological Society as a keeper

---

[32] P. MacDougall, 'The formative years: Malta dockyard, 1800–15', MM lxxvi (1990), 205–14; M. Duffy, 'World-wide war and British expansion, 1793–1815', in P. J. Marshall (ed.), *Oxford history of the British Empire*, II: *The eighteenth century*, Oxford 1998, 197, 206.

[33] ZSL, MC, iii, fo. 367.

[34] *Malta Government Gazette*, 4 May 1836, 145; *The Times*, 9 Jan. 1836, 1.

[35] *Proceedings of the Zoological Society of London* iv (1836), 9; Anon., *A popular description and history of the giraffe, or cameleopard, now exhibiting in the Zoological Gardens, Regent's Park: with an account of their Nubian attendants and the adventures of M. Thibaut, who at a great risk and expenses procured them in Africa*, London 1836.

and catalogue-maker, but he quit after a bitter quarrel about his wages and continued his career with Cross.[36])

The race was on to be the first to exhibit giraffes in Britain. Warwick left Alexandria for London on 9 May 1836, only five days after Thibaut left Malta (*see* Table 1). Fearing that Cross's giraffes would arrive first, the Zoological Society cancelled the naval transport that they had booked and instead chartered, for £2,000, an English steamer the *Manchester*, which was then fitted out for carrying the giraffes.[37] Such extravagant spending sparked a popular rumour, reported in the *Saturday Magazine*:[38]

> It is said that [the] activity and success of this gentleman [Edward Cross] was so great that a steam vessel was employed by the Regent's Park Society, at an expense of a thousand pounds, in preference to the slower mode of conveyance in a brig, which had been already chartered, and by this means they were enabled to land their specimen in England before their rivals.

Thibaut and his giraffes won the race, docking in London a month before their competitors. In the early morning of 25 May 1836 the four giraffes, accompanied by Thibaut and three Nubian and one Maltese attendant, walked from the Blackwall Docks along the canal to Regent's Park. Dawn was the best time to avoid crowds of spectators, but there were none the less many curious bystanders gathering to see the exotic cavalcade.[39]

The daily and weekly papers rejoiced at the first public exhibition of giraffes in Britain. It was now time to forget the early death of the king's giraffe in 1829. The *Saturday Magazine* recollected the popular frustration when that giraffe passed into royal ownership: 'Public curiosity, though excited to the highest degree, was, however, in this country at least, but very partially gratified, for … access to it was very sparingly granted.'[40] The arrival of the four new giraffes thus appeared to be a remedy for Britain's chagrin. Triumphing over the French in the number that they could exhibit was particularly important: 'but our giraffes – our four giraffes!' The number mattered, as Charles Knight, Fellow of the Zoological Society and editor of the *Penny Magazine* emphasised: 'The arrival of four giraffes together in

---

36 ZSL, MC, i. fo. 390. Little information is available about his life. He often contributed reports to Loudon's *Magazine of Natural History* on the animals kept in the Surrey Zoo. His name also appeared as a supporter of its proprietor, Edward Cross: Booth, *The stranger's intellectual guide* 146.

37 Steam power was applied to military ships only after 1850: R. Kubrick, 'British expansion, empire, and technological change', in A. Porter (ed.), *Oxford history of the British Empire*, III: *The nineteenth century*, Oxford 1999, 247–69; A. D. Lambert, 'The British naval strategic revolution, 1815–54', in G. Jackson and D. M. Williams (eds), *Shipping, technology and imperialism*, Aldershot 1996, 145–61.

38 *Saturday Magazine*, 3 Sept. 1836, 92.

39 *Penny Magazine*, 18 June 1836, 233.

40 *Saturday Magazine*, 3 Sept. 1836, 89.

Table 1
Itineraries of the giraffes intended for the London Zoo and the Surrey Zoo

Date	Regent's Park Zoo	Surrey Zoo
15 Apr.1834	Thibaut left Cairo	
5 Dec. 1834	Thibaut capture five giraffes at Kordfan (but four died during the winter); later caught three	
21 Nov.1835	Arrived at Malta with four giraffes	
25 Apr. 1836		Embarked from Cairo for Alexandria with three giraffes
4 May1836	Embarked from Malta on a steamer *Manchester* chartered for £2,000	
9 May1836		Embarked from Alexandria on 300-ton brig
24 May1836	Landed at Blackwall on the Thames	
25 May1836	Arrived at the London Zoo	
30 June1836		Arrived at Stangate Creek (seven days quarantine)
8 July 1836		Arrived at the Surrey Zoo

Source: Anon., *A popular description and history of the giraffe*, London 1836; J. E. Warwick, *Description and history with anecdotes of the giraffes*, London 1836

Europe forms an era in the annals of natural history.'[41] William Broderip could not help but observe, ungenerously, that 'if that in the possession of our French neighbours would die, an event, we regret to find, not unlikely happen, the Zoological Society will be the sole European proprietor of living specimens of this rare and delicate species'.[42]

The news brought throngs of spectators flooding into the zoo to view both the giraffes and their exotic attendants. On the day after the giraffes' arrival, over five hundred children were taken to the zoo from five schools in the neighbourhood; and the following Sunday recorded the exceptional attendance of nearly 4,000 visitors.[43] Spectators were asked to remain in the

[41] *Penny Magazine*, 18 June 1836, 231.
[42] [W. J. Broderip], 'The Zoological Gardens, Regent's Park', *Quarterly Review* (July 1836), 328.
[43] ZSL, OG, 1836.

zoo for as short a time as possible; admission procedures were tightened up to prevent the entry of improper characters; and police officers were called in to relieve traffic congestion at the entrance to the zoo.[44] The almost overwhelming popularity of the exhibition lasted until the end of the summer season, and, although records are not exact, it seems that over the whole year attendance peaked at 260,000. This was figure not exceeded until the year of the Great Exhibition.

Such public interest has significant implications for any interpretation of the zoo as 'a showcase of empire', and also for the broader historiography of imperial science. Certainly, the Zoological Society took advantage of naval and colonial networks.[45] This was demonstrated clearly in *Hints for collecting animals and their products* (1832). This small tract, compiled by William Broderip for the Admiralty's Hydrographic Office,[46] was designed to provide naval officers with practical advice on how to keep records of captured animals and how to bring them back alive. Indeed, a number of zoological specimens was donated, either dead or alive, to the Zoological Society by ships' captains and their accounts of collecting animals were often published in its *Proceedings*. The society regularly received so many specimens that John Edward Gray of the British Museum complained at a parliamentary committee that naval officers were more willing to donate their collections to the society than to the museum.[47] Since the imperial networks clearly contributed to the foundation of institutional science, it might be tempting to regard the successful collection of the giraffes as just one more example of the hegemonic synthesis of science and empire.[48]

Nevertheless, this is an interpretation that confines itself, somewhat crudely, only to factors that were a function of the empire. When events and situations outside the empire are brought into the frame, the animal-collecting networks look very different. In particular, the ascendancy of Mehmed (Muhammad) Ali was decisive. Egypt had long been a province of the Ottoman Empire, but after the French invasion of 1798 the country collapsed into the chaos engendered by rivalries between Mamluk rulers.

---

44 ZSL, MC, iv, fos 447, 462–3.

45 The earl of Derby was instrumental in securing support from naval officers. In one case he asked Lord Auckland, then a former vice president of the Zoological Society and the First Lord of Admiralty, to authorise the conveyance, by naval steamer from the western coast of Africa, of his zoological collector and the captured animals: Auckland to Earl Grey, 5 Nov. 1847, Earl Grey papers, University of Durham Archive, GRE/B76/6/43. The other case is also mentioned in Ritvo, 'Zoological nomenclature', 335.

46 W. J. Broderip, *Hints for collecting animals and their products*, London 1832.

47 *Report from the select committee on the British Museum*, PP vii (1835), q. 3358.

48 Drayton, 'Science, medicine, and the British Empire', and 'Science and the European empire', *Journal of the Imperial and Commonwealth History* xxiii (1995), 503–10; P. Petijean, C. Jami and A. M. Moulin, *Science and empires: historical studies about scientific development and European expansion*, Dordrecht 1992.

From this Mehmed Ali, formerly a commander of the Ottoman irregulars, emerged and by the 1820s had established his own dynasty. Given the title of viceroy in 1805 by the Ottoman sultan, Mehmed Ali was to all intents and purposes functioning independently of Istanbul. After invading and taking control of Sudan,[49] he collected giraffes and presented one each to the rulers of Britain, France and Austria, through the conventional gift-giving protocol. This was not the result of any British control over Egypt, which was not established until much later in the nineteenth century, but rather of Mehmed Ali's aim to establish relationships with European monarchs in pursuit of their approval of his dynasty and hence of his independence.

As far as the London Zoo's giraffes were concerned, Mehmed Ali did not directly support the Zoological Society, but if he had not been in control in Egypt and Sudan, European travellers would have been unable to enter the interior savannah, where the giraffes were to be found. Before Mehmed Ali came to power, the German explorer John Lewis Burkhardt had tried to conduct geographical research in Sudan under the patronage of London's Association for Promoting the Discovery of the Interior Parts of Africa. He had first to spend several years in Syria to master the Arabic language and local customs so that he could pass himself off as a pious Muslim. A decade later, Eduard Rüppell of Frankfurt-am-Main was able to follow in the wake of Mehmed Ali and gather a large number of specimens in Sudan, including a giraffe, which he sent back home to raise the international reputation of the Senkenberg Museum.[50]

Now that the giraffe's habitat could be reached via Egypt, European explorers no longer had to round the Cape of Good Hope as Le Valliant had done some forty years earlier. The shorter voyage also enhanced the giraffes' chance of survival. Indeed, Ignatius Pallme, an Austrian tradesman staying in Kurdufan from 1837 to 1840, commented that almost all the living specimens sent to Europe had so far originally been caught in the plains of this region. Local hunters devised a method of capturing giraffes alive, and then brought them to Cairo or Alexandria, where they could be sold at an extraordinarily high price. A *firman* issued by a local sheikh was needed to hunt giraffes, but he was generally willing to grant one: hunting giraffes, a luxurious exotic commodity, was becoming a business.[51]

---

[49] K. Fahmy, *All the pasha's men: Mehmed Ali, his army and the making of modern Egypt*, Cairo 1997, and 'The era of Muhammad Ali Pasha, 1805–1848', in M. W. Daly (ed.), *Cambridge history of Egypt, II: Modern Egypt from 1517 to the end of the twentieth century*, Cambridge 1998, 139–70; A. Lutfi al-Sayyid Marsot, *Egypt in the reign of Muhammad Ali*, Cambridge 1984.

[50] J. L. Burkhardt, *Travels in Nubia*, London 1819; E. Rüppell, *Reisen in Nubien: Kordofan und den peträischen Arabien*, Frankfurt-am-Main 1829 (extracts from these books appeared in the *North American Review* [Apr. 1835], 477–510); R. Hallett (ed.), *Records of the African Association, 1788–1831*, London 1964.

[51] I. Pallme, *Travels in Kordofan*, London 1844, 239–43.

Adhering solely to the concept of the imperial zoo fails to take into account the subtleties of the animal-collecting networks, as well as the geopolitical contexts within which they developed. Seen from this vantage point, the animal-collecting networks appear more ephemeral and elusive than imperial networks are generally supposed to be. Frequently they were one-off projects and involved non-colonial agents whose contribution was vital to their success. Care should be taken not to regard the British Empire as producing a stable infrastructure ready to be utilised for various scientific projects. It is also erroneous to think that the geopolitical contexts within which collecting activities took place were static. Various agents were involved, from the Zoological Society to Mehmed Ali, and they changed over time. The animal-collecting networks were not merely a product of the synthesis of science and empire: animal collectors negotiated in a range of ways within their own geographical settings and opened up trans- as well as intra-imperial networks.

Cultural domestication

According to cultural historians our understandings of animals have an aspect of cultural construction and have changed contingently. They have rejected whiggish presumptions that zoological knowledge has progressed teleologically to achieve scientific truth by marginalising anecdote, superstition and religious myth. It is instead suggested that the making of scientific knowledge has often engaged with popular tales and fables.[52] This discussion problematises the role played by the London Zoo in framing popular perceptions of animals. On the one hand, the zoo seemed to disseminate the kind of scientific knowledge that could be obtained only through the observation of living specimens. The idea that the zoo epitomised a triumph of science over superstitions was clearly expressed by Edward T. Bennett, author of *The gardens and menagerie of the Zoological Society* (1830–1):[53]

> One great aim of the Society is to diffuse as widely as possible a practical acquaintance with living animals, in order to eradicate those vulgar prejudices which have in too many instances usurped the place of truth, and to substitute just ideas, drawn from actual observation, instead of false deductions from distorted facts, or wild speculation built upon erroneous foundations.

[52] C. Plumb, '"Strange and wonderful": encountering the elephant in Britain, 1675–1830', *JECS* xxxiii (2010), 525–43; S. Sivasundram, 'Trading knowledge: the East India Company's elephants in India and Britain', *HJ* xlviii (2005), 27–63.
[53] [E.T. Bennett], *The gardens and menagerie of the Zoological Society, delineated: published, with the sanction of the council, under the superintendence of the secretary and vice-secretary of the society*, London 1830–1, p. vi. See also Åkerberg, *Knowledge and pleasures*, 144–5.

On the other hand, when spectators tried to interpret their encounters with the animals, they tended to employ ideas and language familiar to them. As one diarist revealed:

After church [I] went to the zoological gardens and saw 4 giraffes. They look healthy and well – are very elegant and gentle creature altho[ugh] so enormously tall. It is difficult to imagine their destined use unless for food either for man or some other animal.[54]

The idea of a giraffe being 'destined' for food seems crude to later generations, but it could be justified in 'scriptural natural history', which described animals mentioned in the Bible and tried to deepen readers' understanding of divine creation. In the section on zoology, animals were classified, for instance, as 'domestic', 'ferocious wild beasts', 'wild inoffensive' and 'dubious' (the leviathan and the unicorn for example).[55] It is not surprising that the diarist took this attitude in attempting to understand why God had created the giraffe. This was the cultural framework into which a new animal had to be slotted and intellectually absorbed.

Another diarist, Sophy Codd, provides further insight into how this cultural framework operated in the everyday life of the family.[56] Nearly a month after the arrival of the four giraffes, Sophy Codd reached her nineteenth birthday and visited the London Zoo with her family. Spectators were still flocking in their thousands to see the giraffes. Like many other spectators, Sophy was amazed at such tall creatures, finding them quite beautiful and elegant as long as they were motionless, but when they were running, she thought that they looked 'extremely ungraceful'.[57] That evening, at home, Sophy looked into Peter Parley's popular natural history book and learned that the real existence of the giraffes had long been doubted on account of their rarity.[58] Extracting a passage from a chapter on the giraffe, she learned a lot more about the animals: their physical character, moral nature, habitat and so forth. In her diary entry Sophy was not just recording her interactive learning process, but was also a piece of her family history. She bore in

---

[54] Diaries of John Biddulph of Ledbury, Biddulph collection, Herefordshire Record Office, Hereford, G2/IV/J/69.

[55] W. Carpenter, *Scripture natural history*, London 1828.

[56] Sophy Shirley Codd journal, 1835–6, London Metropolitan Archive, ACC/2042/002/1, fo. 67. Sophy's father, Harrison Gordon Codd, was deputy lord-lieutenant of Middlesex from 1824 to 1840. The record concerning his involvement in society and government is in the London Metropolitan Archive.

[57] Ibid. fos 68–70.

[58] P. Parley, *Tales of animals: comprising quadrupeds, birds, reptiles and insects*, London 1833, 96. Commenced in the late 1820s by an American writer, Samuel Griswold Goodrich, Peter Parley remained a popular juvenile book series in the nineteenth century. *Tales of animals* went into its 14th edition in 1875: D. Roselle, *Samuel Griswold Goodrich, creator of Peter Parley: a study of his life and work*, New York 1968.

mind the reader of her diary, her father, with whom she anticipated merry conversation about the giraffe, and who she hoped would compliment her on her improved writing.[59] It might be that Sophy and her father discussed her first impressions of the giraffes later.

Sophys's diary shows how science gave shape and meaning to everyday life. Moreover from the 1830s onwards a flood of publications on the sciences, both books and magazines, was available to a reading public that had hitherto been neglected. Recent research on the production, circulation and consumption of scientific books, prints and magazines has therefore explored how the quality and quantity of scientific knowledge changed during this period.[60] Literature was not, however, the only means through which visitors to the zoo could interpret their encounters with exotic animals such as the giraffe. The physical structure of the zoo was also important.

Since tall buildings were banned in the south garden it was inevitable that the giraffe house would be in the north garden: it was situated, next to the elephant and rhinoceros enclosures, in a rather remote corner of the long strip of land outside the Inner Circle. Like many other animal houses in the zoo, the giraffe house was designed by Decimus Burton. Now it could be described, as 'an emphatically functional shed, a "Tuscan" barn'. Decoration was less important than functional completion.[61] When it first appeared, however, it was viewed differently. George Scharf appreciated the beauty of the architecture, although finding it disproportionate. On 12 December 1836 he noted in his diary that 'I saw the New Giraffes House for the first time, nearly finished, which is very handsome, but the windows [are] too high up and too small.'[62]

The design of the structure invited such an impression. The ceiling had to be high enough to accommodate the giraffes, while, for the same reason, the three doors on the south wall were five metres high. A spectator would wonder what strange creature was housed there. In his literary guide to the London Zoo, Charles Knight sought to excite the readers by likening the extraordinary appearance of the giraffe house to the imaginary world of Brobdignag, the land of giants in Jonathan Swift's *Gulliver's travels* (1726). As the giraffe house was at the farthest corner of the north garden, readers were addressed as if they had reached it after travelling through different worlds, in which they had already encountered many exotic creatures. Lastly, they approached 'a remarkably lofty building':[63]

[59] Sophy Codd journal, ACC/2042/002/1, fos 26–7.
[60] Cantor and Shuttleworth, *Science serialized*; Henson and others, *Culture and science.*
[61] Guillery, *Buildings of London Zoo*, 27–8.
[62] Scharf journal, entry for 12 Dec. 1836, Scharf papers, NPG7/3/7/2/1/2.
[63] C. Knight, *London*, London 1843, iv. 270.

[W]ith an enclosed yard on the left, where the trees, fenced to a most unusual height, and with a projecting guard at the top of each fence, seems to imply we have got among some creatures from the scene of Swift's geographical discoveries – the mysterious land of Brobdignag, which not all British skill, capital and enterprise, have yet been able to find the way to.

It was only when they entered the building that visitors realised what they had been looking at. Immediately, they were convinced that 'the almost incredibly tall creatures cannot belong to any part of our planet with which we have been hitherto familiar'. By using the analogy with Gulliver's fabulous adventure, Knight offered a referential frame within which spectators could interpret their first encounter with the animals.[64]

The analogy with *Gulliver's travels* suggests that the physical environment and the narrative device complemented each other. The interaction was encapsulated by another guide, which William Broderip wrote for the *Quarterly Review*. Since the giraffe house was located next to the elephant and rhinoceros enclosures, spectators might be inclined to contrast the slim and gentle giraffes with their slow, clumsy neighbours. Broderip brought out the feminine aspect of the giraffe:

> Few contrasts are greater than that between the heavy masses of flesh and bone, and the light, elegant giraffes, with their sleek, rich, dappled coats, towering swan-like necks, lofty heads, and large brilliant eyes, worthy of Juno herself, and full of a noble expression, such as Edwin Landseer alone could give.[65]

Associating the giraffe with the goddess Juno and her stately beauty, and referring to Edwin Landseer, the renowned animal painter, mattered greatly. While Charles Knight edited his guide in such a way that the general reader would find it helpful and enjoyable, Broderip sought to elevate his writing on natural history into literature, intended for a more limited audience. The *Quarterly Review*, with a circulation of 9,000–10,000 in the 1830s, aimed at the Tory-affiliated upper and professional classes. It supposed that its readers had received a classical education and took an interest in the fine arts.[66] In his literary guide to the London Zoo, Broderip took an antiquarian approach, with overtones of high culture. He sought ancient descriptions of the animals although he avoided obscure jargon and used vernacular names with the corresponding Latin terms footnoted. This could help the cultured reader to enjoy the guide without having to stop to check the nomenclature, while the footnotes confirmed the scholarship of the text. Given that

[64] Although Swift initially wrote the novel as a political satire, by the nineteenth century it had come to be read as an entertaining adventure.

[65] Broderip, 'Zoological Gardens', 324–5.

[66] R. Altick, *English common reader: a social history of the mass reading public, 1800–1900*, 2nd edn, Columbus 1998, 392.

zoologists had often been accused of being unable to communicate with a wider public, Broderip's guide could be a model for an ideal style of writing on animals. His talent was confirmed by the great success of his *Zoological recreations* (1847), which his friend, Richard Owen, acclaimed as ranking with Gilbert White's *Natural history of Selborne*, and Kerby and Spencer's *Introduction to entomology*.[67]

Refining the literary quality of works on natural history was not simply a matter of references to classical texts and limiting technical information. Romanticism also came into play, as exemplified by the poet and literary critic James Henry Leigh Hunt. In his review of the London Zoo, published in the *New Monthly Magazine*, he observed the zoo animals and recorded his reactions as a person of poetic sensitivities and literary talents. This contrasted sharply with Broderip's self-presentation as a zoologist whose role was to offer well-organised information. Their different approaches are shown in how they described the giraffes. Like Broderip, Leigh Hunt feminised the animal, but in different language. Hunt's elaborate word picture is worth citing in full:[68]

> They are extremely interesting from their novelty, and from a singular look of cleanliness, delicacy, and refinement, mixed with a certain *gaucherie* arising from their long, poking necks, and the disparity of length between their fore and hind legs. They look like young ladies of animals, naturally not ungraceful, but with bad habits. Their necks are not on a line with fore legs, perpendicular and held up, nor yet arched like horses' necks, but make a feeble-looking, obtuse angle, completely answering to the word 'poking': the legs come up so close to the necks, that in front they appear to have no bodies; the back sloped like a hill, producing the singular disparity between the legs just mentioned; and the whole animal, being slender, light-coloured, and very gentle, gives you an idea of delicacy amounting to the fragile; the legs looks as if a stick would break them in two, like glass.

Leigh Hunt went further than Broderip, characterising the giraffe with the contradictory attributes of grace and *gaucherie*. The way in which the giraffe walked was, he concluded, 'the strangest mixture in the world of elegance and uncouthness'. This dictum may appear unique, but was in fact an elaboration on what was observed by others. Giraffes were indeed treated as the weakest of creatures. Caroline Owen, Richard's wife and a regular visitor to the giraffe house, believed that the young animals feared the dark. She recorded that when they arrived in London: 'they had to have a light at night as they would not rest quietly without it'.[69] Two months later an extra keeper was appointed 'to aid in the care of the giraffes'.[70] It is not surprising

67 [R. Owen], 'Broderip's *Zoological recreations*', *Quarterly Review* (Dec.1847), 119–42.

68 Hunt, 'A visit to the Zoological Gardens', 483–4.

69 Owen, *Richard Owen*, i. 98.

70 ZSL, MC, iv, fo. 501.

Figure 13. 'The giraffes and Nubian master', *Penny Magazine*, 18 June 1836, 223.

Figure 14. George Cruikshank, 'Giraffes – Granny Dears & other novelties' (1836). Bodleian Library, Oxford, JJC, Animals on Show 2 (28).

that Leigh Hunt thought that the keepers were 'constantly curry-combing them after a gentle fashion'.

The image of the giraffe was therefore a juxtaposition: grace and beauty on the one hand; fragility and awkwardness on the other. This was echoed in popular perceptions of the three Nubian attendants who were an integral part of the exhibition. Although they were all peasants, they were attired in their formal costumes, at least two of them appearing to belong to a superior caste judging by the gashes on their faces and their tattooing. Their presence added to the exotic allure of the scene, as one popular guide to the exhibition commented: 'The appearance of M. Thibaut and the Nubian attendants is very picturesque.'[71] The illustration published in the *Penny Magazine*, which testifies to their presence at the exhibition (*see* Figure 13), places both animals and keeper as if they had been more or less confronting the viewer in the zoo. This layout complied with the editorial policy of the periodical, which aimed to disseminate 'useful knowledge' among its working-class readership. Readers were expected to obtain their information by reading the text, backed up by the illustration.

In this pedagogical illustration, both the giraffes and their keepers were depicted as if objects in a still life. George Cruickshank, however, tried to give them active roles in his comic print (*see* Figure 14). A female visitor in

[71] Anon., *Popular description and history of the giraffe*, 14–15.

Figure 15. George Scharf, 'The giraffes with Arabs who brought them over to this country' (1836).

the foreground has her sunshade bitten by one of the giraffes, while soldiers join civilians in admiring the display. Thibaut on the chair and the Nubian keepers standing around him are observing the scene with pleasure. Unlike the print published in the *Penny Magazine*, this comic print complicated the relationship between the viewer and the viewed by depicting the three Nubian attendants as observers. They were probably asked by the Zoological Society to remain at the zoo, as their presence certainly added to the exotic atmosphere of the exhibition. At the end of the 1836 summer season they were paid, given travel expenses and returned home.[72]

The ambiguous relationships between the various actors – the giraffes, the Nubians, Thibaut, anonymous spectators – were crystallised in George Scharf's lithograph, which was published shortly after the opening of the giraffe exhibition (*see* Figure 15). When he rushed to the scene, he seemed to be captivated by the sight of Thibaut and 'three Arabs' and finished the drawing in two weeks.[73] His lithograph was soon circulated via the print-sellers and had favourable reviews. It sold so quickly that he could not keep up with demand. A month later, on 24 June 1836, he noted in his diary that 'The Prints of the Giraffes sold so much through Printsellers that I could not get them ready fast enough, sold 500 in two weeks.'[74] He also

[72] ZSL, MC, iv, fo. 485.
[73] Scharf journal, entry for 25 May 1836, Scharf papers, NPG7/3/7/2/1/2.
[74] Ibid. entry for 24 June 1836.

presented each of the three keepers with a copy of the print before they left for home.[75]

The *Spectator*'s appraisal, 'A very accurate and picturesque print', encapsulated the integration of scientific and aesthetic perfection.[76] Since Scharf worked as an illustrator for scientific journals, he had mastered the skill of reproducing what was deemed a realistic image of natural objects. In fact, he was well aware of the importance of scientific accuracy, taking the advice of Richard Owen, who was his patron and regular client.[77] This was probably reflected in the picture's close reference to the conventional descriptions of the animal. A giraffe on the left side is shown bending towards the ground, its forelegs splayed, the one on the right raises its neck upright, while the one in the centre demonstrates a unique sitting position. All three poses were held to demonstrate the salient characteristics of the giraffe and had been illustrated in a number of previous prints, albeit of poorer quality. What 'being accurate' meant here was therefore not mere realism, but the faithful portrayal of typical, distinctive and identifiable attributes of the animal.

The other important feature of this picture is the illusion of the exotic. Unlike his previous lithographs of zoo scenery, *Six views of the Zoological Gardens*, Scharf took the giraffes and their attendants out of the physical environment of the zoo and into an imaginary space. The lyre, pictured as being played by one of the Nubian attendants and listened to by the giraffes, added to the exotic atmosphere. There were also other artefacts such as a sabre, a sword, a pot and pipes, which together served to create the overall impression of the exotic. These objects related to each other, but the reference rarely reached beyond the frame of the portrait. It doubtful whether the print expanded the viewer's ideas of the geography of Africa, because it encased rather than opened up a space of visual representation.

Clearly, the peaceful and harmonious appearance of the picture does not necessarily mean that every actor was of equal status. Most significant is the relationship between the dignified upright stance of Thibaut, and one of the Nubian keepers, on his knees before his 'superior'. The lyre-player appeared to be the chief keeper, who might even control the minds of the giraffes. Asymmetrical power relations operated between the actors in the scene and also with the viewer of the portrait, because once printed and circulated it was subject to spectators' interpretations. In this sense the picture hinted at the zoo's role of provoking emotional and intellectual responses to an encounter with unfamiliar animals, and of allowing spectators to understand the meanings of that encounter within multiple frames of reference. One of them was the physical environment within which the animals were actu-

---

[75] Ibid. entry for 2 July 1836.

[76] *Spectator*, 18 June 1836, 590.

[77] Scharf to Owen, n.d. (c.1836?), Richard Owen collection, National History Museum, London, OC62, xxiii, fo. 151.

ally displayed. Another was influenced by a variety of literary and pictorial motifs that helped to describe the size, appearance and moral characters of the animals. These themes – divine creation, romanticism, scientific observation and works of fine art – resonated with each other, without any one dominating. It is therefore inappropriate to assume that the zoo projected one particular view and then to analyse the zoo from that angle alone. The London Zoo had come to offer ample room for a range of ideas and views which might compete with each other in other fields. The 1836 giraffe exhibition did not simply illuminate an imperial vision of the world; rather it made the zoo a cultural device, one that transferred exotic animals into a mixed space of scientific realism and picturesque fantasy.

The concept of 'imperial zoo' uncritically assumes that animals were collected through the communications system of the British Empire, and that this infrastructure was straightforwardly reflected in the realm of animal display. This leads to the further assumption that the exhibition of exotic animals inevitably expanded geographical knowledge and drew the imagination towards the remote corners of the empire. The 1836 giraffe exhibition, however, hardly supports this line of argument. It instead demonstrated that the ideologies and mechanisms that influenced the collecting enterprise were not necessarily transferred onto the public stage. Even though the proprietors of the zoo and the public media claimed that the arrival of the four giraffes symbolised the rise of British zoology in the context of imperial rivalry with France, their claims were not predominantly influential in framing popular perceptions of the animals. The 'imperial approach' that places the London Zoo at a juncture of 'home' and 'colony' is therefore no longer sustainable. An analysis of the exhibition suggests an alternative interpretation: the zoo presented an imaginary realm, disconnected from the everyday world. Scharf's lithograph epitomised the zoo as an enclosed space within which exotic animals could be confined and tamed. While popular guides and prints elaborated on various motifs, spectators combined them to locate the animals within their own frame of reference. The mechanisms of 'cultural domestication' developed as the zoo came to receive exotic animals regularly and to employ the public media to spotlight their exhibitions.

It should finally be noted that as the London Zoo monitored and controlled public access, there was presumably a large number of people who knew of the arrival of the giraffes but could not see them themselves. They experienced the exhibition only indirectly through word-of-mouth and the reading of newspapers and popular periodicals such as the *Penny Magazine*. The exhibition thus highlighted the gap between demand for direct access to the zoo, and the protection of the privilege given only to those affiliated with the Zoological Society. How, then, when entry to the zoo was not open to all, could the benefits of animal display be conveyed to the public at large?

3

The Question of Access

'The characteristic of the English populace – perhaps we ought to say people, for it extends to the middle classes – is their propensity to mischief. The people of most other countries may safely be admitted into parks, gardens, and public buildings, and galleries of pictures and statues; but in England it is necessary to exclude them, as much as possible, from all such places ... This disgraceful part of the English character ... can neither be soon nor easily corrected; but anything tends to correct it that contributes to give the people a taste for intellectual pleasures.'[1]

In principle, the London Zoo was open only to Fellows of the Zoological Society, their families and friends. This policy remained unchanged during the first two decades of the zoo's history. In practice, however, the zoo was accessible even to those who were not acquainted with Fellows. The society carefully regulated its complex admission system, but the illegal entry of those described by the society as 'improper characters' was common. There was also a continuing tension between the society's attempts to expel strangers and the growing demand for open access to the zoo. As a result, the question of access arose not only with regard to the London Zoo, but also other public institutions involved in the arts and sciences. Moreover, it provoked debates on the ideal relationship between learned societies and the public at large – especially concerning their respective roles as providers and recipients of 'culture', meaning the cultivation of intellect, taste and morality. The zoo's case was discussed by a series of parliamentary committees on the reform of the British Museum, the National Gallery and other public institutions, and presented crucial evidence on the provision of wider access. This chapter explores how the social conflict developing at the London Zoo problematised cultural politics and had repercussions for the reform of art galleries and scientific institutions.

The zoo's clientele

On opening in 1828, the London Zoo became popular with high society. Its role as a backdrop for social display is demonstrated in a print by Benjamin

---

1 [R. Southey], 'Fables and other pieces in verse by Marry Maria Colling', *Quarterly Review* (Mar. 1832), 100; also quoted in the *Penny Magazine*, 7 Apr. 1832, 18.

Figure 16. Benjamin Read, 'Display of the present fashion in the London Zoo' (1829). City of Westminster Archives, Ashbridge 129 (Acc 1026).

Read, a tailor and printmaker (*see* Figure 16).[2] The purpose of the print was to advertise the latest gentlemen's fashions: an array of masculine and female elegance is portrayed in the foreground. The print was composed in such a way as to enable the zoo's main attractions all to appear at once: the bear in the left middle ground is noteworthy. This was Toby the Russian black bear, who had once been in the possession of Francis Seymour-Conway, 3rd marquis of Hertford, the former Envoy Extraordinary to Russia. Upon completion of his mission, Hertford returned home with Toby and acquired St Dunston, a sumptuous villa in Regent's Park, which was designed for him by Decimus Burton (and is today the residence of the American ambassador). Hertford was a living legacy of the Regency period: his lavish lifestyle made him the model for the marquis of Steyne in Thackeray's *Vanity Fair* (1847).[3] Toby was said to have a refined taste for ale, a result of the influence of his decadent master. Presented to the Zoological Society, of which Hertford was an early member, Toby captured the public imagination and was patronised by fashionable crowds.[4]

[2] Hyde and Cumming, 'The prints of Benjamin Read', 262–84.

[3] Samuel, *Villas in Regent's Park*, 23–4.

[4] It was often reported, however, that bears were injured by visitors who poked them with sharp pointed umbrellas. Several warning notices were put up in 1836, but by this

The presence of Toby epitomised the zoo's close links with polite society. The council of the Zoological Society was indeed eager to promote the patronage of high-profile figures. In January 1828, prior to the public opening of the zoo, the council resolved to present foreign ambassadors with ivory tickets, which allowed them free admission to the zoo.[5] Later in the same year the council decided to distribute the tickets more widely to 'such individuals as, from their station or service to the society, may appear likely to aid the object of the institution', as well as to 'such foreigners and gentlemen connected with the public press'.[6] When the coronation of Queen Victoria took place in June 1838, the Zoological Society issued admission orders to 114 individuals, foreign ambassadors and aristocrats, who were expected to attend the ceremony.[7] It is difficult to identify all the public figures who were encouraged to become subscribers through receiving complimentary tickets, but it is likely that Prince Christoph von Lieven, the Russian ambassador, was one of them.[8] His correspondence, deposited the British Library,confirms that he received an admission ticket from the Zoological Society when the zoo opened and paid subscription fees for the years 1831 and 1832. His wife, Dorothea, was a talented diplomat in her own right, using her charm and intelligence to become such a prominent figure that she was said to have been the mistress and confidante of everyone at court and in the cabinet.[9] If Princess Lieven accompanied her husband to the zoo, her presence would certainly have confirmed the zoo's enjoyment of aristocratic patronage.

In Benjamin Read's print, the fashionable ambience was stressed by the presence of a long procession of carriages making for the the zoo gates. The size of the crowds was probably no exaggeration: a pilgrimage to the zoo was an integral part of the social round, and the parade of private vehicles caused phenomenal congestion on the Outer Circle. This occurred so regularly that the Zoological Society appointed special constables from the zoo staff, who worked at the direction of the police 'for the preservation of the peace of the gate'.[10] All the same, the parade of luxurious carriages was not totally elimi-

---

time Toby's name had disappeared from guidebooks: he seems to have survived in the zoo for only a few years: ZSL, MC, iv, fo. 484.

5   ZSL, MC, i, fo. 67.

6   ZSL, MC, i, fo. 213.

7   ZSL, BABA, Returns, fos 49–52.

8   Vigors to Prince Christoph Heinrich von Lieven, 23 June 1828, Lieven papers, BL, MS Add. 47294A, fo. 113; Zoological Society to von Lieven, 10 July 1833, MS Add. 47296, fo. 100; Zoological Society to von Lieven, 10 July 1833, MS Add. 47309, fos 110–12. Von Lieven returned to Russia in 1834.

9   J. Charmley, *The princess and the politicians: sex, intrigue and diplomacy, 1812–40*, London 2005; J. L. Cromwell, *Dorothea Lieven: a Russian princess in London and Paris, 1785–1857*, London 2006.

10   ZSL, MC, i, fos 97, 100, 211; G. Vevers, *London's zoo: an anthology to celebrate 150 years of the Zoological Society of London*, London 1976, 25–6.

nated and continued to constitute a scene of conspicuous display. When a carriage passed by, pedestrians were afforded a glimpse of elegant ladies. One record from an obviously masculine viewpoint depicts his reaction to the female beauty on display:[11]

> On our way thither [to the zoo] we saw a great number of very elegant carriages drawn by beautiful spirited horses, with harness of superior description, and the coachmen and servants behind the carriages dressed in liveries of every known colour; within the carriages as they swiftly rolled by, we saw many women, fair and with light hair, many of them appeared to us most beautiful. All of them appeared to have mild blue eyes, and very sweet expression of countenance, and we saw more of female beauty in a few hours, than we had ever beheld in all our lives.

The authors of this record were Jehangeer Nowrojee and Hirjeebhoy Merwanjee, naval architects from Bombay, where for generations their families had served the East India Company. They were visiting London to study the construction of steamships. Shortly after their arrival in 1838, they were taken by their host, Charles Forbes, to the Diorama and then to the London Zoo. Upon arrival they observed a number of animals, from elephants and bears to rhinoceroses. Their descriptions of the animals are similar to those in accounts written by English diarists, and only the passage which likens a bear sliding down the bear pit pole to a sailor descending a ship's mast provides a reminder of their line of work. Their account is none the less unique because of their own self-awareness. They noted that they had become the 'objects of very great curiosity to the visitor – as much so perhaps as winged and four footed inmates of the place'.[12]

Indian shipbuilders were not the only visitors from the East. The journal of three Persian princes also casts light on social engagement within polite society. Staying in London as political refugees in 1836, the princes spent most of their time socialising among London's *beau monde*. Their journal, which was later published in English, indicated that they occasionally visited the zoo. On 30 November 1836, for instance, they noted that 'This morning we were invited by some beautiful houris [sic] to accompany them to the Zoological Gardens; and as it was of importance to accept the invitation of the possessors of such charming eyes, we joined their parties.' In the zoo,

---

[11] J. Nowrojee and H. Merwanjee, *Journal of a residence of two years and a half in Great Britain*, London 1841, 31–2. Charles Forbes had been involved with his family commercial venture in Bombay, and upon returning to England in 1812 entered politics and fought against the East India Company's monopoly. See, for details of this travelogue, M. H. Fisher, 'East Indian travel guides to Britain', in T. Youngs (ed.), *Travel writing in the nineteenth century: filling the blank spaces*, London 2006, 87–106.

[12] Nowrojee and Merwanjee, *Journal*, 34.

they were amazed to watch a large rhinoceros trying to break out of its iron cage.[13]

Although the journal was written from an overtly male perspective, it hinted at the gender pattern of visitors to the zoo. Because the society admitted both female and male subscribers on the same terms, female members were able to secure free access to the zoo.[14] Five per cent of the 1837 membership list was female, ranging from the wives of eminent aristocrats to those whose identities are totally unknown; and the proportion remained unchanged into the 1850s.[15] This is notable given that other scientific societies such as the Royal and the Linnean Societies did not accept females at that time.[16] Yet it does not fully explain the remarkable prominence of fashionable ladies at the zoo. As the privileges of the subscribers included free entrance to the zoo with two companions, the wife of a member could visit the zoo with her husband free of charge.[17] Likewise, the husband could write a letter of introduction, which would allow his wife to go on her own or with companions of her choice. Alternatively, when the subscriber had an immediate family member who wished to visit the zoo regularly, an ivory ticket, which allowed the admission of the holder with one companion, could be obtained at a price of one guinea *per annum*.[18] Among council members, Vigors and Sykes had ivory tickets, while John George Children cancelled his in 1833 on the grounds that it had not been used for the last three years.[19]

The age/gender balance of visitors can be detected in a family letter written by Alleyne FitzHerbert, scion of a well-established Derbyshire family.[20] Writing to his father on 18 March 1828 Alleyne stated that he and his aunt had been invited by his father's uncle, the 1st Baron St Helens, who had once been a diplomat and subsequently a lord of the bedchamber to George III. St Helens was a founding member of the Zoological Society and was therefore able to take them to the zoo on a Sunday. Alleyne took

[13] A. Y. Kayat, *Journal of a residence in England: and of a journal from and to Syria, of their royal highness Reeza Loolee Meerza, Najaf Koolee Meerza, and Taymoor Meerza of Persia*, London 1839, i. 140–1.

[14] Ritvo, *Animal estate*, 212.

[15] Zoological Society of London, *List of the members of the Zoological Society of London*, London 1837.

[16] Bye-laws of the Zoological Society regulated that 'Ladies may be admitted as Fellows upon the same terms, with the same privileges, and under the same regulations in all respects as gentlemen', but female members were not expected to attend meetings of the society. They were instead allowed to vote by proxy at the general meetings of the society: Mitchell, *Centenary history*, 56–7.

[17] Extra persons were allowed by payment of 1s. each.

[18] The holder of the ivory ticket had to be at the residence of the subscriber. The council declined applications that did not comply with this condition: ZSL, MC, iii, fo. 110.

[19] ZSL, MC, i, fo. 348; iii, fos 281, 393.

[20] The father of Alleyne FitzHerbert, Sir Henry FitzHerbert, inherited the property in 1839 on the death of his uncle, the 1st Baron St Helens.

advantage of his great-uncle's privilege. His is one of the earliest records made by a visitor to the zoo: 'Amongst the animals we saw a Lynax [*sic*] which amused us very much because it was so very angry at us & it grouled [*sic*] in a very odd manner.'[21]

Catherine Gore's *Diary of a désennuyée* (1836) gives further insight into the patterns and characteristics of polite society. As the witty author of 'silver fork' novels, Gore satirised the lives and pursuits of the English upper classes; this particular novel was a prime example of the genre, describing their social engagements in the role of an imaginary diarist.[22] Since the London Zoo was a venue for fashionable gatherings, it featured in the novel. In the sarcastic tone that was typical of silver fork novels, she sketched a conversation – a variation of 'the same sapient remarks uttered there Sunday after Sunday':[23]

'What a vastly conjugal couple!' 'Who? Mr. and Mrs. William C.?' 'No! that pair of blue and buff macaws! What a fate; to be caged in eternal fidelity, as an example for ladies and gentlemen!' 'How those chamois remind one of Chamonix! Dear Switzerland! Lord Hilton, were you ever in Switzerland?' … 'And then, people talk of the diffusion of knowledge, and the advantage of penny libraries! Do let us go, Lady Evelyn, and see the kangaroos swallow their young'. 'Do they really swallow them?' 'To be sure – I have seen them a thousand times.'

This dialogue displays a conventional antipathy to the frivolity of the fashionable elite.[24] Subjects for conversation shift quickly from macaws and kangaroos to the other visitors. Although this fictional conversation cannot be read as describing a real situation at the zoo, it certainly developed from the contemporary recognition that the secret of success in polite society was to entertain conversational partners with agreeable, wide-ranging chatter for which the zoo offered an ideal backdrop. Social display, exotic animals and gossipy talk peppered with a hint of science – the gentleman's proposal to witness kangaroos 'swallow' their young – together constituted a pleasurable

[21] Alleyne FitzHerbert to Henry FitzHerbert, 18 Mar. 1828, FitzHerbert papers, Derbyshire Record Office, Matlock, D239 M/F 7012.

[22] A. Kendra, 'Gendering the silver fork: Catherine Gore and the society novel', *Women's Writing* xi (2004), 25–38. For the silver fork novel see A. Alison, *Silver fork society: fashionable life and literature from 1814 to 1840*, London 1983; W. Hughes, 'Silver fork writers and readers: social contexts of a best seller', *Novel: A Forum on Fiction* xxv (1992), 328–47.

[23] [C. G. F. Gore], *The diary of a désennuyée*, London 1836, i. 178–80.

[24] The novel was described by the *Mirror* as 'a running satire upon the heartlessness, follies and vices of what is commonly terms fashionable life' (24 Sept. 1836, 201). It was also reviewed in other periodicals including the *Athenaeum*, the *Literary Gazette*, the *New Monthly Magazine* and the *Quarterly Review*. Stereotyped attacks on aristocratic morals and behaviours were not the invention of the silver fork novel, and could be traced back to the 1770s: D. Andrew, '"Adultery à la mode": privilege, the law and attitudes to adultery, 1770–1809', *History* lxxxii (1997), 5–23.

interlude for a party of the *beau monde*. This was, of course, not confined to outings to the zoo. Members of polite society congregated at opera houses and pleasure grounds to indulge in conspicuous display as well to be entertained.[25] Salons were a semi-public space where scientific conversation was encouraged although the range of topics and the degree of female participation had to be controlled.[26] The London Zoo provided another public space and effectively drew together different leisure habits.

The zoo's primary affiliation to high society, however, by no means excluded visitors from other social groups. Regent's Park was now easily reached by middle-class Londoners. In 1829 George Shillibeer launched the first omnibus service, which connected Paddington and the Bank of England through the New Road, a thoroughfare which ran along the south face of Regent's Park. The fare was 1*s.* compared to the old stagecoach fare of half a crown for the same journey.[27] Regent's Park was a key stop on this route, an important junction in the expanding public transport system. Subsequently, a number of operators followed in Shillibeer's footsteps and pioneered new omnibus routes. In 1831 Robert Durham anticipated a growing demand for public transport to the zoo and applied both to the Zoological Society and the Commissioners of Woods and Forests to run omnibuses between Westminster and the zoo gate. The society favoured his plan, but it was rejected by the commissioners.[28] The fear of congestion on the Outer Circle apparently undermined the scheme, and the proposed route might also have been part of hackney coach monopoly.[29] By the mid-1840s, however, a new route had opened from the Elephant and Castle through Waterloo Bridge, the Strand, Regent Street and Great Portland Place to the York and Albany Tavern on the Outer Circle.[30] This public house, so rumour said, provided its

[25] J. L. Hall-Witt, 'Reforming the aristocracy: opera and elite culture, 1780–1860', in Burns and Innes, *Rethinking the age of reform*, 221–37; T. J. Edelstein, 'Vauxhall Gardens', in B. Ford (ed.), *The Cambridge guide to the arts in Britain. V: The Augustan age*, Cambridge 1991, 202–15; J. D. Hunt, *Vauxhall and London's garden theatres*, Cambridge 1985.

[26] For discussions on science in polite conversation see A. N. Walters, 'Conversation piece: science and politeness in eighteenth-century England', *BJHS* xxxv (1997), 121–54, and Secord, *Victorian sensation*, 162–3, 410–16, and 'How scientific conversation became shop talk', in Fyfe and Lightman, *Science in the marketplace*, 23–59.

[27] A. Major, 'Shillibeer and his London omnibus', *Transport History* x (1979), 67–9.

[28] 'Memorial', 26 Nov. 1831, Zoological Gardens papers, WORK 16/726; Robert Durham papers, TNA, RAIL 989/33; Vevers, *London's Zoo*, 25. Durham later became the director of the Brentford and Hammersmith Omnibus Association.

[29] For the competition between omnibuses and hackney coaches see T. C. Barker and M. Robbins, *A history of London transport: passenger travel and the development of the metropolis*, London 1963, i. 17–24.

[30] It was estimated in 1845 that 4,000 buses were operating in and around London, 11,000 men being employed in the service: Anon., *The omnibus men of London: their occupation, lives and deaths*, London 1851, 11.

customers with zoo tickets.[31] Since the new route stretched into the plebeian inner London suburbs south of the Thames, the zoo could potentially cater for working-class customers.

While the omnibus made an access to the zoo easy and quick, pedestrian access was also possible for many Londoners. This was further facilitated by the opening of the Broad Walk in 1834 which then became the north terminus for an urban promenade starting from the south of the city around Trafalgar Square and Piccadilly Circus. Michael Faraday, the distinguished chemist and member of the Zoological Society, liked this walk to the zoo, as he reported in a letter of 1862.[32] The diary of William Tayler, a footman in the service of a wealthy widow in the West End, gives more insight into what the urban promenader saw at the London Zoo when compared to the other sights and spectacles of the metropolis. On 28 June 1837 Tayler was given a day off and decided to go sightseeing. He started from St James's Park, thence to the National Gallery, where he was excited at the encounter with pictures of naked women – 'plenty of representations of women and men naked and made quite perfect'. After lunch in a nearby coffee house, he went to the British Museum, where he was overwhelmed by the size of the building and the vastness of the collection. He seemed to be wandering around the labyrinthine streets of the city, eager to see and to be astonished by the sights of the metropolis. Tayler then left the museum, passed some time in window-shopping and spotted the street corner scene of a recent sensational murder. After a drink in a public house he found himself in the early evening wandering through Regent's Park. Then to the London Zoo, which was still open in the long summer evenings.[33] Again, just as he had been walking from one sight to another in the city, now Tayler spent two hours in the zoo, strolling from 'one den to another all through the gardens'. The vitality of the animal life amazed him: 'There I saw all sorts of beasts, birds and all sorts of animals all alive.' The rest of the day was spent at a friend's house. It was just an hour before midnight when he arrived home and made a brief record of his exciting day off.[34]

Tayler's diary gives a fascinating glimpse of a leisurely stroll that many might have shared but did not describe. It might be thought that he was excited by his experiences because few people of his social status visited the zoo, but contemporary commentaries suggest the contrary. In April 1832 one self-styled respectable gentleman reported to *The Times* that visitors to the zoo consisted 'chiefly of the class of persons called decent tradesmen, with a

[31] *Punch*, 27 Apr. 1844, 186.
[32] Michael Faraday to George Bernard, 22 Dec. 1862, Michael Faraday papers, RI, F1A/32.
[33] As the zoo opened until sunset, the closing time varied from season to season.
[34] This account is drawn from an authentic manuscript diary, which was later edited by a local historian: D. Wise (ed.), *Diary of William Tayler, footman, 1827*, London 1962, 53–4.

fair sprinkling of servants of both sexes'.[35] Another correspondent, 'Scotus', who had come down from the countryside, despised them: 'a more numerous assemblage of what may be called the vulgar classes I scarcely remember having seen'.[36] This attitude fuelled public debate on the zoo's clientele.

Sunday opening

The debate on how far a cultural institution should be open to the public was not simply about the inclusion or exclusion of the lower orders. As Anne Goldgar has argued, it was essentially about competing views on how culture should be transmitted in the public arena for the purpose of cultivating the intellect, taste and morality. In the era of Enlightenment the British Museum was central to such theories. It promulgated the idea of a 'virtual representation of culture', based on the assumption that 'the public would profit not from their own visits, but from the research done in the museum by its curators'.[37] National ownership of the institution did not necessarily mean public access: rather the museum was the preserve of those who could use it most efficiently. Just as the limited parliamentary franchise – confined to propertied males – by no means excluded consideration of the public good, so monopoly of the museum by the learned elite rarely negated ideas of cultural transmission. In this manner, the public was 'virtually' represented in the operation of the museum.

By the 1830s, however, elite culture was being eroded amidst the rapid growth of public institutions of art and science. As Holger Hoock has demonstrated, the role of the state in relation to the public status of the arts was put on the national agenda.[38] The scope of his study of such institutions can be expanded further, for the art world was just one indicator of the changing relations between politics and culture. Indeed, the flowering of Literary and Philosophical Societies, Mechanics' Institutes, and the Sunday Schools movement, the 1826 foundation of the Society for the Diffusion of Useful Knowledge (the SDUK), the 1836 reduction of the 'tax on knowledge' (the Stamp Duty), and Lord Russell's, ultimately unsuccessful, proposal for the establishment of a non-sectarian school system all suggest that state

---

35 *The Times*, 27 Apr. 1832, 3.

36 Ibid. 5 Sept. 1831, 6.

37 A. Goldgar, 'British Museum and the virtual representation of culture', *Albion* xxxii (2000), 218. The notion of 'virtual representation' is borrowed from the study of the eighteenth-century parliamentary system. See J. Brewer, *Party ideology and popular politics at the accession of George III*, Cambridge 1976, and P. Langford, 'Property and "virtual representation" in eighteenth-century England', *HJ* xxxi (1988), 83–111.

38 Hoock, 'Reforming culture', 254–70, and *The king's artists*; Barlow and Trodd, *Governing cultures*.

and voluntary associations were begining to tackle, either in collaboration or competition, the problem of cultural transmission.[39]

Now that the public was becoming a potential recipient of culture and demanded open access to repositories of knowledge, access to art galleries and scientific institutions could no longer be restricted to a select group of the cultural elite. The London Zoo was in fact one of the first institutions to raise the question of accessibility; political and social controversy ensued. In particular, the problem of Sunday opening was a crucial. The range of visitors and their visiting patterns was obviously influenced by whether the zoo was accessible to them on the traditional day of rest in the Christian week, when ordinary work was suspended. In principle, only subscribers and their guests were admitted on Sundays, and this was perceived to be an exclusive privilege of rank and elegance. Catherine Gore's 1836 satire on an aristocratic outing to the zoo on a Sunday touched upon the divisiveness that the zoo's policy created among the public:[40]

> Away to the Zoological [Gardens]; whose, as it is Sunday, when man and beast, with a reasonable proportion of the female of both, are waiting the good-fellowship of the public; that is, not the very *public* public. The public who privileged themselves by a payment of so much per annum, to evade the payment of such much per diem, are alone permitted to enter the Eden of Northern Marylebone on the Sabbath-day.

Her satire on the privileged public ('not the very *public* public') demonstrated that the exclusivism of aristocratic society was axiomatic to the silver fork novel. The popularity of these novels with middle-class readers resulted from an empathic engagement: they both desired aristocratic privilege for themselves and resented it. In other words, the reading of a silver fork novel involved engagement with elite culture, if only in the imagination, and realising one's exclusion from it.[41] The Sunday zoo was thus a narrative space of encounter and exclusion that aroused both aspiration and antipathy.

Moreover, the ironic label – 'the Eden of Northern Marylebone on the Sabbath-day' – has evidently religious implications. For moral reformers, the kind of instructive amusement offered by the zoo was not specifically irreligious. It could be recommended as an effective tool for deepening understanding of God's design of the world. But it was a different matter when it happened on the Sabbath. In 1831 the council of the Zoological Society was asked by Charles James Blomfield, bishop of London, to close

---

[39] An assumption that Victorian Britain was a *laissez-faire* society has been recently reconsidered in response to a growing body of literature on the role of the state in British history. See, for example, P. Mandler, *Liberty and authority in Victorian Britain*, Oxford 2006.

[40] Gore, *The diary of a désennuyée*, i. 171.

[41] Hughes, 'Silver fork writers', 331, 345.

the zoo on Sundays and Good Friday.[42] As a High Churchman with liberal tendencies, Blomfield had worked energetically for the provision of urban amenities for the rapidly increasing population of the metropolis.[43] Sabbath observance was part of his moral programme as demonstrated in his *A letter on the present neglect of the Lord's Day* in 1830. Blomfield's was not a solitary voice. The Zoological Society had to cope with continuous pressure from an extra-parliamentary lobby group, the Lord's Day Observance Society (1831), against Sunday working and entertainment.[44]

Within the Zoological Society, there were many professional men who thought it important to resist such pressures; their anti-Sabbatarian sentiments were revealed in the correspondence columns of *The Times*. In October 1830 *The Times* published a letter from a 'Spectator', who denounced the society for providing 'public amusement' on the Sabbath: when he was riding around Regent's Park on Sundays, he witnessed a number of carriages parked at the zoo entrance and several groups passing through the gate.[45] In reply to this accusation, a member of the society responded, signing his letter as 'F.Z.S' (Fellow of the Zoological Society). He explained that the zoo opened only to Fellows and their companions (not exceeding two), and defended the admission system as a 'great convenience to many of them, who might otherwise be prevented from visiting the gardens'. As for the accusation of Sabbath-breaking, the editor of *The Times* noted that he had received many angry letters, including those subscribed 'No Hypocrite' and 'an Enemy to Cant'. These letters pointed out the hypocrisy of 'Spectator' 'being on horse-back when he made his criticism'.[46]

Such verbal warfare heralded more serious battles within the Zoological Society itself. At first, the society hesitated to discuss an issue that would inevitably lead to schism, but as sectarian idealists were elected onto the

---

[42] Charles Blomfield, bishop of London, to ZSL, 24 Mar. 1831, ZSL, BADG, Edward Greenaway papers.

[43] A. Blomfield (ed.), *Memoir of Charles James Blomfield, bishop of London: with selections from his correspondence*, London 1863; M. Johnson, *Bustling intermeddler? The life and work of Charles James Blomfield*, Leominster 2001. For church reform in the early nineteenth century see A. Burns, 'English "church reform" revisited, 1780–1840', in Burns and Innes, *Rethinking the age of reform*, 136–62.

[44] See, for the activity of Lord's Day Observance Society, B. Harrison, 'Religion and recreation in nineteenth-century England', *P&P* xxxviii (1967), 98–125; J. Wigley, *The rise and fall of the Victorian Sunday*, Manchester 1980; and M. J. D. Roberts, *Making English morals: voluntary association and moral reform in England, 1787–1886*, Cambridge 2004, 117–19. For Evangelicalism in Victorian society see D. W. Bebbington, *Evangelicalism in modern Britain*, London 1989; H. McLeod, *Religion and the working class in nineteenth-century Britain*, London 1984; E. R. Norman, *Church and society in England, 1770–1970*, Oxford 1976; and especially, B. Hilton, *The age of atonement: the impact of Evangelicalism on social and economic thought, 1795–1865*, Oxford 1988.

[45] *The Times*, 19 Oct. 1830, 5.

[46] Ibid. 20 Oct. 1830, 3.

Table 2
Attendance at the London Zoo on Sundays, March–April 1833

Date	Entries before 2.00 p.m.	Entries after 2.00 p.m.	Total
3 Mar.	42	471	513
10 Mar.	3	174	177
17 Mar.	0	5	5
24 Mar.	0	194	194
31 Mar.	29	603	632
7 Apr.	19	611	630
14 Apr.	25	146	171
21 Apr.	23	418	441
28 Apr.	25	589	614
Total	166	3,211	3,377

Source: ZSL, UAA, Visitor Book, 1833

council to replace founder members such as Auckland and Vigors, the situations began to change radically. On 4 April 1833 the council adopted, and submitted to a general meeting of members of the society, a motion proposed by a new member, Robert Hodgson, dean of Carlisle, that the zoo be closed during the time of morning service on Sundays. This motion was not only rejected, but elicited a counter-suggestion that the zoo should remain open from eight o'clock on Sunday. As the meeting was so divided, discussion was adjourned to the anniversary meeting on 29 April 1833.[47] Reports of that meeting in the public media revealed the bitter dispute within the society. Hodgson explained that his intention was not to prevent the 'cheerful enjoyment of the people'. Referring to Agnew's bill to prohibit work on Sundays, he emphasised that he would be opposed to it: 'If such a bill were passed it would throw them back to the worst days of Puritanism.' His speech was greeted with a lusty cheer, yet it was not persuasive enough to change the minds of the majority of the attendants. No compromise being possible, the issue went to a vote: sixty-nine for the council's motion, eighty-nine against it.[48] The reasons for such strong objections is noteworthy. It might be assumed that the opposition tended to visit the zoo on Sunday mornings, but the registration book kept at the zoo gate contradicted this: of the 3,377 subscribers and their guests who visited the zoo during nine consecutive Sundays in March and April 1833 – the weeks of the controversy over Sunday opening – only 166 (4.9 per cent) were recorded before 2.00 p.m. (*see* Table 2). This suggests that few of the opponents of Sunday closing themselves considered visiting the zoo in the morning. Their opposition

[47] ZSL, MM, i, fos 287, 293, 289–9, 310.
[48] *The Times*, 1 May 1833, 2; *Athenaeum*, 4 May 1833, 283.

stemmed from antagonism towards the council, which had challenged the will of the majority in the general meeting.

The ballot at the 1833 anniversary meeting did not settle the dispute. In May 1838 the council of the Zoological Society received a memorial from thirty-four clergymen of St Marylebone and St Pancras parishes, who requested closing the zoo on the Sabbath. As the zoo was located on the border between the two parishes (although mainly within St Marylebone), the clergymen were afraid that the sight of cheerful zoo visitors would have a harmful moral influence on their parishioners. Attached to the memorial was a statement from Blomfield expressing his full support. The council decided to distribute a circular among the society's members to make them aware of the feelings of the neighbouring religious communities, although this did not happen immediately.[49] In June 1840 the council again tried to abolish Sunday opening, but due to the allegation that it had irregularly distributed a circular that justified its proposition, the motion was rejected by a large majority in the general meeting.[50]

Furthermore, the labour and leisure pattern of professionals was an underlying reason for the objection. For those who worked during the normal weekday business hours, Sunday opening was probably their only chance to visit the zoo. A letter from William Broderip, metropolitan magistrate, to Charles Babbage in March 1831, encapsulated the ethos of such non-leisured devotees: 'My hours of relaxation have not been hours of idleness. I do not mean to say that I have done much for science but I may assert that all the time which had not been employed in my official duties, and all the money I could spare has been cheerfully devoted to the advancement of it.'[51] Broderip had become interested in natural history while at Oxford, and despite heavy official duties he maintained his youthful interests and joined the Zoological Society.[52] In 1829, with the assistance of Joseph Sabine and Nicholas Vigors, he compiled the first official catalogue of the zoo animals.[53] Like Broderip, many lawyers joined scientific societies and spent their spare time in the associational activities. The earnest message from Broderip to Babbage thus expressed the views of many non-leisured naturalists.

His close friend, Richard Owen, also realised the importance of Sunday opening. Although Owen himself was a zoologist at the Royal College of Surgeons (appointed Hunterian Professor in 1836) and had time to do his own research during weekdays, he encouraged his medical students to visit

[49] ZSL, MC, v, fos 316–19, 322.

[50] ZSL, MM, ii, fos 295, 300–1, 303; *The Times*, 6 June 1830, 5.

[51] W. J. Broderip to C. Babbage, 25 Mar. 1831, Charles Babbage papers, BL, MS Add. 37185, fos 510–11.

[52] Broderip was also elected a Fellow of the Linnean, the Royal and the Geological Societies.

[53] Broderip was first commissioned to work on the project alone, but was later joined by Sabine and Vigors: ZSL, MC, i, fos 98, 194, 200, 215.

the zoo on Sundays, when they could find time more easily. Moreover, he occasionally supplied Sunday admission tickets to 'journeymen and others of the weekly-wage class', because he recognised 'their inability to profit by the collection of the Zoological Society, on any day but Sunday'. Thus, when one wealthy London resident asked Owen for several Sunday tickets, Owen politely declined the request and recommended this noble client to join the society as a subscriber.[54]

Indeed, natural history had an appeal that transcended class, although it did not necessarily diminish class difference. Working-class naturalists had their own collections, venues for meeting and manner of discussion, and occasionally solicited professional help in the identification of their specimens.[55] On a provincial tour, preparing a report on the reform of the British Museum, John Edward Gray was asked by an artisan in Manchester to compare his own specimens with the collection of his local natural history museum, which was closed to non-subscribers.[56] Likewise approached by artisans in need of professional help, Owen believed that zoos should admit people from a wider social range as long as they shared a taste for natural history. Both Broderip and Owen sat on the council of the Zoological Society, and an anti-exclusionist reformer, Nicholas Vigors, was secretary until 1832.[57] This indicates that even when the council submitted the plan for Sunday closure, all its members were not behind it and it could not therefore take a united stand on Sabbath observance.

Independently of council members, radical reformers supported resistance to the Sabbatarian movement. They criticised its excesses which would deprive the labouring poor of the opportunity to enjoy healthy exercise in public places, even though the zoo would remain open for the leisured classes. The radical Thomas Wakley was a strenuous parliamentary opponent of the Sabbatarianism.[58] In June 1837, opposing Andrew Agnew's bill to prohibit labour on Sundays, Wakley argued that the bill would have 'the worst possible effect on an enlightened and happy population' and would 'convert … [a] happy population into a body of sectarians and mock saints'.

---

[54] Owen, *Richard Owen*, i. 401–2.

[55] A. Desmond, 'Artisan resistance and evolution in Britain, 1819–48', *Osiris* 2nd ser. iii (1987), 77–110.

[56] Secord, 'Botany on a plate', 28–57, and 'Corresponding interests: artisans and gentlemen in nineteenth-century natural history', *BJHS* xxvii (1994), 383–408; G. R. McQuat, 'Species, rules and meaning: the politics of language and the ends of definitions in nineteenth-century natural history', *Studies in History and Philosophy of Science* xxvii (1996), 473–519.

[57] In parliament Vigors voted against Andrew Agnew's bill to ban open labour on Sundays: *Hansard* 3rd ser. xxxviii, 1243, 7 June 1837.

[58] Sprigge, *Thomas Wakley*; I. A. Burney, 'Medicine in the age of reform', in Burns and Innes, *Rethinking the age of reform*, 163–81.

One of his colleagues suggested that many proponents of the bill frequented Regent's Park on Sunday. In the eyes of the radicals this revealed the blatant hypocrisy of Evangelical reformers and patronising aristocrats.[59] Wakley went so far as to criticise the subscribers of the Zoological Society for monopolising the zoo on Sundays and excluding those who could not afford the annual membership.[60]

Although his speech against Sabbath observance would be cheered by the society's members, especially by professional men like Broderip and Owen, his demand for public access on Sundays was unlikely to gain their consent. In a general meeting of the Zoological Society in March 1830, Robert Gordon proposed Sunday opening, but the opposition, led by Robert Hodgson and other members, forced him to withdraw the motion.[61] Outside the society the proposal would garner the support of significant public figures. John Claudius Loudon, who advocated the reform of scientific societies and announced his plans through the medium of his own publications such as the *Magazine of Natural History* and the more successful *Gardener's Magazine*, argued that servants and petty-tradesmen would benefit if the zoo admitted the public on Sundays.[62] *The Times* also published many letters that demanded extensive access to the London Zoo. Among them all, an open letter from an anonymous member to the president of the Zoological Society is notable for its plain speaking:[63]

> The dealing with a man as if he were a thief is the surest way to make him one … notwithstanding the immense numbers admitted to the gardens in the Regent's Park, there has been no one instance of misconduct: so that, independent of the advancement of science which will result from the society, I think its menageries may be made the means of working considerable good in the character of the people, and at the same time afford them a rational and cheap amusement.

The language of moral reform and self-improvement was also deployed by working-class reformers. In 1829 William Lovett, a leading working-class radical, presented to parliament 'a petition for the opening of the British Museum, and the other exhibitions of Art and Nature, on Sundays'. It was one of the earliest attempts of this kind, and influenced the foundation of the

59 *Hansard* 3rd ser. xxxviii, 1237–8, 7 June 1837.
60 Sprigge, *Thomas Wakley*, 394.
61 *The Times*, 8 Mar. 1830, 5.
62 *Magazine of Natural History* ii (1829), 371–2; E. McDougall (ed.), *John Cladius Loudon and the early nineteenth century in England*, Washington, DC 1980; M. L. Simo, *Loudon and the landscape: from country seat to metropolis, 1783–1843*, New Haven 1988.
63 *The Times*, 22 Jan. 1830, 2.

National Sunday League.[64] Lovett clearly identified museums and libraries as educational resources for the public:[65]

> No more effectual means for the removal of drunkenness could be provided than the opening of our museums, our mechanic and scientific institutions, our libraries, and all our exhibitions of art and nature on Sunday, the only day our working population have to enjoy them, and by giving every facility and encouragement for persons delivering scientific, historical, and every description of instructive lectures to the mass of the people on that day.

In the social history of leisure, this statement has been dismissed as simply urging that the cultural hegemony of the middle classes be extended to include a group of self-improving working-class men, who represented only a small minority of the social category to which they belonged.[66] But it should not be assumed that William Lovett and his like were merely absorbing the values of middle-class reformers. Lovett's petition should rather be read in the light of various contemporary changes surrounding public access to knowledge. From the 1820s onwards, the flood of unstamped newspapers led to an excited parliamentary debate on whether stamp duty – criticised by its opponents as 'tax on knowledge' – should be repealed. By that time it had become obvious that the Stamp Act could no longer control the provision of political news, and it was finally reduced from 4d. to 1d. Sunday opening and a tax-free press were part of the same move towards 'open access' to knowledge. The radical Weekly Times called for the zoo to be open on Sundays, repeating that Sunday was the only day of the week when labourers could visit the place.[67] In parliament, Thomas Wakley advocated the promotion of Sunday recreation and the repeal of the tax on knowledge with equal eagerness.[68]

The question of Sunday opening was at the heart of a complex web of competing views about the control and monitoring of public access to culture. While moral reform was at work, the Zoological Society came to be recognised as a national institution that should bring scientific discoveries and activities directly to the public – 'directly' in the sense of the public being the primary recipients of its benefits. There was, however, another question concerning access to zoo, one that was even more difficult of deal with.

---

[64] Harrison, 'Religions and recreation', 109; D. Stack, 'William Lovett and the National Association for the Political and Social Improvement of the People', HJ xlii (1999), 127–50.

[65] W. Lovett, The life and struggles of William Lovett, London 1876, 57–8.

[66] D. Vincent, Bread, knowledge and freedom: a study of nineteenth-century working class autobiography, London 1981, 155–6.

[67] Weekly Times, 5 June 1836, 4.

[68] Sprigge, Thomas Wakley, 394.

Public admission

While the zoo was still under construction in 1827, the council of the Zoological Society began to discuss the entrance fee and the number of days in a week that non-subscribers should be admitted. It was only in May 1828, when the society finally obtained government permission to open the zoo to the public, that it was able to reach agreement on the issue.[69] In the summer of 1828 the regulations on public entry were finally drafted. The non-subscribing public was required to obtain an order of admission from a member of the society. This could be done either in writing or on a printed form prepared by the society. The order of admission applied not only to its holder but also to his whole party, host and guests. At the zoo gate a copy of the order plus 1s. entry fee per person was presented to a clerk, whose post was in a booth to the left of the gate. In return visitors were given a receipt which was shown to an attendant in another booth.

For the first few years after the zoo opened, the council of the Zoological Society allowed the clerk to hand out admission orders so that non-subscribers were able to gain entry even if they were not acquainted with a member of the society.[70] In August 1831, however, the council seems to have recognised that this system contradicted the principle that personal acquaintance was a requirement for admission and ceased to distribute admission orders at the zoo gate.[71] The sudden change in policy angered the non-subscribing public and led to a fierce debate in *The Times* in April 1832. It began with a complaint from an anonymous correspondent, 'Enemy of All Humbugs', who had frequented the zoo and had therefore understood that the production of an admission order was a mere 'matter of ceremony'. At his latest visit, however, he had been denied entry on the grounds that his party did not possess an order, and therefore determined to write to *The Times* and rouse public opinion against the Zoological Society. The letter was followed by an unusually long editorial, which castigated the procedure as working against the society's original intentions: 'The necessity of an order implies a certain respectability among the company, which is peculiarly gratifying to the "eminent" tallow-chandlers and tripe-sellers who, with their wives and daughters, visit these places of fashionable resort, and who cannot bear any thing "as is low".'[72] This comment suggests that admission tickets were widely circulated beyond the control of the society, especially among the

---

[69] Vigors to Milne, 5 May 1828, and Milne to Vigors, 14 May 1828, Zoological Gardens papers, WORK 16/724; circular addressed to the members of the Zoological Society of London, 14 May 1828, Bodl. Lib., JJC, London Play Places 8(67); ZSL, MC, i, fos 40–1, 52–3, 56–9.

[70] In April 1830 the council ordered 10,000 copies of the order to be printed, many of which were likely to be distributed at the zoo gate: ZSL. MC, i, fo. 369.

[71] ZSL, MC, ii, fo. 258.

[72] *The Times*, 23 Apr. 1832, 3.

lower middle classes, and that this was publicly remarked upon by cynical observers.

The protest letter and the sarcastic editorial were soon rebutted by James Whishaw, a Fellow of the Zoological Society who supported the council in taking an exclusionist stance.[73] He argued that admission orders served to filter the zoo's clientele and thereby to protect the animals from troublesome behaviour on the part of 'illegitimate' strangers. This argument was not at all new, but his concluding remarks are noteworthy. Whishaw stated that the current procedure was 'conducive not only to the interests of the society, but also to those of its best patrons and most liberal supporters – the public at large'.[74] Here the focus of the debate was shifting from the zoo's admission policy to the reciprocal relationship between the Zoological Society and the public. Protest letters swiftly responded. They justified their intervention by arguing that the society's finances relied largely on the 1s. admission fee paid by the non-subscribing public. The authors of these letters confidently acted as the representatives of the 'public at large', whose opinions, they considered, should be reflected upon by the management of the society and the zoo.[75] In their view the problem was rooted in the enclosed scientific community, and the solution lay in increased efficiency, transparency and accountability. John George Children, keeper of the zoological department at the British Museum and a Tory-affiliated member of the council, argued to the contrary: Fellows of the society alone were entitled to discuss its business. Children accused the reformers of attempting to provoke public animus against the society, and warned the Fellows to ignore this demagogue. None the less Children felt himself bound to respond to the challenges of the non-subscribing public. With a tacit sense of dilemma, he made an excuse in a postscript: 'where gross misstatements are made, they must be contradicted'.[76]

The debate in *The Times* signalled a growing awareness of relations between the scientific community and the public and presented the two competing interpretations of that relationship. One rested on the principle of virtual representation, which the council barely sustained. The zoo's status as a public institution neither automatically guaranteed public access nor entitled the non-subscribing public to discuss its affairs: the object of the Zoological Society was to benefit the public, but the means by which this was achieved was its own affair. The other interpretation was that the non-subscribing public funded the society by paying admission fees, and that the society should therefore serve public interests by listening to what they said. The latter argument was apparently more convincing not only to those who

[73] ZSL, MM, i. fo. 321. Little is known about James Whishaw; he was appointed to a number of different committees of the society, and was later elected to the council.

[74] *The Times*, 23 Apr. 1832, 3.

[75] Ibid. 25 Apr. 1832, 2.

[76] Ibid. 27 Apr. 1832, 3.

ZOOLOGICAL SOCIETY.

ADMIT   AND PARTY,

TO THE GARDENS, REGENT'S PARK,

BY ORDER OF *Jn. Sabine*

ADMIT   AND PARTY,

TO THE MUSEUM, 33, BRUTON STREET,

BY ORDER OF *Jn. Sabine*

EXTRACT FROM REGULATIONS—'Strangers may be admitted either to the Gardens
or Museum, by Orders from Fellows, upon payment of 1s. by each Person.'
No Admission, except to Fellows, on Sundays.

Catalogues of the Museum and Menagerie may be obtained at the respective
Establishments.

Figure 17. An early printed form of the order of admission, ZSL.

were disadvantaged by the restrictive entry procedure, but also, ironically, to the members of the society who bitterly observed that the current procedure could not prevent 'illegitimate' strangers from flooding into the zoo.

While the challenge to 'virtual representation theory' took place within the pages of *The Times*, it was moved forward within the confines of the London Zoo itself. Although the admission policy remained unaltered until the late 1840s, the society's attempts to implement it struggled to succeed. First of all, subscribers who prioritised their own personal interests did not necessarily follow proper procedures. One Fellow supplied his friends with extra admission tickets that he had obtained at the entrance booth, knowing that it was prohibited, so that they would enter the zoo in his absence without paying admission fees.[77] Compared with this, signing for strangers was a minor violation although a more common means of circumventing the regulations. To accommodate a request from an unacquainted person who sought to become 'company' when passing through the zoo gates was a customary manner of showing generosity. Many strangers took advantage of this custom, which worked to the satisfaction of all parties. It was occasionally reported to the council, but there were probably many more undocumented instances.[78]

Moreover a large number of admission orders seemed to be in circulation, way beyond the personal networks of Fellows. When a Fellow filled in the printed from he was expected to specify the name of the recipient, but that space often remained blank (*see* Figure 17, an order signed by Joseph Sabine, the treasurer of the Zoological Society). Of the sixty-eight copies of

---

[77] ZSL, MC, iii, fos 154–5; iv, fo. 353.

[78] ZSL, MC, i, fo. 376; iii, fos 59, 178, 447; v. 365; vi, fos 160, 178–9.

printed admission orders in the society's archive, thirty-seven fail to specify the recipient's name. A few others simply note 'this party'.[79] The evidence suggests that admission orders could be obtained easily by a third party, who often came from a lower social background: a common example would be a servant or customer being given an order by their master or a tradesmen. Although William Tayler did not say how he obtained his zoo admission order, it might be that his mistress had provided it for him. Indeed, a self-fashioned 'respectable' reader of *The Times* complained that the orders could be possessed not only by servants but also 'by almost any description of persons who have any knowledge of a Fellow of the Society'.[80]

While subscribers regularly violated the official regulations, the staff of the zoo showed little enthusiasm for monitoring the admission procedure. A handful of staff was skilful and loyal, rewarded with a wage rise and a pension after long service to the society.[81] But, in fact, nothing was in place to motivate them to check that there was no irregular conduct on the part of the visitors. It is understandable that they hesitated to ask a question that might offend an irritable guest. In the case of trouble with one of the Fellows, they were obviously in a weak position unless the council aimed at a thorough, fair investigation. Insolence and insulting language on the part of the staff was a common accusation made by Fellows to the council, after some unpleasant experience, and the accusation often resulted in dismissal of the person in question.[82]

Above all, Londoners knew that admission tickets could be obtained easily in nearby public houses or from drivers of the omnibuses. So many tickets were in circulation that there were rumours that the society circulated them deliberately among those to whom it could not officially admit to providing tickets. A reader of *The Times* sent to the editor an advertising card, presumably of the York and Albany Tavern, Regent's Park. It included the words: 'Tickets to be had for the Zoological Gardens'.[83] Since the public house was at the terminus of one omnibus route starting from the Elephant and Castle, travellers could use it as an unofficial ticket office. Moreover, tickets were openly sold in the park even on Sundays, and forgeries were allegedly very common.

At the general meeting in July 1838, the council of the Zoological Society officially conceded that 'the admission of improper characters could not

[79] ZSL, UAA, Visitor book.
[80] *The Times*, 27 Apr. 1832, 3.
[81] ZSL, BABA, Returns, memoranda; Vevers, *London's Zoo*, 34.
[82] In July 1834, following a proposal from Robert Gordon, the council set up a committee to discipline the zoo staff: ZSL, MM, iii, fo. 458.
[83] *The Times*, 26 Apr. 1832, 2.

be prevented'.[84] Five years later, in his guide to London, Charles Knight described the typical strategy of an 'improper character':[85]

> Two young genteel-looking females have been waiting for some time, looking with a peculiar air of curiosity in the faces of those who enter; at last, seeing a party of ladies and gentlemen stop for the same purpose – one of them modestly steps up and begs permission to enter as part of their company. Surprise appears on the face of the lady addressed, but another steps forward, remarking, 'O yes! It is a common request;' and the whole party enter; the money-taker at the lodge, who could hardly avoid seeing what passed, making no comment.

To visitors from the countryside, Knight advised that tickets could be obtained from a nearby tavern, or that an intending visitor to the zoo could sneak in under the cover of a group of 'legitimate' visitors. It is remarkable that this mode of illegal entry was not only known by word-of-mouth but also appeared in print, in a reputable guidebook published by a Fellow of the Zoological Society.

By that time the admission policy had already ceased to invite polemics. As the council became less enthusiastic about vetting the zoo's clientele, the momentum for reform abated. Knight recognised that the council would not dare to ban the informal market for zoo tickets. The penalty for circumventing the society's regulation came along some ten years later, however, when he fell victim to a shrewd trick by one Charles Surrey Knight of King's Street, Covent Garden. In 1852, this otherwise unknown man sent letters in the name of Charles Knight to a number of renowned figures of the Zoological Society including the marquis of Lansdowne, Henry Brougham, William Henry Sykes and Michael Faraday, and requested free admission tickets for the zoo. Although he successfully obtained several tickets, the application was seen to be somewhat strange. Not surprisingly, suspicion fell on Charles Knight, the well-known publisher, and he had to protest his innocence by writing to *The Times*.[86] In the meantime, the council of the Zoological Society dispatched a messenger to the address given by Charles Surrey Knight, and then discovered that his wife was running a milliner's shop at that address.[87] The tickets were probably either sold directly to her customers or distributed as free gifts.

In a letter to *The Times* published in February 1836, one anonymous reformer argued that the zoo was 'so essentially national' that it should not 'suffer through corrupt or negligent management'.[88] As the reform of scien-

---

84 Ibid. 6 July 1838, 6.
85 Knight, *London*, v. 258–9.
86 *The Times*, 2 Mar. 1852, 7.
87 D. W. Mitchell to Faraday, 22 June 1852, Faraday papers, F1k/p.28.
88 *The Times*, 26 Feb. 1836, 6.

tific societies was directed towards the enhancement of efficiency, transparency and accountability, the public began to evaluate them according to these barometers. The changes surrounding the status of the public were irreversible: the public was no longer mere recipients who commissioned the learned elite to represent their interests in the institutionalisation of 'culture'. This can be more clearly understood in the light of the national debates on public access to art galleries and scientific institutions.

Repercussions

In March 1833 William Cobbett spoke in parliament against state subsidies of £16,000 towards the annual expenses of the British Museum. As a representative of distressed rural communities, Cobbett asked: 'Why should tradesmen and farmers be called upon to pay for the support of a place which was intended only for the amusement of the curious and the rich, and not for the benefit or for the instruction of the poor? If the aristocracy wanted the Museum as a lounging place, let them pay for it.'[89] This was a conventional criticism of the theory of virtual representation of culture, defining the British Museum as a manifestation of 'old corruption', but it had already become stale by the 1830s. Although Cobbett made a determined yet vain effort to cut spending on what he denounced as 'a lounging place' for the aristocracy, an increasing number of people distanced themselves from his view and instead demanded wider access to the rapidly expanding collections of the museum. Attendance figures had indeed multiplied from 24,000 to 210,000 over the previous ten years.

Eventually, in 1835, parliament set up a select committee, but as its proceedings ended rather abruptly and without making any recommendations, another committee was appointed in the following year.[90] Topics for discussions varied, ranging from the make-up of the body of trustees to the mode of displaying and cataloguing objects, but among them all, the question of accessibility was noteworthy.[91] The committees summoned various staff and external specialists to the hearings and asked them whether they would agree to open the museum in the evenings and on public holidays. Senior officials were highly reluctant to acknowledge the advantage of longer opening hours. Henry Ellis, principal librarian, protested that it would only benefit people 'of a very low description' and would offend 'the more important class of the population', for which he believed the museum was

[89] *Hansard* 3rd ser. xvi, 1003, 25 Mar. 1833, quoted in Goldgar, 'British Museum', 195.
[90] For details of the select committee on the reform of the British Museum see Wilson, *The British Museum*, 85–92.
[91] D. Cash, *Access to museum culture: the British Museum from 1753 to 1836* (British Museum Occasional Papers cxxxiii, 2002), 165–96.

essentially intended.[92] This statement did not contradict his belief in the educational value of the museum's collections. He wrote on the Elgin and Phigaleian marbles for the SDUK's *Library of Entertaining Knowledge*, which aimed to advance working-class education.[93] Ellis espoused the ideology of virtual representation, which his assistant, James Forshall, explained: 'it [the Reading Room of the British Museum] is not intended to be a library of education, but a library of research; and its use must ever be confined, or ought to be confined, chiefly to persons of literary or scientific pursuits, who have some serious objects in view in coming to consult its collections'.[94]

Likewise, other staff members expressed anxieties that opening on public holidays would cause a great confusion in the museum space. George Samouelle, assistant keeper of the zoological department, was advised to 'have a good watch at the door, that no one in a state of the slightest inebriation or not decently attired should be admitted, for it is under those circumstances that we might expect mischief'.[95] Samouelle's colleague in the zoological department, John George Children, also testified that no drastic change was required, as the collections were satisfactorily arranged for use by 'each of those respective classes of people'.[96] Their statements were, however, contradicted by many external scholars, who in their answers approved the extension of opening hours. Apart from the range of prospective visitors that they had in mind (ranging from medical students and junior clerks to petty-tradesmen and interested artisans), references to the London Zoo in support of opening on public holidays were particularly notable. James De Carle Sowerby, naturalist and later a co-founder of the Royal Botanic Gardens at Regent's Park (1838), remarked that it was 'evident from the circumstances of the Zoological Gardens' that the British Museum could expect even larger attendance on Easter Monday and Whit Monday. When asked if that would be 'beneficial, not only to scientific men, but to the public at large', Sowerby firmly replied that it would be advantageous to 'the people at large'.[97] Nicholas Vigors, summoned as the former secretary of the Zoological Society, expressed his keen support for the widest possible access to the British Museum. Concerning fears that the collection would be damaged by the unruly conduct of vulgar visitors, Vigors confirmed that no injury had ever occurred at the London Zoo on public holidays, when it admitted those thousands of visitors who were otherwise unable to come.[98]

---

92   *Report on the British Museum* (1835), qq. 1328–30.
93   [H. Ellis], *The British Museum: Elgin and Phigaleian marbles*, London 1833.
94   *Report on the British Museum* (1835), qq. 1280–90.
95   Ibid. qq. 3917–20
96   *Report from the select committee on the British Museum*, PP x (1836), q. 2791.
97   Ibid. q. 142.
98   Ibid. qq. 1432–4.

Consequently, on the recommendation of the select committee of 1836, the Trustees of the British Museum were forced to extend opening hours as well as to admit visitors on certain public holidays.[99] It is reasonable to think that the experience of the London Zoo had a certain impact on this decision. As the zoo had recorded larger visitor numbers than the British Museum until the last few years, it was held to be a successful test case for controlling access to public institutions of art and science. In May 1835, a few months before the museum committee was launched, William Cobbett, in the last year of his life, had again expressed his opposition to state subsidies for the British Museum. His speech contrasted sharply with that of Joseph Hume, radical leader of the new generation, who asserted that the state should fund the museum on condition that it should be a more accessible.[100] The Cobbetian criticism of the British Museum had by this time been replaced by the growing belief that it should be managed under parliamentary supervision for the purpose of providing intellectual interest for the wider public.

From the late 1830s the reform of cultural institutions was championed by Joseph Hume, who founded the Society for Obtaining Free Admission to National Monuments and Public Edifices Containing Works of Art in 1837, and demanded free access to St Paul's and Westminster Abbey, both of which exhibited military monuments.[101] The accession to the throne of Queen Victoria was advantageous, as the government tried to make cultural institutions more accessible on coronation day in order to add to the festive mood. As the London Zoo was listed as a popular destination, Lord John Russell, the Home Secretary, was consulted on the plausibility of opening the zoo 'gratuitously' to the public on that day.[102] Victoria herself was in favour of the plan and exercised her influence to allow public access to the royal residences and collections such as Hampton Court Palace.

Accordingly, the continuing efforts of Joseph Hume and his allies led to the appointment in April 1841 of a select committee on National Monuments and Works of Art. Chaired by Hume himself, the committee recommended that St Paul's and Westminster Abby should admit the public free of charge, especially on Sundays. The committee went on to gather supporting evidence by examining the cases of Hampton Court Palace and the Naval Gallery of Greenwich Hospital, both of which were already open on Sunday afternoons, and established that visitors to these institutions benefitted in

[99] *Minutes of the Trustees of the British Museum*, PP xxxix (1837), p. 4.

[100] *Hansard* 3rd ser. xxvi, 186–7, 18 May 1835.

[101] [G. Foggo,] *Report of the proceedings at a public meeting, held at the Freemasons Hall, on the 29th of May, 1837, to promote the admission of the public, without charge, to Westminster Abbey, St Paul's Cathedral, and all depositories of works of art, of natural history, and objects of historical and literary interest in public edifices*, London 1837; T. Nakamura. 'Rulers of the sea: naval commemoration and British political culture, c.1780–1815', unpubl. PhD diss. Osaka 2007, 179–85.

[102] J. K. Cook to John Russell, 16 June 1838, Home Office papers, HO 44/31, fos 459–60.

taste and morality by seeing works of fine art. Senior officials at the British Museum remained vigorous opponents. Henry Ellis opposed Sunday opening on the grounds of Sabbath-breaking. Edward Hawkins, keeper of the department of antiquities, also pointed out the difficulty of employing attendants, as he had 'less confidence in a man who would be willing to have his Sunday occupied in that way than in one who had scruples upon the subject'.[103]

The only exception was John Edward Gray, who called for reform from within the museum. He presented the committee with the information that he had collected from a number of cultural institutions in Europe, many of which admitted visitors on Sundays. Moreover, he referred to the case of the London Zoo, where visitors arrived after the time of morning service, as evidence that Sunday opening would not necessarily encourage Sabbath-breaking. When Henry Goulburn, representing Tory Sabbatarians on the committee, observed that Sunday access was limited to the subscribers and their guests, Gray retorted that 'the lower class of the population' would imitate the conduct of those who could afford to subscribe for their privilege.[104] These statements invited hostility from his colleagues, especially from Henry Ellis. In June 1841 Gray informed Francis Place, a leading working-class reformer, that he had been warned by Ellis that he would submit a petition against Sunday opening with the assistance of Charles Blomfield, *ex-officio* trustee of the British Museum.[105] Gray angrily wondered why the British Museum was so staunchly against reform, while the zoo and other institutions were already opening on Sundays.[106]

When it came to it the recommendations of the select committee were rejected, as Robert Peel returned as premier and appointed Goulburn as Chancellor of the Exchequer in September 1841.[107] When the Tory government fell in July 1846, Joseph Hume again tabled a motion for free access on Sunday, but was not supported by Peel's successor. Lord John Russell made it clear that he was happy to leave the matter in the hands of the Trustees of the British Museum.[108] Russell's decision marked the limits of state intervention on the question of Sabbath observance.[109] Apart from Sunday opening, however, access to cultural institutions was significantly widened. By the 1850s, the fears of crowds and mobs in public spaces had finally receded, and a new spirit of reform was abroad, symbolised by the opening of

103 *Report from the select committee on National Monuments and Works of Arts*, PP vi (1841 sess. 1), qq. 3091–4.

104 Ibid. qq. 3121–76.

105 The bishop of London was an *ex officio* trustee of the British Museum.

106 J. E. Gray to Francis Place, 23 June 1841, Francis Place papers, BL, MS Add. 37949, fos 424–5.

107 *Return from the Trustees of the British Museum and the National Gallery*, PP, xxv (1846).

108 *Hansard* 3rd ser. lxxxviii, 718–25, 14 Aug. 1846; *The Times*, 15 Aug. 1847, 2–3.

109 Russell, however, decided to open Kew Gardens on Sundays in 1847: Wigley, *The rise and fall*, 91.

the 1851 Great Exhibition and further boosted by the establishment of the South Kensington Museum, which displayed its decorative art collection as an educational resource.[110] Meanwhile, as will be discussed in chapter 4, the London Zoo had opened its door to the general public and taken on some of the features of a scientific amusement park.

A visit to the zoo became a familiar form of recreation for a far wider range of people than its proprietors had initially conceived. This was not the direct outcome of the original scheme of the Zoological Society or evidence of the total failure of its admission system. It turned out that the society was flexible in controlling public access, although its compromises may have seemed to be the result of public pressure. The range of visitors now served to create an amphitheatric atmosphere, where spectators were keen to observe their similarities and differences, admiring the elegance of fashionable crowds or regarding with suspicion the behaviour of vulgar flocks. Their mutual visibility, either appreciated or despised, encouraged them to realise how widely the enjoyment of the zoo was shared among very different members of the public. When critical debates arose over the issue of the zoo's admission system, this diversity was transmuted into the comprehensive image of the public, which as a subjective agent claimed to evaluate the administration of the Zoological Society. The real diversity of the public, which was visually recognised, was still virtually embraced by the language of the public.

It is hard to overestimate the role played by the London Zoo in guiding discussions on cultural politics. As a large-scale, pioneering institution that admitted thousands of visitors on a daily basis, the evidence that it presented in support of widening access was crucial. In the discursive arena of parliamentary debate, the London Zoo offered a successful model of direct transmission, and it certainly affected the actual changes that occurred in the public institutions of art and science in the 'age of reform'. All the same, the idea that accessibility was a basic function of public institutions presented new questions. Defending the restrictive admission policy of the London Zoo, James Whishaw had stated that the council of the Zoological Society acted for the interests of 'its best patrons and most liberal supporters – the public at large'. How a scientific society could best communicate with this 'public at large' remains a question.

---

[110] E. Bonython and A. Burton, *The great exhibitor: the life and works of Henry Cole*, London 2003, 172–89.

4

Between Science and Commerce

Of all the scientific institutions in Britain the Zoological Society had the largest funds. Charles Babbage remarked in his *Reflections on the decline of science in England* (1830) that the enormity of the society's income was 'a frightful consideration'.[1] The society's affluence placed it in a different category from other scientific institutions and also drew public attention to its spending patterns. Whereas most scientific institutions were funded by voluntary subscriptions, the Zoological Society had an additional source of income: receipts from admission to the London Zoo. The potential was clearly identified by William Swainson, naturalist and external critic of the society, who explained its two principal aims in his *A preliminary discourse on the study of natural history* (1834): promotion of 'legitimate science' and provision of 'popular recreation'. He hoped that the society would unite these spheres:[2]

> Where there are ample funds, as in the present case, a judicious management may unite, in equal proportions, popular recreation with the encouragement of legitimate science; for the attraction of the former would raise funds for paying the latter, and thus the highest objects might be combined with those that were more ornamental than useful.

His proposals questioned the public rationale of the Zoological Society, but their importance hardly registered at a time when the society had such confidence in the popularity of the zoo. The time for reflection only came in the early 1840s when the society faced a financial crisis, when it had to make a choice between legitimate and recreational science.

Financial restructuring

The Zoological Society was not a commercial exhibitor of animals, but a voluntary society. In the early nineteenth century there emerged a new genre of institutions, each pursuing a specific branch of the natural sciences; the Zoological Society was one of these, modelled on the Horticultural Society

[1] C. Babbage, *Reflections on the decline of science in England and on some of its causes*, London 1830, 46.
[2] W. Swainson, *A preliminary discourse on the study of natural history*, London 1834, 439–40.

(1804), and following in the steps of the Geological Society (1807) and the Astronomical Society (1820). Admission fees and annual subscriptions were £5 and £3 respectively, not particularly high in comparison with other institutions.

In terms of the size of its membership and funding, however, the Zoological Society was exceptional. In the 1830s the society recorded over 3,000 subscribers, whereas the smaller Entomological Society listed less than 200 and even the relatively large Geological Society had only around 300 at the same period.[3] Moreover, the annual income of the Zoological Society was twice that of the Horticultural Society and nearly ten times that of the Geological Society: the result of the popularity of the London Zoo. During its first ten years, gate receipts were the largest source of income, accounting for around 40–70 per cent of annual revenue. In 1836, the year of the giraffe exhibition, gate receipts amounted nearly to £9,500, and the amalgamation of admission fees and annual subscriptions together came to £6,600, together constituting three-quarters of the gross revenue of over £21,000. This proportion was extremely high in comparison to the Horticultural Society, which received from its botanic garden only one-eighth of its gross income. The Zoological Society thus broke through the principle of voluntary contribution; it could not have operated without an external source of income.

The society's *raison d'être* was the exhibition of the widest possible range of living species and it was this that produced its extraordinary fiscal structure. The collection of natural objects such as minerals, insects, shells, plants and fossil remains was equally the object of different scientific societies, but it was far more costly to collect animals in foreign lands and then keep them alive in an alien climate. Feed costs were extremely high, often exceeding £2,000 *per annum*, and the wages bill was even larger during the years from 1828 to 1838. Besides, the Zoological Society had to pay for expensive construction works, which cost not less than £1,400 *per annum*. On the whole, during this period, the London Zoo accounted for 70–80 per cent of the gross expenditure of the Zoological Society.

As the society's financial accounts were published in its annual report, they were subject to public scrutiny. In the aftermath of the council election of 1835, the disenchanted reforming members were radicalised and strengthened their resistance to the Tory coterie. In April 1836 they criticised the council's decision to liquidate a portion of the society's funded capital via bond disposal.[4] This was needed to defray the extra costs of the giraffe exhibition, but when announced at a general meeting of the society, James Pope requested detailed explanation.[5] As communications with the council

---

[3]   *Reports of the council and auditors* (1837), 3; H. B. Woodward, *The history of the Geological Society of London*, London 1907, 245; S. A. Neave, *The history of the Entomological Society of London, 1833–1933*, London 1933, 14.

[4]   ZSL, MC, iv, fos 354–7.

[5]   ZSL, MC, iv, fos 404–5, 428–9.

Table 3
Staff numbers and their salaries, 1837, 1845, 1850

	Office		Zoo		Museum		Total	
	staff	£ salaries	staff	£ salaries	staff	£ salaries	staff	£ salaries
1837	6	596	31	2,126	8	698	45	3,412
1845	5	598	28	1,618	4	265	32	2,418
1850	4	524	23	1,347	1	54	28	1,926

Source: ZSL, GAAW, Reports of the Receipts and Expenditure Committee

proceeded unsatisfactorily as far as Pope and his allies were concerned, he disclosed the society's balance sheet and cast doubts on its accuracy in his correspondence to *The Times*.[6] This invited suspicions of fraud and greatly alarmed the council. When financial scandal at the Horticultural Society was publicised in 1830, many subscribers withdrew, fearing that they would be made responsible for the society's debts.[7] Fearing a similar *débâcle*, the council of the Zoological Society decided to draft a counter-report, but delay in its publication meant that Pope's insinuations prevailed.[8] Although, in the event, there was no sudden decline in membership of the society, the council recognised the need for financial restructuring.

In 1837 the newly-appointed Receipts and Expenditure Committee suggested that contracts for construction and maintenance work in the zoo be revised, subscriptions be collected more efficiently and, above all, staffing costs be reduced.[9] The latter was pursued the most radically (*see* Table 3) in the museum department; its drastic downscaling pointed to significant changes in the institutional structure of the Zoological Society. The Zoological Museum had continued to develop since its establishment at Bruton Street in 1828, and the collection had been further expanded by the purchase in 1836 from Hugh Cuming, conchologist and dealer in natural history specimens, of a large shell collection of around 6,000 species estimated to be worth more than £3,000. Named the 'Cumingian Shell Collection', it was an important addition to the museum.[10] In the same year, under pressure from pro-museum lobbyists, the council agreed to move the collections to more

6   *The Times*, 18 May 1836, 7.
7   Fletcher, *Story of Royal Horticultural Society*, 120–4.
8   ZSL, MC, iv, fos 458, 466; MM, ii, fos 87–8.
9   ZSL, MC, v, fos 212, 223–4.
10 Edward T. Bennett to Owen, 30 Dec. 1835, Owen collection, OC62, iii, fos 189–9; George B. Sowerby to Owen, 31 Dec. 1835; 'agreement', 13 Jan. 1836, ZSL, BADC, H. Cuming papers; *Reports of the council and auditors* (1836), 19; S. P. Dance, 'Hugh Cuming (1791–1865): prince of collectors', *JBNH* v (1970), 369–88.

extensive and convenient premises in Leicester Square.[11] Nevertheless, few people visited the new museum, a fact which soon came to the attention of the Receipts and Expenditure Committee. In 1838 the committee proposed that visitors to the zoo be given free tickets to the museum and and suggested exhibiting some living animals at the site. It recognised that a collection of shells and inanimate animals had little popular appeal. The council adopted the first suggestion, but attendance at the museum was hardly affected.[12]

In 1840 the council of the Zoological Society began to discuss how to make the museum 'a popular attraction', and in the following year a special general meeting was summoned 'for the purpose of considering and determining on the ultimate abstraction of the Society's Preserved Collection'.[13] The meeting agreed that the museum was 'a necessary and intrinsic part of the scientific establishment which it is essential should be perpetuated'. However, it had become obvious that the society's declining resources could no longer fund the museum. Thus James Pope's suggestion that the council should take actions to retain the Leicester Square Museum was rejected by a large majority. Instead, the society resolved to consider how to preserve its collection without the need for a museum.[14] Simultaneously, John Edward Gray had suggested that the collection should be transferred to the British Museum, but this was rejected by the council, presumably because the gross value of the collection (estimated at £10,565) made negotiations difficult.[15] Instead, in 1842, the Zoological Society resolved to downgrade the museum and then to move its collection to premises at the London Zoo. It also abolished the office of curator and discharged George Waterhouse, who had been in post since the beginning. Informed of his preremptory dismissal, he wrote to Charles Darwin that he understood that it was 'entirely upon the grounds of economy', yet still resented the fact that the council had steamrollered financial retrenchment to such a degree.[16] At that time there were few full-time jobs available for vocational zoologists without a private income. The reduction in salaried posts therefore gave grounds for the fear that the society's scientific foundations were being undermined.

It was not only the museum that had its expenses scrutinised more tightly. The number of zoo staff was trimmed from 31 in 1837 to 23 in 1850, with the major achievement of a saving of £779 in salaries. Unlike the museum,

[11] Desmond, 'Making of institutional zoology', 232–3.

[12] ZSL, MC, v, fos 340, 347; MM, ii, fo. 209.

[13] ZSL, MC, vi, fos 325, 410.

[14] ZSL, MM, ii, fos 338–44.

[15] ZSL, MC, v, fo. 96; A. C. Wheeler, 'Zoological collections in the early British Museum: the Zoological Society's museum', *Archives of Natural History* xxiv (1997), 89–126.

[16] George Waterhouse to Charles Darwin, 9 Aug. 1843, *CCD*, ii. 381–2.

however, the zoo had not completely lost its allure, as a Swedish traveller noted in the summer of 1840:[17]

> Going on through this labyrinth of paths that wound between many bushes, groups of trees and flowerbeds, we soon found ourselves surrounded by rare animals from all zones of the world ... In this way we passed several hours in this incomparable establishment wandering amongst thousands of animals and enjoying one surprise and delight after the other. Even on weekdays it is filled with visitors and on Sundays it is a meeting place for the society of London.

As this account shows, a Sunday visit to the zoo continued to be popular with polite society, even though the Zoological Society was still under pressure from the Sabbatarians. The question was therefore how the council could use its declining recourses to enhance the attractiveness of the zoo. The answer was a new Carnivora Terrace. Originally designed by Decimus Burton, work began in 1842 on what was to be a 150ft extension of the existing terrace walk.[18] The new promenade, with an ornamental balustrade on each side, started from the bear pit and continued over the roof of the carnivora terrace. The walk ended with a flight of stone steps leading to the open field at the centre of the south garden. The picture (*see* Figure 18) shows a couple of spectators ascending the steps in order to return to the promenade. Underneath the terrace, six cages were arranged on each side for the display of large carnivores such as lions, tigers and leopards. The council proudly announced that the carnivore terrace provided a healthier environment for the animals in that it adopted a new open-air system and natural ventilation for the caged areas, although the effectiveness of this system soon came into question.[19]

The grassy open field began to be used for promenade concerts. With the arrival of the summer season in 1843, the council resolved to introduce a series of musical performances, such as had already proved successful in attracting large crowds to the Royal Botanic Gardens in Regent's Park and the rival Surrey Zoo.[20] These marked the zoo as an exclusive venue for social pleasures. A reporter for the *Literary Gazette* emphasised the elegant ambience in which the music in was performed: 'Another brilliant reunion of the fellows of this Society and their friends took place at the gardens ... when the fineness of the weather drew together a more than usually large and fashionable party to enjoy, *al fresco*, the performance of an admirable

---

[17] L. Hansen (ed.), *Impressions of London from the late summer of 1840: the thoughts and experiences of a Swedish gentleman*, London 2001, 65.

[18] Mitchell, *Centenary history*, 132.

[19] *Reports of the council and auditors* (1843), 10–11; Knight, *London*, v. 29; *Illustrated London News*, 22 Apr. 1843, 278; Scherren, *The Zoological Society*, 108.

[20] *Reports of the council and auditors* (1843), 5.

Figure 18. Frederick William Hulme, 'View of the new carnivore terrace' (1848). LMA, Main Print Collection, p538818x.

selection of music.'[21] Any social mingling was absent from the zoo on prom-enade days; the ticket price of 3s. 6d. was self-selecting.[22] The council was aiming for a wealthier clientele rather than for a wider general audience by providing extra privileges for subscribers and thereby restoring an ambience of fashionable exclusivity to the zoo.

This policy was reflected in Frederick William Hulme's *Views in the gardens of the Zoological Society of London* (1848). Although Hulme was a professional landscape painter and contributed to exhibitions at the British Institution, the Royal Manchester Institution and later the British Academy, he occa-sionally drew for engravings, especially for the *Art Journal*. His work on the zoo, of the five key locations – the terrace walk, the carnivore terrace, the clock tower, the tunnel and the avenue – conveyed a sense of semi-secluded tranquillity. In 'The view of the new Carnivora Terrace' (*see* Figure 18), the figures of two children playing on the grass in the foreground are particularly noticeable. Their father is calling them, presumably because the group is heading for the lions and tigers. This picture differed from orthodox urban

[21] *Literary Gazette*, 3 July 1847, 495.

[22] The Fellows themselves were allowed to exercise their normal privilege of free entry to the zoo. The ticket price was reduced to 2s.6d. in the season of 1848. Children were also admitted at 1s.: ZSL, MM, iii, fo. 45.

Figure 19. Frederick William Hulme, 'View of a tree-lined avenue' (1848). LMA, Main Print Collection, p5388109.

topography in the way in which it populated the scenery. The audience is relatively sparse, and even the animals are invisible. Clearly, the main motif is not the spectators, nor the animals or their interaction: it is the landscape itself. 'The view of a tree-lined avenue' (*see* Figure 19) is most remarkable: the picture shows a pathway where elephant rides was introduced in the late 1840s. An elephant with a chair on its back – the only animal shown in any of the five pictures – is coming along the path and draws the attention of the pedestrians. The shrubs and trees are designed to form a green tunnel and the promenade stretches underneath. This peacefully enclosed space contrasts with the open field next to the carnivore terrace. Such spatial structures had been absent from the zoo some ten years earlier. Hulme gave a nuanced interpretation of the zoo's unique landscape, highlighting its secluded tranquillity.

The new attractions were slow to make their mark. In 1836, the year of the giraffe exhibition, zoo attendance peaked at 260,000, the highest in the first two decades of its existence, but in the following year, it decreased by 100,000 and by 1848 had shrunk to 80,000. Membership of the society dwindled from 3,050 in 1836 to 2,478 in 1843. In that year the council introduced promenade concerts, but they cannot have helped to recruit new subscribers, as membership declined further to 1,710 in 1848. The annual income of the Zoological Society consequently fell, from £19,123 (£9,463 from gate receipts) in 1836 to £8,165 (£4,040 from gate receipts) in 1848. Although the Zoological Society endeavoured to cut expenditure – from £19,637 to £9,822 in the corresponding period – this was not enough to cover the shortfall. The society ran at significant deficit, of over £3,000 in 1843 (when construction costs for the new carnivore terrace were incurred). As a result, the funded capital of the society decreased by nearly £2,500 to £10,642, reaching £3,826 in 1848.

The deteriorating situation infuriated specialist zoologists, who complained that the council had made sacrificed the museum to the zoo. Their indigna-tion erupted in Lovell Reeve's open letter to the earl of Derby, president of the society, which was published as a tract in 1846. Reeve denounced the 'indolence' and 'inability' of successive councils which had tarnished the society's scientific reputation.[23] Reviewed in the *Athenaeum*, his protest reverberated beyond the society and led both subscribers and the public to reflect upon the ideal constitution of scientific societies.[24] Reeve's career explains why he had taken a stand. The son of a draper and mercer in the City, he had been apprenticed to a grocer at Ludgate Hill in London. One day he purchased shells from a sailor and these inspired him to become a conchologist.[25] Since shells were the kind of natural object that could be traded inexpensively, conchology was an accessible entry into the world of zoological science for the novice. By the 1840s Reeve cut a conspicuous figure in the Zoological Society, regularly presenting papers at the scien-tific meetings and joining the editorial board of the society's *Proceedings* and *Transactions*. Reeve owed his key publication, *Conchologia iconica* (1843–78), to the Cumingian Shell Collection held at the Leicester Square Museum.[26]

---

[23] L. Reeve, *Letter to the right honourable the earl of Derby, K.G., D.C.L., on the management, character, and progress of the Zoological Society of London*, London 1846, 17.

[24] *Athenaeum*, 6 June 1846, 580–1.

[25] J. C. Melvill, 'Lovell Reeve: a brief sketch of his life and career', *Journal of Conchology* ix (1898–1900), 348.

[26] S. P. Dance, *A history of shell collecting*, Leiden 1986.

He deplored the fact that the council had downsized the museum's collections and transferred them to Regent's Park.

In his letter of protest to the president, Reeve proposed the centralisation of the scientific departments of the society – the museum, the library, the venue for scientific meetings and the office – at a site in central London: 'It is not the luxurious appurtenances of the Meeting Room, nor an entertainment of *jeux d'esprit*, that will bring scientific men together; there must be a collocation of those objects which they are invited to discuss, and whenever a comparison suggests itself, the facilities for making it should be at hand.'[27] This plan endorsed the idea of 'juxtaposition': the word used to express the most accessible and efficacious method of locating scientific institutions in mid nineteenth-century London.[28] Indeed, Reeve envisaged that the Zoological Society would provide a research forum open to all devotees of zoology, irrespective of their social backgrounds. He argued that 'many worthy naturalists, fully competent and willing to contribute to the Society's publications' were currently excluded by the high admission costs and membership fees. In order to recruit plebeian zoologists, Reeve proposed a new scientific fellowship, with a subscription of one guinea *per annum*, which would offer free access to the museum, the library and scientific events, but not to the zoo.[29] This proposition defined the zoo as the subordinate institution, its purpose being to secure financial resources for the scientific work. He suggested that spending on the zoo should be limited to three-quarters of the society's gross income, reserving the remainder for the museum, the library and other scientific matters. To stabilise cash flow, the council would have to abandon high-risk enterprises for the acquisition of rare species. Reeve criticised the extravagant charter of a steamship to bring the giraffes to London in 1836; he thought that this had been a disastrous blow to the society.[30] Ideally, the zoo should be managed economically so as to provide a regular surplus to support the scientific business of the society.

The impact of Reeve's diatribe is difficult to gauge. In August 1846 he wrote to his old colleague on the publication committee, John Gould, formerly curator of the ornithological collection at the museum. 'The agitation that I have made already had some beneficial effect', Reeve noted with confidence and asked Gould to attend a general meeting to support his motion 'for the amelioration of the Scientific Business'.[31] But Gould sided with the council, whose patronage had enabled him to climb the career

---

[27] Reeve, *Letter*, 18.

[28] S. Forgan '"But indifferently lodged …": perception and place in buildings for science in Victorian Britain', in Smith and Agar, *Making space for science*, 195–215.

[29] Reeve, *Letter*, 24.

[30] Ibid. 9.

[31] L. Reeve to John Gould, 5 Aug. 1846, in G. C. Sauer (ed.), *John Gould, the bird man: correspondence*, London 2001, iv. 61.

ladder from backstage taxidermist to renowned ornithologist.[32] At the meeting Reeve's proposals were eventually referred back to the executive on the grounds that 'the matter be left to the direction of the Council, without any recommendation'.[33] It was a polite but definitive rebuff. Despite Reeve's protest, the council continued to prioritise the zoo and finally agreed to transfer its collections to the British Museum in 1850.[34] The *Proceedings* were downsized, and the costly *Transactions* ceased publication. Scientific meetings faded away, leaving John Edward Gray to lament that they attracted only a handful of zoologists.[35]

Reeve's open letter was the swan-song of the pro-museum element at the Zoological Society. Revisiting Swainson's agenda, Reeve had re-stated the dual nature of the society and urged that the provision of public recreation and the funding of scientific transactions should be rebalanced. To his mind, three initiatives were necessary to help the society to recover its scientific role and reputation: consolidation of the scientific departments in central London; maximising the zoo's function as a stable source of finance; and an egalitarian research forum. This was not, however, the route that David Mitchell took when he was appointed secretary in 1847.

The 'charm of novelty'

Little is known about David Mitchell, an Oxford graduate and ornithologist, apart from his twelve-year service with the Zoological Society, although his letter to George Robert Gray, younger brother and colleague of John Edward Gray at the Natural History Department of the British Museum, gives some insight into his ambitions within the scientific community. Since Mitchell was responsible for the illustrations for Gray's *The genera of birds*, he was eager to persuade the maddeningly indecisive Gray to publish: 'Your reputation as an ornithologist is only half made … it affords you a most glorious opportunity not only of establishing yourself in the republic of letters (as it could) but of invigorating the whole scene of Zoology.' His advice to Gray was to 'take a tea spoonful of ambition'.[36] *The genera of birds* finally came out in 1844 and made Mitchell's name in the international zoological commu-

[32] I. Tree, *The bird man: the extraordinary story of John Gould*, London 1991.

[33] ZSL, MM, ii, fos 465–6; iii, fos 1–4.

[34] Zoological Gardens papers, WORK 16/729.

[35] Gray to the council, 18 Apr. 1855, ZSL, BADG, John Edward Gray papers, ZSL, GAAW, Report of the Receipts and Expenditure Committee, 23 Mar. 1849; Scherren, *The Zoological Society*, 123; M. A. Edwards, 'The library and scientific publications of the Zoological Society of London: part ii', in S. Zuckerman and others (eds), *The Zoological Society of London, 1826–1976 and beyond*, London 1976, 224.

[36] Mitchell to George Robert Gray, 6 Aug. 1843, George Robert Gray papers, BL, MS Egerton 2348, fos 163–6.

nity. It seems to have been about this time that he became a member of a zoological dining coterie that centred around John Gould, William Jardine, the famous editor of *The Naturalist's Library* (1844–5), and William Yarrell, self-made naturalist and a former secretary of the Zoological Society.[37]

It is not clear why the council of the Zoological Society appointed Mitchell to the post of salaried secretary, but it certainly valued not only his zoological expertise but also his management skills. Mitchell's first action upon appointment was to abandon the exclusive admission system to the zoo and to introduce open access days: on Mondays and Tuesdays throughout the year and any day over Easter and Whitsun (excluding Saturdays). No order of admission was required. In the following year the council agreed to open the zoo to the general public on every weekday and reduced the fees for the admission of children to 6*d*. On Mondays adult visitors were charged the same. The aim was to cultivate a working-class clientele, which still observed St Monday.[38] A contemporary witness recorded that many of the 'Saint Mondayites' went on outings, and there was no reason to exclude the zoo from their list of favourite destinations if they could afford half a shilling per head.[39]

The council also catered for a wealthier clientele. It decided to introduce a discount membership of £3 *per annum*, which gave subscribers free personal access to the zoo with one companion. Later, transferable ivory tickets were introduced at a price of £10, and subscribers could buy admission tickets in bulk.[40] Clearly, this was a very new step for the council, which since the early 1840s had attempted to foster an air of exclusivity, rank and elegance. Generally the change was welcomed by the media. In 1849 one newspaper article remarked that 'There is no institution in the Metropolis so easily accessible, so instructive, and so productive of rational amusement as the menagerie of the Zoological Society.'[41] In June 1852 *Bentley's Miscellany* also praised Mitchell for having achieved 'the breaking up [of] the old system of exclusiveness'.[42]

It was the right time to widen access, mirroring other developments in the leisure market. In 1851 London hosted the Great Exhibition and was full of sightseers who planned to visit not only the Crystal Palace but also many other metropolitan sights. In order to attract them to the

[37] Sheets-Pyenson, 'War and peace in natural history publishing', 50–72; T. R. Forbes, 'William Yarrell, British naturalist', *Proceedings of American Philosophical Society* cvi (1962), 505–15.

[38] ZSL, MM, iii, fos 17–18; D. A. Reid, 'The decline of saint Monday, 1766–1876', *P&P* lvvi (1976), 76–101, and 'Weddings, weekdays, work and leisure in urban England, 1791–1911: the decline of saint Monday revisited', *P&P* cliii (1996), 135–63.

[39] T. Wright, *Some habits and customs of the working classes*, London 1867, 118–20.

[40] *Reports of the council and auditors* (1848), 27; ZSL, MC, xi, fos 285, 289.

[41] ZSL, GACP, Newspaper cuttings, i, fo. 7.

[42] *Bentley's Miscellany* (June 1852). 622.

Table 4.
The number of animals and new species displayed in the Zoo, 1829–65

	Number of captive animals				Number of new species imported			
	Total	Mammals	Birds	Reptiles	Total	Mammals	Birds	Reptiles
1828								
1829	627	152	475					
1830								
1831					70	27	43	
1832					51	25	26	
1833	1,002				21	9	12	
1834	1,034	296	717	21	38	12	26	
1835	995	269	704	22	21	11	10	
1836	1,025	307	704	14	17	9	8	
1837	931	268	645	18	15	8	7	
1838	933	303	592	38	28	10	18	
1839	910	303	587	20	43	22	21	
1840	894	352	524	18	25	14	11	
1841								
1842					26	12	14	0
1843					27	18	5	4
1844					46	22	24	0
1845					3	1	2	0
1846	905	341	557	7	17	5	11	1
1847	1,086	359	714	13	63	15	45	3
1848	1,335	383	851	101	55	13	33	9
1849					66	16	28	22
1850					51	18	26	7
1851					86	16	59	11
1852					50	21	18	11
1853					25	8	13	4
1854					19	7	8	4
1855					19	7	8	4
1856					33	6	11	16
1857					35	6	15	14
1858					33	10	12	11
1859	1,320	364	819	137	29	7	14	8
1860	1,590	467	931	192	34	7	16	11
1861	1,414	450	843	121	32	8	15	9
1862	1,748	485	1,114	149	36	14	16	6
1863	1,730	567	1,063	100	69	12	35	22
1864	1,858	498	1,255	105	33	8	23	2
1865	1,956	490	1,365	101	75	21	50	4

Source: ZSL, MC; *Reports of the council and auditors*; Scherren, *Zoological Society*

zoo, Mitchell engaged with commercial advertisement and the tourism industry.[43]Advertising expenses doubled, reaching £700, and arrangements were made to allow passengers arriving in the city on excursion trains to visit the zoo.[44] In the meantime, the council of the Zoological Society proposed to the government, which was planning to move the Marble Arch from Buckingham Palace, that the north terminus of the Broad Walk in Regent's Park – close to the entrance to the zoo – would be an ideal site.[45] This glorious monument would enhance the zoo's national status and would attract even more sightseers. Although the government rejected the proposal, another attempt to attract publicity succeeded. In October 1852 Mitchell negotiated with W. H. Smith to exhibit two advertising boards at each of 250 railway stations across the country.[46]

The changes initiated by Mitchell were not only to the admission policy but also in the scale and diversity of the animal collection, During the two years after his appointment, the number of the zoo animals increased from 804 to 1,335 (*see* Table 4). Although the overall size of the collection stayed unchanged during the remaining decade of his position as secretary, he added more than 500 new species. Mitchell established the Committee for the Purchase of Animals, which was responsible for adding to the range of animals exhibited. A letter from John Gould, who later joined the committee, suggests how keenly they sought after new species.[47] In July 1850 Mitchell and Gould visited the *Muséum national d'histoire naturelle* in Paris. They wanted to buy one of their tigers for £100–£150 plus some animals worthy of attention. When negotiations failed, they decided on a budget of £100 to complete their purchases, but there were still problems. Whereas Mitchell was interested in an onager (wild ass) priced at £20, Gould yearned for cranes. He wrote from Paris to Owen in London: 'I was very anxious to see the cranes in London because I had never before even seen a skin of [the] bird.'[48] Their price was £80 – £20 higher than his estimate, which put Gould in a dilemma: should he abandon the idea of cranes or forgo other animals to the value of £20.

[43] ZSL, Report of the Receipts and Expenditure Committee, 23 Mar. 1849.

[44] ZSL, MC, x. fo. 41. In April 1859, for instance, a party of Sunday School teachers and pupils from Yorkshire visited the London Zoo: ZSL, MC, xiii, fo. 174.

[45] Advertising expenses began to feature from 1848 and were to be itemised in the accounts of the Zoological Society for the year 1850: ZSL, Report of the Receipts and Expenditure Committee, 23 Mar. 1849; ZSL, MC, x, fos 32–3.

[46] ZSL, MC, x, fo. 320. Space for advertising was rented by the firms that had a franchise to sell books on stations: J. Simmons, *The Victorian railway*, New York 1991, 249.

[47] The original members were David Mitchell, Richard Owen and William Yarrell. Owen was replaced by John Edward Gray in 1854, and John Gould filled the vacancy caused by the death of Yarrell in 1856: ZSL, MC, xi, fos 80, 169, 263.

[48] Gould to Owen, 14 July 1850, Sauer, *John Gould*, iv. 267.

Apart from new species displayed in the zoo, the Animal Purchase Committee recognised the need to keep regular attractions such as lions and tigers in the carnivore terrace. Since large felines rarely survived long, a steady supply of healthy replacements was required.[49] Thus Mitchell wrote to an unknown trader in March 1854: 'I have changed my mind respecting the Tigress and if she is really a good animal and still is unsold, I shall be disposed to treat for her. I think therefore your best plan will be to bring both the Tigress and the Leopard up to town when I can see them and we can, I have no doubt, succeed in coming to terms for both.'[50] In 1855 Mitchell auctioned off surplus animals. The most expensive was an adult female giraffe at £450, followed by a female elephant at £350. Mitchell listed two lion cubs for sale, but decided to keep all of the three tigers in the zoo. During the next two years, however, the society obtained more than enough replacements.[51] In March 1857 Mitchell declined an offer of tigers from Edward Blyth of the Museum of the Asiatic Society in Calcutta (present Kolkata): 'you will not ship any Tigers for me. We have six, and it is quite impossible for me to do anything with others however fine'.[52] The sale of surplus animals and the purchase of healthy replacements had to be carefully balanced.

In March 1854 William Yarrell, self-made naturalist and former secretary of the Zoological Society, wrote excitedly to Edward Charlesworth, curator of the Yorkshire Philosophical Society Museum, on the flourishing state of the zoo:[53]

> I have little Zoological news to mention – the Pasha of Egypt has given the Zoological Society another Hippopotamus different from the former in sex, and we expect it will arrive in May – We have now two Great Brasilian Anteater, that eat anything but ants; and the Fish House is bringing more money than did the Hippopotamus. Last year's receipts exceeded any former year – except the Crystal Palace year – and 1854 at present promises to exceed 1853.

In this letter Yarrell sheds light on the new management policy, to which council members had been successfully converted by Mitchell. In his view,

[49] Broderip, 'Zoological Gardens: Regent's Park', 318–19; Crisp, 'On the causes of death of the animals', 179–80.

[50] Mitchell to unidentified recipient, 15 Mar. 1854, ZSL, BADM, D. W. Mitchell papers.

[51] In July 1855, at the recommendation of Yarrell, the council resolved to purchase two male tigers for £310.

[52] Edward Blyth to Mitchell, 10 Mar. 1857, ZSL, BADB, Edward Blyth papers.

[53] William Yarrell to Edward Charlesworth, 16 Mar. 1854, BL, MS Add. 50849, fos 80–1. Charlesworth had once been a candidate for the curatorship of the Leicester Square Museum, but the council of the Zoological Society elected Waterhouse by ballot and appointed Charlesworth to the new post of assistant scientific secretary in 1837. He had already left the Zoological Society when the Leicester Square Museum was demolished: ZSL, MC, iv. fos 410, 418; v. fo. 112.

visitors would only return to the zoo if its main attractions were renewed every season. At council meetings he articulated his marketing strategy: 'the charm of novelty has a never failing effect in the attraction of visitors'.[54] As Yarrell testified, 'the charm of novelty' started with Obaysch the hippopotamus in 1850, followed by the introduction of a dam and infant elephant, and then a special exhibition of John Gould's Hummingbird Collection in 1851. The society opened an aquarium and obtained a great Brazilian anteater in 1853. In the following year, Dil the female hippopotamus was added to make a pair with Obaysch.

Certainly, innovation brought visitors and their friends back to the London Zoo. On 22 June 1850 Henrietta Halliwell-Phillips, daughter of Sir Thomas Phillips, noted in her diary that she had visited the zoo to see the hippopotamus, knowing that he was 'the first ever brought alive to Europe', and had found herself amongst tremendous crowds. Her impression of Obaysch was 'a short thick heavy animal something like a pig about the mouth & head & of a dark brownish colour'.[55] Not surprisingly, his comical appearance was an ideal subject for *Punch*, which regularly reported on his sleepiness, 'sea-bathing', wedding and so forth.[56] Gideon Mantell, surgeon and geologist of Clapham Junction, south of the Thames, had kept up with the events in the zoo since its opening in 1828. He named a particular variety of the kiwi *Apteryx Mantelli* (North Island Brown Kiwi), when he examined a specimen sent to him from New Zealand. In 1851 the opportunity came to see a living specimen and Mantell frequented the zoo to make observations of this 'wingless' enigma of ornithology.[57]

The 'charm of novelty' had to be ready in time for the summer season. The popularity of the zoo – and hence attendance – varied greatly from one year to the next: high in 1850, fairly good in 1830 and 1835, and unpopular in 1840 and 1845 (*see* appendix). Statistically, admission figures hardly changed between late autumn and early spring, but a large attendance could be expected during the summer months.[58] A rapid increase during the two months from May to June 1850 is explained by the arrival of Obaysch the hippopotamus in late May. Mitchell certainly realised the importance of timing, as is shown in a particular case, the purchase of a pair of elephants. In spring 1851 the celebrity equestrian William Batty contacted Mitchell: he had a dam and an infant elephant for sale.[59] Elephants were no longer

---

[54] ZSL, MC, x, fos 332–4.

[55] M. Spevack (ed.), *A Victorian chronicle: the diary of Henrietta Halliwell-Phillips*, Hildesheim 1999, 48.

[56] Blunt, *Ark in the park*, 106–12, 117–21.

[57] E. C. Curwen (ed.), *The journal of Gideon Mantell: surgeon and geologist covering the years 1818–52*, London 1940, 69, 79, 254, 259, 269, 278, 288.

[58] ZSL, MC, x, fos 332–4.

[59] At that time Batty was holding equestrian shows in Kensington: T. Frost, *Circus life and circus celebrities*, London 1881, 139–40.

valued for their rarity, but the calf elephant, which had been born on board a ship from Calcutta, was an exception as so small an elephant had rarely been seen in Europe.[60] Mitchell proposed a lease: £25 per week for the animals so that in case of their early deaths no further costs would be incurred.[61] Batty, however, stipulated a £500 payment upfront for the five summer months (the weekly rate was still calculated at around £25) and £300 for the purchase of the elephants at the end of the term. He also implied that he would sell them to a rival circus manager unless this was agreed.[62] Neither party wanted to take a risk on the unpredictable health of the elephant calf. As a member of the Animal Purchase Committee, Richard Owen advised Mitchell to reject Batty's demand as too high: 'I would rather let Batty walk off with them. An elephant grown beyond infancy is a hobbletehoy [sic] & not worth its keep – and we don't want to be saddled with another female during winter.'[63] Mitchell none the less agreed to Batty's terms.[64] He did not want to 'let Batty walk off with them' and for them to be hugely popular at a rival venue.

Mitchell was right, as the mother elephant demonstrated her maternal tenderness to the young calf in front of throngs of excited spectators. A story was circulated to the effect that the calf elephant was fed with zebu's milk (the zebu is a humped species of bovine animal) as the fatigue of the voyage from Calcutta had reduced the mother's supply. Another rumour suggested that the calf had actually been born in the zoo, even though elephants rarely breed in captivity. Popular fancy was accordingly stirred. Named Betsey and Butcher, the mother and child were featured in *Punch:* the baby elephant, dressed as a human baby, is held on his mother's lap, the centre of a circle of curious children and parents (*see* Figure 20). On the other side of the picture, the hippopotamus looks on enviously, his nose 'put out of joint by the young elephant'. His attendant whispers consolingly, in a pseudo-African accent: 'Nebber mind den! Him shall be a lubly'potamus – For all um great ugly elflint.' At the back one of the giraffes, once an icon of the zoo's reputation, glumly observes the fickleness of the crowd. This satirical illustration implies how quickly the audience lost interest in previous attractions in the presence of new arrivals.

The other message implicit in the print is the zoo as a powerful story-telling device. As various rumours, gossip and stories emerged for public consumption, the zoo became a narrative space.[65] The zoo's literary association is most clearly identified by the media coverage of an accident in the

---

[60] Scherren, *The Zoological Society*, 110.

[61] Mitchell to W. Batty, 17 Apr. 1851, ZSL, BADB, W. Batty papers.

[62] Batty to Mitchell, 17 Apr. 1851, ibid.

[63] Owen to Mitchell, 17 Apr. 1851, ibid. Mitchell papers.

[64] Batty to Mitchell, 23 Apr. 1851, ibid. Batty papers.

[65] In May 1859 free admission was granted to the editors and writers of newspapers to encourage them to visit frequently: ZSL, MC, xii, fo.18.

Figure 20. 'The nose of the hippopotamus put out of joint by the young elephant', *Punch*, 10 May 1851, 92: ZSL, Newspaper cutting, i, fo. 29a.

zoo. In October 1852 a zoo keeper named Girling died from a cobra bite in the reptile house. It happened when Girling aroused the cobra by trying to imitate the performance of Arabian snake charmers, which he had watched in the zoo some time earlier.[66] Mitchell was urged to investigate the accident and to confirm that the zoo had provided sufficient protection for its workers and spectators.[67] The coroner's inquest, which was reported in the principal morning papers, revealed that a group of zoo keepers including Girling had been drinking together to say farewell to one of their colleagues, who was emigrating for Australia.[68] In the eyes of moral reformers such as members of the temperance movement, Girling was therefore a stereotype, a victim of the working-class culture of heavy drinking.

[66] The performance of the Arab snake charmers was held in the summer months of 1850. The society gave them a gratuity of £21 when they returned to Alexandria: ibid. x, fos 30–1. The details of the performance were described in the *Illustrated London News*, 15 June 1850, 424.

[67] ZSL, MC, x, fos 306–7.

[68] ZSL, Newspaper cuttings, i, fos 43–5; *Weekly Times*, 24 Oct. 1852, 688; *Sun*, 21 Oct. 1852, 1.

It was at this time that Charles Dickens asked Richard Owen to write on the cobra for his *Household Words*, the aim of which was to refine middle-class taste for reading. Accepting the offer, Owen began his article by explaining the accident as 'one of the countless calamities befalling the weekly-wage classes plainly referable to intoxication'.[69] While his work satisfied Dickens's need for a familiar piece on natural history, the tragic story of a working-class drunkard also served the needs of the Zoological Society, which had denied any responsibility for his death.[70] This was not the only story, however, that was going around the reading public. A number of weekly magazines drama-tised the story.[71] The most sensational version was that 'all the serpents in the Zoological Gardens are kept, like the happy family in Trafalgar Square, in one large case', and that Girling worked 'in the ordinary course of his duty' until 'the screams of the victim to the hazardous duty attracted the instant attention of William Cocksedge, another keeper, who thereupon rushed to the serpent-case and drew his companion out'.[72]

As the virtual proprietor of the London Zoo, Mitchell was alerted by the spread of rumours and took immediate measures to enforce discipline among the zookeepers.[73] In the meantime, however, the story went so far as to cause a series of debates on the accident. It centred upon whether the urgent medical treatment given to Girling at University College Hospital was appropriate, and deepened the mystery of cobra venom.[74] Much taken with the story, Francis Buckland, son of William Buckland and a naturalist, experimented with the effect of the venom on rats. By mistake, however, he poisoned himself, and nearly died. Only the knowledge obtained from reading about Girling's case saved him. This dangerous episode was narrated in his *Curiosities of natural history* (1858) and was referred to by many other writers.[75]

---

[69] [R. Owen], 'Poisonous serpents', *Household Words*, 6 Nov. 1852, 186. Owen received £3.3s. for this article. Dickens met Owen first in 1843 and occasionally visited his family: A. Lohrili, *Household Words: a weekly journal, 1850–9, conducted by Charles Dickens*, Toronto 1973, 393.

[70] Dickens suggested that Owen should write on the zoo animals under the title 'Private lives of public friends?', although Owen could not find time to continue his writing: *Richard Owen*, i. 389–90, 92. For Dickens's fondness for Owen's writing see Charles Dickens to Owen, 15 Dec. 1863, Southgate collection, BL, MS Add. 39554, fo. 426.

[71] *Illustrated London News*, 23 Oct. 1852, 335; *Bell's Weekly Messenger*, 24 Oct. 1852, 5.

[72] Owen, 'Poisonous serpents', 188.

[73] The council directed that experiments with venomous serpents were to stop and discharged one keeper for drunkenness: ZSL, MC, x, fos 310–14.

[74] *The Times*, 25 Oct. 1852, 8; 26 Oct. 1852, 3; 25 Oct. 1852, 3, 7–8; 2 Nov. 1852, 3; *Medical Times*, 30 Oct. 1852, 441–4; *Legal Examiner*, 30 Oct. 1852, 671–2, 688–9; *Lancet*, 23 Oct. 1852, 389; 30 Oct. 1852, 397–401, 410.

[75] F. T. Buckland, *Curiosities of natural history*, London 1858, 153; [A. Wynter], 'The Zoological Gardens', *Quarterly Review* (Dec. 1855), 237–8; P. H. Gosse, *Romance of natural history*, London 1860, 264–6.

In terms of offering a stream of stories, the zoo's strength, and its difference, for example from popular literature, was that enjoyment of a visit there was activated not only by observing and by the imagination but also by the other physical senses. In 1847 William John Broderip published *Zoological recreations*, which compiled scientific findings and anecdotes on various animals with reference to the living specimens in the London Zoo. He aimed to improve the middle-class taste for natural history and his efforts were favourably reviewed in the literary journals.[76] The announcement of its forthcoming publication was welcomed by *Punch*, which deliberately misinterpreted the title as 'a series of sports and pastimes for the brute creation', with an illustration of crocodiles jumping over the head of a hippopotamus. Broderip enjoyed the idea and excitedly wrote to Richard Owen that his '*Zoological Recreations* have got in *Punch*'.[77] In 1852, when he published another book *Punch* responded by commenting on his previous publication: 'he has left out a few of the most popular recreations in zoology, which are known to and indulged in by the inhabitants of the Metropolis'. These recreations were, the reviewer noted, 'riding on the elephant's back', 'throwing bits of stale bun to the bear', 'pelting the ducks at nightfall' and, above all, 'making a donkey of one's self, a recreation which is much indulged in by certain persons at all places of public amusement'.[78]

'Making a donkey of one's self' was illustrated in *Punch* (*see* Figure 21) by Richard Doyle, a pioneer of the graphic novel, who produced the famous series on the comic trio Brown, Jones and Robinson as they unsuccessfully tried to enter fashionable society.[79] On visiting the London Zoo, they visited the usual attractions. At the bear pit they peered into the bottom of the den to catch a sight of the animal, which was watching them from the pole over their heads. Afterwards Brown strayed into a noisy aviary, while Robinson was frightened by the aggressive cranes. Jones was brave enough to attempt the challenge of riding a camel and only just managed to hang onto its hump. They encountered an elephant and eventually enjoyed riding on its back. Finally, they discovered Obaysh, who, with one eye open, is pretending to be asleep to disappoint them.

The pleasures of physical exertions were complemented by musical fantasies. One remarkable example was *The hippopotamus polka* (1850), a set of variations for the piano, dedicated to Obaysh. The scorebook contained a short story in which a lady explained the origin of the music: 'I had last night the oddest dream imaginable ... that night when I retired to sleep,

---

[76] [Owen], 'Broderip's *Zoological recreations*', 119–42.

[77] *Punch*, 7 Nov. 1847, 169; Broderip to Owen, 4 Nov. 1847, Richard Owen collection, OC62, v, fo. 144.

[78] *Punch*, 14 Aug. 1852, 85.

[79] The series later developed into a book: R. Doyle, *The foreign tour of Messrs. Brown, Jones, and Robinso: being the history of what they saw and did in Belgium, Germany, Switzerland and Italy*, London 1854.

BROWN, JONES, AND ROBINSON GO TO THE ZOOLOGICAL GARDENS.

THEY INSPECT THE BEARS.

ROBINSON FEEDS THE WATER-FOWL.

BROWN HAVING RASHLY STRAYED INTO A ROOM FULL OF MACAWS,
WE SEE THE CONSEQUENCE.

JONES VOLUNTEERS TO RIDE THE CAMEL, AND, TO A CERTAIN EXTENT,
HE DOES IT.

IN A LONELY PATHWAY THEY SEE SOMETHING COMING.

THEY ARE PERSUADED TO MOUNT THE ELEPHANT.

THEY GO IN QUEST OF THE HIPPOPOTAMUS.

THEY SEE THE HIPPOPOTAMUS!

Figure 21. 'Brown, Jones and Robinson go to the Zoological Gardens', *Punch*,
10 Aug. 1850, 64: ZSL, Newspaper cuttings, i, fo. 29.

but not to rest – I fancied the strains of a polka somewhat resembling the grave growl of the Hippopotamus, but still more the heavy polka-step of our Friend Lord A——.'[80] This was a joke at the expense of an unnamed aristocrat who was evidently not light on his feet. The polka, lively and rhythmical dance music, rendered it even more comical. The score instructed that the initial part should be played 'meditatingly and slow' to herald the entrance of the bulky aristocrat into the ballroom (see Figure 22). Another example of lively musical association with everyday life was *Walking in the zoo*, a 3s. popular song published in 1869, in which a young man tells of how he took his lovely cousin to the zoo on Sunday, with the frank confession: 'It's jolly with a pretty girl walking in the Zoo.' In an aviary, however, a horror awaited them as he sang:[81]

> For the cheerful Cock a too,
> Rudely caught my ear a nip and bit it through and through.
> Oh! that cheerful Cock a too
> That awful Cock a too
> That horror and agony that Sunday at the Zoo
> …
> My cousin bolted off without any more ado,
> And I skedaddled also looking very blue
> So sympathising friends I bid you all adieu
> Don't mention this occurrence if you meet me at the Zoo,
> If you meet me at the Zoo
> You meet me at the Zoo
> I'm as great a swell as ever on Sunday at the Zoo
> Walking in the Zoo
> Walking in the Zoo
> The OK thing on Sunday
> is walking in the Zoo.

This song testifies to how deeply the zoo featured in the cultural pattern of everyday life. By this time it had become such a familiar place for recreation that people began to refer to it simply as 'the Zoo'. As the last two lines of the song indicate, a Sunday outing to the zoo had become 'the OK thing' – an apparently acceptable form of cultural consumption – for an even wider social range of people than could have been imagined in the 1830s. Although advocates of Sabbath observance still maintained their influence on certain aspects of social life, they had negligible effect on the proprietors and customers of the London Zoo.

Amidst the rapid development of the leisure market, the zoo regained its prosperity. The effect of weekday opening to the general public soon led to an increase in attendance. In 1850, the year of Obaysh's arrival, the number

---

80 L. Saint Mars, *The hippopotamus polka as a pianoforte duet*, London 1850.
81 H. W. Sweny and A. Lee, *Walking in the zoo*, London 1869.

THE HIPPOPOTAMUS POLKA.

Figure 22. L. Saint Mars, *The hippopotamus polka as a pianoforte duet*, London 1850, frontispiece.

of visitors recorded was over 360,000, and in the following year, when the Great Exhibition galvanised the leisure market, it soared to 660,000. Although attendance dropped to 300,000 in 1852, it maintained a long-term upward trend for the next two decades. The income of the Zoological Society increased accordingly, beginning in 1848, and by 1850 had exceeded outgoings by £1,800. A further rise in 1851 was a happy surprise to William John Broderip, who heard the most recent financial report from Mitchell. On 2 January 1852 he wrote to to his friend, Richard Owen, that 'Yesterday I presided at the winding up of our Zool[ogical Society's] accounts for the year. Our income £26,600!!'[82] The society had a surplus of £4,000 in that year, but Mitchell invested it to enhance the 'charm of novelty'. By so doing, he maintained the zoo's rising momentum throughout his period in office. When he resigned as secretary in 1859, the society officially acclaimed him as an efficient manager and granted him a gratuity of £500 in appreciation.[83]

Mitchell's policies brought their own problems however. Attendance soared, the range of visitors diversified, and the ways of having fun in the zoo were significantly expanded. But the new attractions offered at the zoo appeared little different from other forms of commercial entertainment. As the Zoological Society was defined as a voluntary association for the advancement and application of zoology, close association with profit-seeking ventures could undermine its public role and reputation. This was highlighted by a lawsuit during the years 1852–4, which debated whether it could still be defined as a legitimate scientific institution.

Separate spheres

Under the Scientific and Literary Institutions Act of 1843 (the Exemption Act), the Zoological Society of London was exempt from paying the parochial rates. This legislation granted immunity from local taxation to institutions established exclusively for the purpose of science, literature or art. The act was an instance of pioneering state intervention designed to foster the nationwide development of public institutions. George William Wood, promoter of scientific institutions in Manchester, explained its rationale in parliament: 'this exemption would have the most salutary effects upon the population, by encouraging the dissemination of scientific, moral, and religious instruction in all places where institutions literary or scientific were already or might hereafter be established'.[84] Similar assistance had benefited charity schools and foundling hospitals, which provided the basic needs of

---

[82] Broderip to Owen, 2 Jan. 1852, Owen collection, OC62, v, fo. 201.

[83] ZSL, MC, xiii, fos 169, 175. Mitchell died soon after taking up his appointment as director of the *Jardin zoologique d'acclimatation* in Paris. It has been suspected that he committed suicide, but the truth has remained unknown. After his sudden death, the society discovered that he had appropriated £577 of the society's receipts, largely from the sale of duplicate animals: memorandum, 20 Oct. 1854; extracts from the report of the committee to examine into the state of the account between Mitchell and the Society, 14 Nov. 1859, ZSL, Mitchell papers; Blunt, *Ark in the park*, 85.

[84] *Hansard* 3rd ser. xix, 920, 25 May 1843.

life such as medical treatment and primary education.[85] The Scientific and Literary Societies Act aimed at extending this limited financial support to include the new category of voluntary associations – not only metropolitan learned societies but also provincial Literary and Philosophical Societies and Mechanics' Institutes – which offered cultural services to the public. It was indeed a valuable concession, especially for institutions that occupied expensive urban property.[86] In October 1843 the Exemption Act passed into law without any substantial objections.[87] The scope of the act and the process of applying for exemption from the rates may be summarised:[88]

1. Exemption may be granted to 'any Society instituted for Purposes of Science, Literature, or the Fine Arts exclusively, either as Tenant or as Owner, and occupied by it for the Transaction of its business, and for carrying into effect its purposes'.

2. Exemption may be granted on the condition that 'such Society shall be supported wholly or in part by annual voluntary Contributions, and shall not, and by its Laws may not, make any Dividend, Gift, Division, or Bonus in Money unto or between any of its Members'.

3. Applications are to be submitted to the Barrister at Law in England (the Lord Advocate in Scotland) who is in charge of judging whether or not the constitution of applying society complies with the act.

4a. If the application is rejected, the society may appeal to the quarter sessions, where the grant with the same legal effect as certification from the Barrister at Law can be obtained.

4b. Person(s) assessed to any rate from which any society shall be exempted by this act may appeal to the quarter sessions.

During the first year after the legislation, 183 organisations including the Royal, Zoological, Horticultural, Astronomical and Geological Societies obtained certificates of right to exemption in England, and in the next

---

[85] Poor Law Board, *Official circulars of public documents and information*, 30 Nov. 1843, 154; M. Daunton, *Trusting Leviathan: the politics of taxation in Britain, 1799–1914*, Cambridge 2001, 211.

[86] The Exemption Act of 1840 established that local rates were to be levied on the annual value of real property: Daunton, *Trusting Leviathan*, 285.

[87] W. G. Lumley, *The Literary and Scientific Institutions Act, 1854 [17&18 Vict. c. 112] and the Act [6&7 Vict. c. 36] which exempts such institutions from rateability with notes and index and an introduction, containing a commentary upon both acts, and all the decisions of the courts of law in the construction of the Exempting Act*, London 1855, 23.

[88] 'An act to exempt from county, borough, parochial, and other local rates, land and buildings occupied by scientific and literary societies', in *A collection of the public general statutes passed in the sixth and seventh year of the reign of her majesty Queen Victoria*, London 1843, 318–20.

five years a further 105 bodies were exempted from local rates, with only a handful of applications declined.[89] Examination was easy, as it focused only on the documented constitution of the societies concerned. A record regarding the assessment of the Zoological Society's application, deposited at London Metropolitan Archives, implies that the examiner merely looked through the society's prospectus and bylaws.[90]

Nevertheless, a backlash started in the late 1840s. As parochial appeals against exempted societies increased, the courts came to reassess not only their official documents but also the ways in which they transacted their business. It was at this point that the parish of St Marylebone appealed to the quarter session against the certificate of exemption granted respectively to the Marylebone Literary Institution, the Royal Botanical Society and the Zoological Society. In 1852 all three institutions lost their cases. The council of the Zoological Society resolved to appeal to the Queen's Bench.[91] By that point litigation on the Exemption Act has produced confusion. A surveyor commissioned by the Society of Arts to investigate the matter reported in 1853 that the act contained 'many seeds of litigation' and was therefore 'a puzzle to the Courts'.[92] In an attempt to sort matters out William Golden Lumley, a lawyer and assistant secretary to the Poor Law Board, analysed precedents and issued official guidelines in 1855. The court reports suggest why, in the light of this publication, the Zoological Society failed to qualify under the narrowing rubric of the Exemption Act.

There were two reasons why the Zoological Society should pay the parochial rate. The first concerned the definition of 'voluntary associations'. The Exemption Act specified that exempted societies should be funded by voluntary contributions and should return no profit to members. The interpretation of 'voluntary contributions' was crucial, because it defined the legitimate range of those benefits, whether material or immaterial, that the subscribers could expect to obtain in return for their contributions. In the case of the Linnean Society, a point of debate was whether the free distribution of the society's transactions to its members was apposite.[93] The courts judged that the contributions to the Linnean Society were 'voluntary within the meaning of Act', but the case of the Zoological Society was

[89] *Returns of all applications to the certifying barristers, under the Act [6 & 7 Vict. c. 36], for certificates of exemption from parochial rates by literary and scientific institutions stating the name and locality of each society, and whether the certificates were granted or refused, and specifying the grounds of refusal in each*, PP xlii (1844); xlv (1849).

[90] Middlesex Sessions Records, Literary and Scientific Societies and Libraries, Exemption from Rates, 1843–85, the Zoological Society of London, 20 Oct. 1843, LMA, MR/SL/R/009.

[91] ZSL, newspaper cuttings, i, fo. 49: *Observer*, 7 Nov. 1852, 2; MC, x, fos 283, 308–9.

[92] A. Ryland, 'To the Council of the Society of Arts', *Journal of the Society of Arts and of the Institutions in Union* i (1852–3), 138.

[93] Lumley, *Literary and Scientific Institutions Act*, 32–3.

different, because it returned a completely different kind of benefit to its subscribers. One of the three magistrates in charge of this case happened to be a Fellow of the Zoological Society, who was described by *The Times* as 'a great promoter of science'. He understood the fellowship to have more than returned 'the advantage which he himself, as well as his family and friends, would gain thereby'. He therefore thought that 'he had made a good bargain'.[94] Subsequently, the chief magistrate, Lord Campbell, agreed with his colleague and defined the contributions as a way of gaining access to the London Zoo: 'these enjoyments are bargained for, and the bargain is a good one'.[95]

The decision was predictable. Mitchell had adapted the admission system to accommodate the differing needs of different consumers, and in tandem with the public media and advertising agents, promoted a visit to the zoo as a respectable form of cultural consumption. The provision of animal attractions at the zoo, however, was no longer compatible with the assumption that subscribers acted upon disinterested motives. This judgement raised an essential question as to the legitimacy of the ways in which the Zoological Society fulfilled its own claims to be transmitting scientific knowledge to the public, i.e. by means of animal exhibition in the zoo. This was the second point at issue: how far did the society engage exclusively in scientific activities and was therefore compliant with the Exemption Act, and how far, in providing public entertainment, was it not. In the eyes of the vestrymen of St Marylebone, the bands, the horticultural displays, the Arab snake charmers, and various other exhibitions at the zoo were entirely irrelevant to scientific pursuits.[96] The lawyers acting for St Marylebone argued that the zoo offered the kind of entertainments that were outside the the spectrum of services allowed by the Exemption Act. Accepting this claim, the magistrates concluded that 'the exhibition of the hippopotamus, snakes, humming-birds, and monkeys, which had attracted so much public interest, showed that rational amusement, more than science, was the end contemplated'.[97]

The exhibition of John Gould's hummingbird collection gives further insight into the significance of this judgement for the Zoological Society. In May 1851 John Gould suggested preparing a special exhibition of his ornithological collection, which consisted of '2,000 specimens of 300 species with in many cases nests and eggs'. He argued that the collection would attract a great number of the sightseers who were in London for the Great Exhibition.[98] The council of the Zoological Society approved the plan and

---

[94] *The Times*, 1 June 1854, 11.
[95] *Justice of the Peace, and County, Borough, Poor Law Union, and Parish Law Recorder*, 5 Aug. 1854, 490.
[96] Ibid. 489.
[97] *The Times*, 1 June 1854, 11.
[98] Gould to the council, 5 Feb. 1851, ZSL, BADG, John Gould papers.

permitted a temporary building to be constructed for the exhibition. The room and the displays were designed to give spectators not only a scientific but also an aesthetic overview of the world of hummingbirds. Gould's carefully grouped and positioned his specimens, as noted in *Bentley's Miscellany*:

> Not the least remarkable point is the marvellous ingenuity displayed, not merely in the general arrangements of the content of each case, but in the attitudes of the birds themselves, every individual being placed in just that position best adapted to exhibit his especial beauty.[99]

Gould used hexagonal glass cases to enable the spectators to command a single view of his collection. Impressed with the diversity of the display, Queen Victoria noted in her diary entry for 10 June 1851 that 'It is impossible to imagine anything so lovely as these little Humming Birds, their variety & the extraordinary brilliancy of their colours.'[100] The exhibition was profitable too: in the six months between May and November 1851 more than 80,000 people visited the exhibition, and the revenue from admission fees amounted to nearly £1,600.[101] The exhibition was a microcosm of the zoo in the sense that it created and commodified 'zoological recreations' by combining the pleasures of science and spectacle.

As the synthesis of science and spectacle constituted the zoo's attractiveness, a statement that overstated the entrepreneurial aspects of their exhibitions was unacceptable to the Zoological Society. The society's lawyer insisted that science had to be made entertaining to the public. In his opinion, the activities and attractions offered by the zoo differed little from the pleasures that could be obtained from other types of intellectual engagements: 'Amusement and recreation, however, may be afforded by lectures on chemistry, and are the effect of natural philosophy. This society does not cease to be a scientific society, because it imparts knowledge in a manner that is entertaining as well as instructive.'[102] He argued that any definition of 'the *exclusiveness* of the literary or scientific purposes' was very much contextual. The statute could not uniformly explain why the pleasures of watching chemical experiments in a public lecture stayed within the scope of the act, whereas the pleasures of feeding bears in the zoo were not. Realising that he was fighting a losing battle, the society's solicitor remarked in despair: 'the argument for the rate proves too much: no science is pursued without something being done which is not directly an act of scientific investigation'.[103]

---

99 *Bentley's Miscellany*, June 1852, 625.
100 Blunt, *Ark in the park*, 60.
101 Sauer, *John Gould*, ix. 523–4.
102 *Ellis and Blackburn's Report of the Judges of the Court of Queen's Bench*, iii. 90.
103 Ibid. iii. 820.

The problems facing scientific and literary institutions were related to the controversial system of local taxation.[104] The Poor Law Amendment Act of 1834, which aimed to establish a uniform, centralised bureaucratic organisation for the provision of poor relief under the control of the Poor Law Commissioners, redefined the duties of parochial officials. Their responsibilities involved not only examining paupers' claim to relief, but also raising funds from ratepayers. Thus the Parochial Assessment Act of 1836 included standard instructions on how to assess rateable values.[105] A weekly journal, which aimed to provide parochial officials with the latest judicial information, was launched in 1837 under the title of *The Justice of Peace and Local Government Review*. Moreover, the Poor Law Commissioners disseminated information about relevant court cases through their *Annual Reports* and *Official Circulars*. These publications indicate that the rules of valuation were so inconsistent that individual cases frequently needed to be tried in the courts.[106] In 1844 William Golden Lumley issued *The law of parochial assessments*,and brought out revised editions until 1882. It was in these circumstances that litigation in 1846 against a teacher-training school in London established that a certificate of right to exemption issued by a barrister could be annulled by a court.[107] In an attempt to ameliorate confusion, a bill of amendment to the act was prepared in 1849, with the sanction of both provincial and metropolitan societies as well as of Robert Peel, Lord Russell and George Grey, but it failed to pass during the current parliamentary session. In the meantime cases, in 1851, concerning the Royal Manchester Institution and the Manchester Concert Hall, in which both institutions lost their right to exemption, made parochial officials realise that the likelihood of their recovering their right to tax was very high.[108]

Inevitably the courts judged the exempted institutions to have placed financial burdens upon their parishes, not least because the economic crisis of 1847–8 had caused a rapid increase in expenditure on poor relief.[109] A subsequent recession in the 1850s unmasked the sharp inequality between

---

[104] For local taxation see E. Cannan, *The history of local rates in England: in relation to the proper distribution of the burden of taxation*, London 1912; Daunton, *Trusting Leviathan*, 256–301.

[105] *Annual Report of the Poor Law Commissioners* iii (1837), 91–4, 312–16; iv (1838), 54–5; R. N. Hyde, 'The act to regulate parochial assessments (1836) and its contribution to the mapping of London', *Guildhall Studies in London History* ii (1976), 54–68.

[106] F. W. Showers, 'Anomalies and inequalities in local rating', *Public Administration* xxi (1943), 145–57.

[107] This interpretation was confirmed in the case of a newspaper library in Birmingham: *Justice of the Peace*, Aug. 1844, 551–3; 1 Apr. 1848, 217–18; Lumley, *Literary and Scientific Institutions Act*, 24–5.

[108] G. Tayler, *The law as to the exemption of scientific and literary societies from the parish and other local rates*, London 1851.

[109] After the Poor Law Amendment of 1834, which created unions of parishes as the unit for the provision of poor relief, the parochial basis for raising revenue from the

the poorer and wealthier districts of the metropolis.[110] Arguments for rate equalisation were developing and had an adverse effect on many institutions in London. Since the discussion was concerned with relationships both between and within parishes, it raised public awareness that ratepayers should contribute to local finance on an equal and fair basis.[111] Both national and metropolitan circumstances explained why there was pressure to adjust fiscal structures in the localities and recover the parishes' right to tax those bodies whose properties were of significant rateable value.[112] The appeal against the Zoological Society was no exception. When the society's lawyer made a final attempt to gain concessions by claiming that parts of the zoo ground should not be liable he was told by the chief justice that 'You are, in fact, claiming to exempt from rateability these three acres, and so to burthen the parish.'[113]

As the rateable value of the society's property was estimated at £1,040, it was crucial to determine whether the society had to pay the poor rate.[114] The parish's lawyer stressed the recreational aspect of the zoo by comparing it to a Roman amphitheatre. He cited Gibbon's *History of the decline and fall of the Roman Empire* in order to strengthen the judges' impression that the animal attractions in the zoo were designed not to promote science, but simply to provide 'amusement for the populace':[115]

> While the populace gazed with stupid wonder on the splendid show, the naturalist might indeed observe the figure and properties of so many different species, transported from every part of the ancient world into the amphitheatre of Rome. But this accidental benefit, which science might derive from folly, is surely insufficient to justify such a wanton abuse of the public riches.

Accusations of abusive consumption and moral degradation were, however,

rates had remained: D. R. Green, *From artisans to paupers: economic change and poverty in London, 1790–1870*, Aldershot 1995, 236.

110 Ibid. 212–15, 236–41; Daunton, *Trusting Leviathan*, 281. The rating crisis of the mid-1860s resulted in the creation of the Metropolitan Common Poor Fund, which was intended to raise funds from individual unions according to their rateable value and to build a framework for the administration of comprehensive social services – through a widening range of institutions from asylums and hospitals to workhouses – under the direction of the Poor Law Board: A. Tanner, 'The casual poor and the City of London Poor Law Union, 1837–69', *HJ* xlii (1999), 183–206.

111 Green, *From artisans to paupers*, 238.

112 Lumley, *Literary and Scientific Institutions Act*, 29.

113 *Ellis and Blackburn's Report* iii (1852), 818.

114 St Marylebone parish, vestry minutes 2nd ser. lxxiv, 2 Mar.–7 Oct. 1854, Westminster City Archives, TI/84a, fos 207–8, 227–8, The rates of the Zoological Society for the year 1859 was assessed at £32 10s. per quarter. This was equivalent to the salary of one of the society's office clerks: ZSL, MC, xiii, fo. 7.

115 E. Gibbon, *The history of the decline and fall of the Roman Empire* (Milman's edn), London 1838, ii. 100, as cited in *Ellis and Blackburn's Report*, iii (1852), 820.

too harsh a verdict on the zoo of modern Rome. Although the magistrates agreed that the pleasures offered by the zoo were not drawn from 'the pure pursuit of science', they rejected the implication that the zoo staged vulgar entertainment which was dangerous to public morality and discipline. Instead, they opined that the zoo provided 'amusement of a most innocent and laudable kind'. The chief justice concluded by stating that 'It has, I have no doubt, essentially contributed to the advancement of natural science; and I hope that it maybe long flourish.' Another magistrate echoed this sentiment, remarking that 'I am not sure that the additional object which is attained, that of bringing people together for rational amusement and recreation, is not more important than scientific objects.'[116]

The court case was a catalyst in defining the separate spheres of legitimate and recreational science: and it placed the attractions of the zoo in the latter category. Access to the zoo was no longer perceived as the complementary privilege granted to disinterested subscribers to the Zoological Society. It had become a kind of commodity – materialised in the different forms of admission tickets which were widely circulated in the commercial leisure market. The policy of the 'charm of novelty', which introduced to the zoo a series of attractions such as John Gould's hummingbird exhibition, accelerated the commodification of zoological recreations. If a pedagogical justification was yet to be given, it would be that the pleasure of knowing something about nature need not necessarily be presented in a purely scientific manner. Such pleasures were in essence enmeshed with the pleasures of music, literary imagination and physical exercise. The courts agreed that the Zoological Society played a prime role in offering these mixed pleasures to the public at large, but considered none the less that the pursuance of this role deprived the society of any eligibility to exemption from local rates. This was the price that the society had to pay for having rehabilitated its public role and reputation.

By the mid-nineteenth century, a variety of urban entertainments had gained legitimacy through negotiations with the competitive leisure market and public authorities, and a commercial sector had developed supplying rational recreation for the public. In the light of the legitimatisation and commercialisation of leisure activities, court debates over the Exemption Act demonstrated that provision of social welfare was a priority when set against cultural services since the latter could be assigned to the mixed agency of the voluntary and commercial sectors. All the same, it was still necessary to distinguish between these two sectors and to establish a legitimate framework within which voluntary associations could offer cultural services to the wider public. Informed of the judgement at Queen's Bench, the council of the Zoological Society swiftly contacted politicians and other institutions to

[116] Ibid. 823.

lobby for the recovery of their exemption.[117] At that time, parliament had already debated the matter and accordingly passed a revised Scientific and Literary Institutions Act in August 1854. This expanded the range of institutions eligible for exemption from the parochial rates and allowed them to obtain land not exceeding one acre as a site for their buildings. A wide range of institutions from scientific societies to subscription libraries fell within the rubric of this act, even though the Zoological Society did not.

The legal status of the society, in particular its liability to taxation, remained uncertain. In 1856 it was assessed under Schedule D (profits from trade, commerce and the professions) as liable to £100 in income tax; this was instantly annulled on appeal to the Commissioners of Inland Revenue.[118] Although the framework within which the zoo operated for the public good was already clear in the mid-nineteenth century, it was still ill-defined and the zoo was therefore vulnerable. There were to be further twists and turns to the story. The zoo did not completely withdraw from its scientific mission: behind the scenes of public worship of the 'charm of novelty', Mitchell was seeking to establish a new, legitimate, science at the zoo.

---

[117] ZSL, MC, xi, fos 92, 95–6.
[118] ZSL, MC, xi, fos 241, 249.

5

Illusionary Empire

The zoo and science interacted with each other in various ways. The zoo was a platform for rising zoologists who sought to authenticate their scientific activities, but it also problematised relationships between science and its public by raising the question of accessibility. It has also been argued that the London Zoo embodied the boundary between the separate scientific spheres: as a site of 'recreational science', it formed a bridge between the scientific community and the non-specialist public, and provided financial and material resources for 'legitimate science'. Yet this book has not explored exactly what kind of science was being engaged in at the London Zoo. This chapter thus contemplates the question of science by tracing David Mitchell's attempt to reconfigure the zoo as an institute of 'acclimatisation' – a new form of science that he believed would employ the knowledge and materials available at the zoo.

The validity of the concept of 'imperial zoo' can also be tested through a study of acclimatisation. It can be seen as a particular form of the science/empire symbiosis that demonstrated the dynamic interactions between home institutions and the colonial field.[1] The trajectory of acclimatisation at the London Zoo, however, does not necessarily underline this interpretation. Certainly, it appears to be a manifestation of the British imperial intervention in colonial nature. It was indeed an ambitious attempt to regenerate the zoo as a centre of 'zoological empire', which would use animals as colonial resources on an unprecedentedly large scale. Nevertheless, acclimatisation failed to be recognised as a disciplinary science when the professionalisation of science developed towards the end of the nineteenth century. The eventual failure of acclimatisation poses a question as to the place of empire in the historical narrative of the London Zoo.

Science at the zoo

The advancement of zoological science was one of the goals of the Zoological Society. At first glance, however, it is hard to see how the zoo contributed to achieving this goal. When the society was founded, Nicholas Vigors and

---

[1]   M. A. Osborn, *Nature, the exotic and the science of French colonisation*, Bloomington 1994, and 'Acclimatizing the world: a history of the paradigmatic colonial science', *Osiris* 2nd ser. xv (2000), 135–51; Ritvo, *Animal estate*, 239–42.

his allies expressed enthusiastic interest in taxonomy and nomenclature and endeavoured to universalise the quinerian system of classification, but their discussions were primarily based upon the anatomical study of dead specimens. There was also a mixed group of career zoologists and administrative reformers who intervened in the management of the zoo, but in their view it was the museum that exemplified the society's serious commitment to science; animals were only useful when dead and dissected. The *Proceedings of the Zoological Society* published many articles that recorded the characteristics and behaviours of zoo animals, but on the whole they were a random mixture of records and ideas, with no attempt at the comprehensive organisation of knowledge. Although experiments in animal physiology and pathology were occasionally carried out, they lacked continuity and produced little substantial result.[2] Since mainstream zoology centred on classification and nomenclature, especially in the early nineteenth century, the zoo appeared to make little contribution to the development of the zoological sciences. From the perspective of specialist zoologists, it barely figured in their studies.

By contrast, from the perspective of gentleman breeders and menagerists, the zoo was a focal point of expertise in the care and domestication of ornamental animals. Prior to the opening of the London Zoo, there were around forty private menageries in England, and hence a steady demand for exotic animals. The opening of the London Zoo seemed to satisfy these demands, and the collection of exotic animals increasingly became a cultural pursuit, part of the world of fashion and conspicuous display. The newly 'discovered' kangaroo, which Queen Charlotte, the wife of George III, kept in her menagerie in the Windsor Great Park, was an example.[3] As kangaroo 'mania' was still raging when the Zoological Society was founded, its aristocratic sponsors expected the zoo to breed many specimens which could be distributed among them. The preference for ornamental animals was also reflected in the original zoo collection. It began with a variety of avian and bovine species such as peacocks, fowls, swans, geese, ducks and cattle, and then gradually increased the stock of showy animals.

The breeding of exotic animals was indeed one of the Zoological Society's priorities, as is borne out by the establishment of the Kingston Farm in 1829. Although it ceased to function within a few years, a number of breeding experiments were conducted under the supervision of Joseph Sabine, who endeavoured to realise the late Humphry Davy's vision of 'ornamental and practical zoology'. While kangaroos began to be bred freely at the farm, the collection constituted chiefly of game birds and antelopes that were imported from various countries. Among them were the wapiti (a species of deer indigenous to North America), the sambar (a large deer native to

---

[2] Åkerberg, *Knowledge and pleasure*, 170–96

[3] C. Plumb, 'In fact, one cannot see it without laughing': the spectacle of the kangaroo in London, 1770–1830', *Museum History Journal* iii (2010), 7–32; C. Lever, *They dined on eland: the story of the acclimatisation societies*, London 1992, 17–18.

south and south-east Asia), the axis deer (native to South Asia, notable for the white spots on its skin) and the nilgai (also collected from South Asia). A variety of cattle, sheep and horses was also bred on the farm to test their agricultural utility. Although the Zoological Society reported its intention to advance the study of the 'physiology' of these animals without clarifying the content and meaning of the term, there was a particular aspect to the breeding programme on the farm: excessive attempts at crossbreeding. For instance, zebras were mated with asses, sheep with goats and Wallachian rams with Dorset ewes. A rabbit-hare hybrid was produced and its cadaver was examined by Richard Owen, who testified that the animal combined the anatomical structures of both species.[4]

Although the breeding project at Kingston came to an end amidst loud protests from the pro-science lobby, the gentlemen menagerists regained their influence after the Tory triumph at the 1835 council election of the Zoological Society. The society's emphasis on breeding is most evident in the creation of the premium award. In 1833 the council appointed a Premium Committee at the request of Joseph Cox, who probably expected the society to honour specialist zoologists who had contributed to the advancement of their field of study.[5] In the course of further discussions, however, Joseph Sabine joined the committee and expressed the view that the premiums – a medal designed by Thomas Landseer – should be awarded to those who successfully introduced 'new and curious animals'. In 1837 the Zoological Society announced the categories for the competition: the importer of a hippopotamus or a platypus; the breeder of 'the greatest number of curassows' in the next breeding season; the collector of a new species of Indian pheasant; the breeder of 'the best specimens of Indian fowls'; the breeder of the most rare, or most interesting foreign animal'; and the presenter of the best essay 'on the care and treatment of the species of the genus Felis in confinement'.[6] Clearly, this list reflected the interests of gentlemen menagerists and zoo promenaders. Specialist zoologists could have no expectation of winning the medal, other than by writing the prize essay on a subject that was clearly influenced by the interests of the breeders.

Gentlemen menagerists continued to use the London Zoo as a reservoir of breeding stock. The kind of animals that were most frequently exchanged and loaned were game birds such as curassows, ducks, pheasants and partridges, and the breeder who most took advantage of this custom was the earl of Derby. His life's work was the the breeding of antelopes and various kinds of birds: one of his successful experiments was the breeding of the Wild American Turkey, for which John Thompson, a keeper at Derby's

[4] Scherren, *The Zoological Society*, 41–3, 69–71; Mitchell, *Centenary history*, 93–5; Desmond, 'The making of institutional zoology', 227–8.

[5] ZSL, MC, iii, fos 224, 233.

[6] ZSL, MC, iii, fos 281–2; v, fos 68–9, 76; *Magazine of Popular Science and Journal of the Useful Arts* iii (1837), 472; *Magazine of Natural History* i (1837), 333.

Knowsley menagerie, won a first prize in the poultry breeder's competition organised by the Zoological Society in 1847. At the time of his death in 1851 Derby's collection ran to more than 1,600 specimens (exclusive of poultry), many of which were Knowsley-bred.[7] The extensive scale of the Knowsley collection testified not only to Derby's personal enthusiasm but also to the networks of gentlemen menagerists which allowed him to collect a wide range of breeding stock. At this stage, however, the zoo's role in the breeders' networks was limited to providing duplicate specimens, since the Zoological Society had no intention in taking any initiative in coordinating the individual efforts of gentleman breeders.

At request of the Zoological Society, Prince Albert replaced Derby as president. Albert's generous patronage of the arts and industry is generally noted, but he was also interested in the study of natural history and entrusted Richard Owen, by then vice-president of the Zoological Society, with educating the royal children on the subject. Albert's presidency (1851–60) overlapped with the ascendancy of David Mitchell, a coincidence which precipitated a dramatic growth in 'ornamental and practical zoology'. This stemmed originally from Queen Victoria's desire for breeding stock of the Himalayan monal (see Figure 23), which was acclaimed as the most beautiful gallinacean of the world.[8] The monal was more commonly known as the Impeyan pheasant, named after Lady Impey (1749–1818), wife of the Chief Justice of Bengal, who was said to have, albeit in vain, attempted to introduce the bird into England. The queen's wish to have this particular bird in her collection could partly be explained by her personal interest in India. As Miles Taylor suggests, the public image of the British monarchy began to be closely associated with India, as was epitomised by the display of the Koh-i-noor diamond at the Great Exhibition of 1851. Exotic artefacts and natural objects were integral to Victoria's concept of the British Empire, even before she became the Empress of India in 1876.[9]

Once Victoria's request had been conveyed through Prince Albert to the Zoological Society, David Mitchell drew up a plan for collecting breeding stock of the Himalayan monal. He expected that the project would attract the attention of gentleman breeders, since many of their circle were eager to acquire a monal too; it had great rarity value due to the extreme difficulty of bringing it back alive to London. When a captain of the Bengal Cavalry returned home with some living specimens and exhibited them at the Surrey Zoo in 1847, they were claimed to be 'the only living examples ever seen in

---

[7] *The Times*, 31 July 1847, 7; *Illustrated London News*, 7 Aug. 1847, 91–2; A. C. Stevens, *Catalogue of the menagerie and aviary at Knowsley formed by the late earl of Derby, K.G.*, Liverpool 1851.

[8] Scherren, *The Zoological Society*, 118; J. M. Mackenzie, *The empire of nature: hunting, conservation and British imperialism*, Manchester 1988, 38.

[9] M. Taylor, 'Queen Victoria and India, 1837–61', VS lxvi (2004), 264–74.

Figure 23. William Skelton (after Charles Reuben Ryley), 'Himalayan monal'. Wellcome Library, London, no. 43235i.

England'.[10] Such was their rarity and consequent popularity with ornithological collectors that between 1,000 and 1,500 monal and trapogan plumages (the trapogan was another ornamental pheasant) were sent from Mussoorie to England every year.[11] Meanwhile, the breeding of monal pheasants had been successful in only a few menageries and in the private collection of Queen Victoria.[12]

[10] *Illustrated London News*, 3 July 1847, 5.
[11] A. Hume and C. H. T. Marshall, *The game birds of India, Burmah, and Ceylon*, Calcutta 1879, i. 130.
[12] Mitchell to Blyth, 8 Nov. 1856, ZSL, Blyth papers.

The original aim had been to collect this particular pheasant, but Mitchell expanded this to include other gallinaceans including the trapogan, the argus and the snow partridge, which rivalled the monal in colour and rarity.[13] Mitchell envisaged that the Zoological Society would initiate the breeding programme, using the facilities and resources of the London Zoo. This was clearly reflected in his letter to a prospective collaborator in India, which expressed his desire to obtain 'all the Himalayan Game Birds which inhabit zones in the range where the temperature at all resembles that of Europe'.[14] As the queen's desire for the monal evolved into an extensive breeding project, its importance changed significantly. The Impeyan pheasant became more than a gem of nature that would embellish the private collections of the queen and of gentlemen menagerists. Rather, it bore witness to the potential for the Zoological Society to manipulate animals and birds as natural resources by collaborating with royal and aristocratic sponsors.

Mitchell emphasised the innovative aspects of his project, using the term 'acclimatisation' when it was still unknown to many of his contemporaries. He sought to establish that acclimatisation was a new kind of science that gathered breeding expertise and applied it to the systematic propagation of foreign animals in Britain, but he had to be cautious for the term had problematic connotations. The study of acclimatisation began in France: it involved investigation of the effect of the physical environment upon the constitution of organisms, and was promoted by the foundation of the *Société zoologique d'acclimatation* in 1854. Isidore Geoffroy Saint-Hilaire, director of the society, considered that the shapes and functions of animals changed over time due to environmental conditions such as climate. This theory was at odds with Georges Cuvier's hitherto orthodox 'fixism', which argued that that the functions of an organism were biologically fixed to suit the physical environment that it encountered when it first appeared on earth. According to this view, any organic evolution that occurred would have destroyed its functional integration into its surroundings and rendered the organism unable to survive. 'Fixism' thus complemented natural theology, which regarded eternal unity as a sign of divine creation.[15] In Britain, the theory of acclimatisation was held to undermine the authority of natural theology, and if applied to social hierarchy could even have endangered the aristocratic establishment. Acclimatisation was therefore detached from evolutionary theories and presented as a systematic attempt to domesticate foreign animals within a climate that was not their natural habitat.[16]

---

[13] Mitchell to Charles Canning, 24 Aug. 1856, ZSL, BADC, Charles John Canning 1st Earl Canning papers.

[14] Mitchell to J. B. Hearsey, 19 Aug. 1856, ZSL, BADH, J. B. Hearsey papers.

[15] For the theoretical basis of acclimatisation see Osborn, *Nature, the exotic and the science of French colonisation*, 63–98.

[16] W. Anderson, 'Climates of opinion: acclimatization in nineteenth-century France and England', VS xxxv (1992), 136–7.

Clearly, the reason why Mitchell explained his project as acclimatisation was not to advance evolutionary theories. His intention was to emphasise that the project would depart from 'ornamental and practical zoology', which only aimed at the propagation of exotic animals for gentlemen menagerists. In fact, the ultimate goal of the acclimatisation programme was to domesticate Himalayan game birds in the Scottish Highlands and thereby add to the familiar diversity of the British landscapes. Mitchell believed that this was viable, principally because both the Himalayas and the Highlands were located in the temperate zone and hence should be able to support the same species. The strength of his belief suggests that the Zoological Society had already gathered a certain amount of knowledge regarding the fauna and climatic conditions of the Himalayas. Indeed, the acclimatisation project required not only the sponsorship of the queen and aristocratic menagerists, but also the help of those who searched the hill countries to collect information and specimens for the Zoological Society. How the Himalayas came to play a part in the project is therefore worthy of further analysis.

Hunters and naturalists in the Himalayas

The momentum for the acclimatisation project may have sprung from the collection of Himalayan specimens that John Forbes Royle, former superintendent of the botanic garden at Saharanpur, brought back with him in 1831. As zoology was not his main field, the specimens were examined by William Ogilby, ornithologist and secretary (1837–47) to the Zoological Society, who wrote on Himalayan mammalogy for Royle's *Illustrations of botany and other branches of the natural history of the Himalayan mountains* (1839). In this brief note Ogilby suggested investigating the geographical distribution of animals in the various temperate zones, as he questioned 'whether similar regions, wherever situated, or however separated from one another by intervening seas and deserts, produce kindred or analogous species of Mammals?'[17] Although this suggestion came to nothing, it could have justified the concept of acclimatisation.

Growing interests in the Himalayas coincided with the expansion of British India into the hill countries. In the aftermath of the Gurkha war (1814–16), the development of Simla, Kullu and Mussoorie began in the north-west provinces, followed a decade later by Darjeeling to the north of Calcutta. These hill stations provided a summer refuge free from the burning

---

[17] J. F. Royle, *Illustrations of botany and other branches of the natural history of the Himalayan mountains*, London 1839, i, p. lvii. Royle himself wrote on the acclimatisation of plants and vegetables: S. Sangwan, 'From gentlemen amateurs to professionals: reassessing the natural science tradition in colonial India, 1780–1840', in R. H. Grove, V. Damodran and S. Sangwan (eds), *Nature and the orient: the environmental history of South and Southeast Asia*, Delhi 1998, 218–21.

heat and indigenous multitudes in the plains, and also drew the attention of physicians and naturalists who discussed the impact of climate upon the vegetation, diseases and intelligence of the local population.[18] Medical and topographical literature was prone to describe the climate of India as damp, humid and harmful to the physical and mental constitution, but the Himalayas was different and was perceived instead as a sanctuary within 'tropical India'.[19] Edward Archer, who trekked through the Himalayas on a hunting trip, thus linked the familiar plants that he saw with his native land and declared that 'The climate of the hills, according to our feelings, is the most delicious and agreeable in the world.'[20] His sentiments can best be understood when the distances that he travelled are taken into consideration. As he climbed into the hills, Archer realised that the surrounding topography seemed familiar, and he elaborated on his feeling of nostalgia:[21]

> The recollections of home, and the many kindred associations which possess the mind, and arouse those indefinable feelings of love, of hope, desire, and regret, and which are not the less forcible by being called into existence through the medium of such humble instruments as simple wild flowers; – these make the heart yearn with tenfold eagerness to retrace the distance between it and the objects of its earliest and best remembrances.

It was not just the flora that evoked Archer's nostalgia: 'The cuckoo, blackbird, and thrush are common, and again reminded us of our native country.'[22] In fact, the unique fauna of the Himalayas attracted the attention of two zealous zoologists: Brian Hodgson and Edward Blyth. Hodgson served the East India Company at Kumaon and Katmandu, and after retirement settled at Darjeeling in 1845. While ornithology was his particular interest, he researched Himalayan mammals extensively with the assistance of local staff, whom he trained at his own expense. He made sketches and compiled descriptions of numerous species and delivered many of them to the Zoological Society of London.[23] By contrast, Blyth remained in Calcutta, where

---

[18] D. Kennedy, *The magic mountains: hill stations and the British raj*, Delhi 1996; Q. Pradhan, 'Empire in the hills: the making of hill stations in colonial India', *Studies in History* xxiii (2007), 33–91.

[19] J. T. Kenny, 'Climate, race, and imperial authority: the symbolic landscape of the British hill station in India', *Annals of the Association of American Geographers* lxxxv (1995), 694–714; David Arnold, 'India's place in the tropical world', *Journal of Imperial and Commonwealth History* xxvi (1998), 1–21.

[20] E. C. Archer, *Tours in upper India and in parts of the Himalayan mountains with accounts of the courts of the native princes*, London 1833, i. 337.

[21] Ibid. i. 207.

[22] Ibid. i. 234.

[23] W. W. Hunter, *Life of Brian Houghton Hodgson: British resident at the court of Nepal*, London 1896; M. Cocker and C. Inskipp, *A Himalayan ornithologist: the life and work of Brian Houghton Hodgson*, Oxford 1988; D. Waterhouse (ed.), *The origin of Himalayan studies: Brian Houghton Hodgson in Nepal and Darjeeling, 1820–1858*, London 2004.

he was appointed curator of the Museum of the Asiatic Society. His heavy official duties rarely allowed him to leave the city, but he had a broad knowledge of the animal geography of the Himalayas and assisted Charles Darwin with his *Variation of plants and animals under domestication* (1868).[24] While both Hodgson and Blyth brought the London-based zoological community to recognise the significance of the study of Himalayan fauna, they had the disadvantage of geographical distance from the metropolis. A 'sense of isolation' is an umbrella term that describes the anxieties of many colonial scientists, but what it really meant became clear when the two colonial zoologists were asked to help with the Zoological Society's project.[25]

A further source of information was Joseph Hooker, botanist and close friend of Charles Darwin.[26] With the help of Brian Hodgson, Hooker arrived in the Himalayas in 1847 and spent two years exploring the central and eastern regions. On returning home with a collection of approximately 7,000 specimens, he published his *Rhododendrons of the Sikkim-Himalaya* (1849–51), which produced a rhododendron craze among British gardeners. His subsequent publication, *Himalayan journals* (1854), also mentioned the distribution of animals in different areas of the hill country and described some of the gallinaceans that he had encountered including the kalij and the tragopan, both on David Mitchell's wish-list[27]. When, therefore, Mitchell began to make preparations for his acclimatisation project, information on the climate and natural history of the Himalayas could be obtained from published work on its natural history as well as from specialist zoologists who had lived or travelled in the hill country.

Hunting travelogues also had information to give since the knowledge required for hunting was very similar to natural history. The hill country enchanted the British military officers and civil servants on hunting expeditions. On the plains they generally preferred big game, but in the hills the main quarries were goats and birds. Hunting styles were different too. Big-game hunting was a matter of showy symbolism and male bravado, increasingly so in the course of the late nineteenth century, while game-hunting in the Himalayas was regarded as an individualistic sport that required

[24] C. Brandon-Jones, 'Long gone and forgotten: reassessing the life and career of Edward Blyth, zoologist', *Archives of Natural History* xxii (1995), 91–5, and 'Edward Blyth, Charles Darwin, and the animal trade in nineteenth-century India and Britain', *Journal of the History of Biology* xxx (1997), 145–78.

[25] David Arnold, *Science, technology and medicine in colonial India*, Cambridge 2000, 25–6.

[26] J. Enderby, *Imperial nature: Joseph Hooker and the practices of Victorian science*, Chicago 2008, and 'Sympathetic science: Charles Darwin, Joseph Hooker and the passions of Victorian naturalists', *VS* li (2009), 299–320.

[27] For example, J. D. Hooker, *Himalayan journals, or notes of a naturalist in Bengal, the Sikkim and Nepal Himalayas, the Khasia Mountains, &c*, London 1854, i. 25, 55.

advanced skills and stoicism.[28] Authors of hunting travelogues acknowledged the challenges of the terrain. Rocks and ridges made it hard to stalk or to get within shooting range of the quarry without being perceived. The anonymous writer of *A summer ramble in the Himalayas* (1860) noted plainly that 'No country can possibly be conceived better adapted for stalking than the Himalayas.'[29] Shooting in the hills was also demanding because of the complexity of measuring the distances, compounded by the physical effort of negotiating the steep terrain.[30] The tahr (an ungulate, similar to the wild goat), was particularly prized by British hunters as the finest target in the Himalayas. Captain Mathias, author of *Five week's sport in the interior of the Himalayas* (1865), vowed not to shoot any animal until he had killed a tahr.[31]

British hunters also shot a variety of partridges, kalijes and pheasants. Enthusiasm for game birds resulted from a dramatic transformation in British practices in the early nineteenth century. With the invention of the cartridge in 1808, new sporting rules prescribed that a bird had to be shot on the wing, not haphazardly on the ground. Pheasants then became the prime quarry and their popularity promoted the introduction of many species from Japan, China and India.[32] Thus, in terms of the variety of prizes, as well as the unique terrain, the hill country seemed to be the perfect hunting ground. Many hunters agreed that of all game birds the most beautiful was the monal pheasant, memorably described by Allen Hume in his *Game birds of India, Burmah, and Ceylon* (1879):[33]

> I have shot many Monual [sic] in my time, and have seen a vast number more. There are few sights more striking, where birds are concerned, than that of a grand old cock shooting out horizontally from the hill-side just below eye, glittering and flashing in the golden sunlight, a gigantic rainbow-tinted gem and then dropping stone-like, with closed wings, into the abyss below.

The information contained in hunting travelogues was not limited to

---

[28] MacKenzie, *The empire of nature*; W. Beinart, *The rise of conservation in South Africa: settlers, livestock, and the environment, 1770–1950*, Oxford 2003; M. S. S. Pandian, 'Gendered negotiations: hunting and colonialism in the late nineteenth-century Nilgiris', in P. Uberoi (ed.), *Social reform, sexuality and the state*, New Delhi 1996, 239–64; W. K. Storey, 'Big cats and imperialism: lion and tiger hunting in Kenya and Northern India, 1898–1930', *Journal of World History* ii (1991), 135–73; J. Sramek, "Face him like a Briton": tiger hunting, imperialism and British masculinity in colonial India, 1800–1875', VS xlviii (2006), 659–80.

[29] Anon., *A summer ramble in the Himalayas with sporting adventures in the Vale of Cashmere*, London 1860, 52.

[30] H. V. Mathias, *Five week's sport in the interior of the Himalayas: together with a description of the game found there*, London 1865, 36.

[31] Ibid. 33

[32] MacKenzie, *The empire of nature*, 18–19.

[33] Hume and Marshall, *Game birds of India*, i. 129.

hunting. They also described the value of the game birds to local shikaris as well as the efficient method of hunting that they had invented. During a hunting expedition in the Himalayas, Mathias came across a snaring system that could catch a large number of monal pheasants at once. This involved constructing a light fence along the crest of the hill, about a mile long and three feet high. At regular intervals it had small openings into which monals were enticed by food. Many monals were caught in this manner, generally killed for their flesh and the preservation of their beautiful skins, but sometimes they were sent alive to Mussoorie, where there was a ready market for them.[34] Mathias bought the skins of different pheasants, including monals, from a villager, and was delighted to accept his offer of as many as he liked at one rupee a piece, because Mathias knew that monal skins fetched far higher prices at Mussoorie.[35]

This account implies that the increasing presence of British hunters came to have a crucial impact on the indigenous hunting economy. Even before British influence expanded into the Himalayan interior, game birds were being traded for food and ornament. After the full moon in November, for instance, Nepalese traders came down to sell Himalayan game birds at a fair near Patna. The British demand for animal skins, however, together with the development of hill stations, changed both the scale and structure of the trade. In the 1840s an annual fair began to be held at Darjeeling, where travelling vendors traded in food, clothing and animal products.[36] At Sabathus, a cantonment town near Simla, Kashmiri immigrants came to peddle the skins of various animals from snow leopards and pine martens to monals.[37] These fairs and markets provided useful information and desirable objects for British collectors.

Analysis of hunting travelogues suggests why Himalayan game birds were crucial to the acclimatisation project. Once they were successfully bred in the London Zoo, they could be sold to gentleman menagerists as ornamental quarries, and if it were possible to acclimatise them in the Scottish Highlands, it should theoretically be possible to produce a version of the Himalayan hunting grounds. The monal pheasant thus linked together the Zoological Society, gentlemen menagerists, specialist zoologists and hunting enthusiasts and led them to cooperate in the acclimatisation project.

[34] Mathias, *Five week's sport*, 80.
[35] Ibid. 68.
[36] Pradhan, 'Empire in the hills', 45.
[37] Ibid. 84.

The mechanism of scientific enterprise

While David Mitchell communicated with prospective collaborators in India, Prince Albert proposed a subscription scheme whereby each sponsor would share in the profits of the enterprise – when the birds were successfully introduced – in proportion to the size of her/his subscription. Subsequently, Queen Victoria, the marquis of Breadalbane and Viscount Hill each donated £100 towards the expenses of the project.[38] Their donations covered the extra costs, but its actual operation required scores of rank-and-file collectors who travelled to capture the quarry. The capacity of the East India Company to mobilise its manpower was hard to overestimate, but the company was not usually a generous patron of science for it judged the value of scientific enterprise chiefly from a utilitarian perspective.

Botany was at something of an advantage as it was relatively easy for botanists to impress on the company the commercial profits that it would gain from agricultural products. The botanic garden, which had been founded at Calcutta in 1786, created salaried posts for vocational botanists and encouraged them to collaborate with the Royal Botanic Gardens at Kew.[39] By contrast, zoology remained a leisure activity, although Calcutta benefited from the rich local fauna as well as from extensive trade with south-east Asia, south India and Ceylon (modern Sri Lanka). Many servicemen and civilians of the Company were encouraged to devote their spare time to the collection of exotic animals. In 1801 Francis Buchanan of the Bengal Medical Service had already launched the Barrackpore Menagerie in the neighbourhood of Calcutta.[40] Emily Eden, who accompanied her brother, Lord Auckland, upon his appointment as Governor-General of India in 1834, was fond of animals and enjoyed her visit to the Barrackpore Menagerie.[41] She was also constantly being given animals by the officers: one of these men appeared in Emily Eden's diary. He came to take his leave as he was returning to England after thirty-two years of service in India and expressed his interest in the Zoological Society of London, which had not been in existence when he left home.[42] Many officers collected animals and sent them to the society. One of them, Alexander Elphinstone, an East India Company serviceman, wrote to the society in 1849 and promised donations of Indian animals, adapting Nelson's famous signal at the battle of Trafalgar: 'England has a right to expect from her sons in the colonies contributions to our National Zoolog-

---

[38] ZSL, MC, xi, fos 288–91; Scherren, *The Zoological Society*, 118.

[39] Drayton, *Nature's government*, 180–201; Arnold, *Science, technology and medicine*, 46–9.

[40] V. N. Kisling, Jr, 'Colonial menageries and the exchange of exotic faunas', *Archives of Natural History* xxi (1994), 312–14.

[41] Emily Eden's fondness for animals could have been influenced by her brother. After the disastrous failure of the Afghan campaign, Auckland was recalled by Robert Peel in 1845 and rejoined the Zoological Society briefly before he died in 1849.

[42] E. Eden, *Letters from India*, London 1872, i. 301–2, 333.

ical Society in London.'[43] In his view the society appreciated what they were doing and therefore motivated them to continue collecting. Prince Albert sought to boost the morale of these voluntary collectors, writing to Canning to convey his wish to promote the acclimatisation project. In response, Canning ordered the authorities at the hill stations to send Himalayan game birds down to Calcutta. He was also personally interested in the project and suggested producing a breeding stock at the hill stations by collecting eggs and young birds: this seemed a troublesome yet promising measure. Mitchell, however, clung to his original scheme, because what he anticipated from the Company was not their taking initiatives, but mobilising its manpower to further his own plans.[44]

Mitchell seemed to be concerned that support from the Company might not be enough and contacted Rajendro Mullick of Calcutta, the founder of the Marble Palace, India's 'first museum of western art'.[45] Mullick was also an enthusiastic animal collector. He established a zoo next to the palace and opened it to the public in 1854. His taste for fine art and natural history was nurtured by his early education. Born into a wealthy merchant family, the untimely death of his father placed him under the guardianship of James Weir Hogg, who was then registrar to the supreme court of Calcutta and later became a Director of the East India Company. Mullick's biographer remarked that it was Hogg 'who created in the Rajah an interest for taming birds and animals which resulted in the establishment of a menagerie in the house of the Rajah'.[46] Mullick also inherited his mother's firm Hindu faith and rigidly disciplined his everyday life according to its tenets. It was one of his daily practices to feed between 500 and 600 paupers, a number which was increased to 5,000 when famine struck in 1865. His contribution was appreciated by the government, which conferred on him the title of 'Raj Bahadur'.[47]

Just as Mullick's public *persona* was formed through the combination of his European tutor's guidance and his Hindu faith, so the Marble Palace Zoo was a hybrid, demonstrating not only the influence of European ideas, but also the significance of the indigenous network of animal traders. Mullick donated many Indian animals to zoological societies in Europe and Australia, and in return obtained foreign species that were valued for their rarity in India. His ornithological collection was particularly notable, as one British visitor recorded: 'Animals and birds fill the garden, and his collection contains the feathered tribes of every land, from the Ostrich to the Emu, the Mandarin

[43] *Proceedings of the Zoological Society of London* xvii (1849), 106.

[44] ZSL, MC, xii, fos 304–5.

[45] M. Jasanoff, *Edge of empire: lives, culture and conquest in the East, 1750–1850*, New York 2005, 317–18.

[46] D. Chatterjee, *A short sketch of Rajah Rajendro Mullick Bahadur and his family*, Calcutta 1917, 23.

[47] Ibid. 24.

duck of China to the bird of paradise.'[48] Mitchell solicited Mullick's support with a gift of macaws and curassows. Since they were relatively common in Europe, Mitchell instructed his agent, whom he dispatched to Calcutta, not to underestimate their value in India: 'You will take care not to depress the value of Maccaws [sic] & Curassows to him. They are valued excessively in India'.[49] Mullick appreciated the gift and sent his agents off in search of the animals that Mitchell had requested.[50]

The involvement of influential patrons and participants, from Victoria and Albert to the Governor-General of India and Rajendra Mullick, seemed promising, but the scheme was not yet up and running. In fact, the most difficult aspect of the project was the employment of the agent who would take responsibility for collecting a large number of animals in Calcutta and transporting them to London. Mitchell offered the job to James Thompson, who had superintended Earl Fitzwilliam's menagerie at Wentworth, Sheffield, for ten years. The offer covered a weekly wage of two guineas – very high for a menagerie keeper – plus a bonus of one pound per head for animals brought home safely.[51] It was indeed an appealing proposal and, after discussing health matters with a doctor at Sheffield, Thompson accepted and moved down to London.[52] In September 1856 he sailed for India on a ship specifically fitted out for the conveyance of birds. He was due to arrive at Calcutta in December 1856, and to return home by May 1857 with the animals and birds collected in the hill country.

When Thompson was still on board ship, the collecting began, with a number of hill stations as gathering centres: Darjeeling, Simla, Kullu, Kumaun, Mussoorie and Dehradun. It was doubtful, however, whether everyone involved understood the aim of the project. There seemed to be many officers who simply assumed that Prince Albert wanted curious beasts and birds from the Himalayas. Reginald Ouseley of the 34th Regiment of Infantry of the Bengal Army regarded the campaign as a good opportunity for him to demonstrate his devotion to natural history as well as to Prince Albert. He was determined to present to Albert a young specimen of the tahr, which he had domesticated, with a note containing an exhaustive description of the habitat and character of the animal. He believed that it was a new species of goat and therefore a worthy gift to Albert.[53] A gift of rare animals to the royal family was a more or less common custom. Perhaps Ouseley, in his remote hill station, dreamt of his gift and name

---

[48] Ibid. 35.

[49] Mitchell to James Thompson, 26 Nov. 1856, ZSL, BADT, James Thompson papers.

[50] Rajendra Mullick to Mitchell, 23 Jan. 1857, ibid. BADR, Rajendra Mullick papers.

[51] After returning from Calcutta, Thompson was employed by the Zoological Society and was promoted to head keeper in May 1859: ZSL, MC, xii, fo. 183.

[52] Mitchell to Thompson, 11 July, 12, 19 Aug. 1856, ibid. Thompson papers.

[53] Reginald Ouseley to Gerald Chetwynd Talbot, 21 Jan., 12 Feb. 1857, ibid. BADT, Gerald Chetwynd Talbot papers.

being sent to Prince Albert in England.[54] Canning observed the proprieties and commended Ouseley in his report to Albert.[55] Thompson was, however, unhappy to hear of the imminent arrival of the tahr. He confessed to Mitchell that 'I have but little hope of being able to bring this animal home as it is said to inhabit only the highest and coldest parts of the Himalayas.'[56] What Ouseley's misunderstanding revealed was not the incapacity of the field collectors to understand the acclimatisation project, but that Mitchell preferred to let them interpret the project on their own terms. Although this sometimes led to people being at cross-purposes, it did mean that they could participate for their own reasons.

It was therefore rather surprising that Captain James at Darjeeling acted completely within Mitchell's original scheme. He obtained ninety-four specimens, of which thirteen were monals, and identified all of them with Latin terms, attaching a brass wire ring to each so that the Darjeeling specimens could be easily recognised upon arrival at London. James noted that this would help further investigations into variations of the same species in the Himalayas, and reported his failure to capture the snow partridge, which he considered would be 'easily domesticated in the Northern parts of Scotland'.[57] Obviously, James understood that at the heart of the project was a plan to acclimatise game birds of the Himalyas in the Scottish Highlands, not merely their safe transport to London. What enabled James to make such exceptional contributions was the expertise offered by Brian Hodgson, who acted independently of Canning. To obtain his support, Mitchell wrote to Hodgson and suggested that the Zoological Society would publish an illustrated catalogue of the Himalayan mammals which Hodgson had previously presented to the East India Museum. Since it was important for field naturalists like him to have their discoveries acknowledged by the metropolitan scientific community, Mitchell's message was very welcome.[58]

Hodgson did not share Mitchell's optimism. He questioned the feasibility of the project, as in 1833 he had once failed in an attempt to send a hundred pheasants from Nepal to the Zoological Society. No matter how keen the London Zoo was to have them, no bird could survive the long journey as the society had reported: 'Of nearly a hundred of them dispatched from Katmandu, many perished in the sultry plains of India, and nearly the whole of the remainder died in Calcutta. Of the few that were embarked

---

[54] Talbot to Ouseley, 3 Jan., 15 Mar. 1857, ibid.

[55] Canning to Charles Phipps, 24 Mar. 1857, ibid. Canning papers.

[56] Thompson to Mitchell, 10 Feb. 1857, ibid. Thompson papers.

[57] Mitchell to H. C. James, 25 Aug., 10 Dec. 1856; 26 Mar. 1857, and James to Mitchell, 3 Feb. 1857, ibid. BADJ, H. C. James papers.

[58] Mitchell to Brian Hodgson, 26 Nov. 1856, ibid. BADH, Brian Hodgson papers. It was generally assumed that the metropolitan societies had the authority to publish papers: Sangwan, 'From gentleman amateurs to professionals', 224–5.

for England not one survived the voyage.'[59] Hodgson would therefore have agreed with Charles Canning that the best thing to do was to prepare a breeding stock at the hill stations, where the birds could begin to adapt to different climatic conditions before they had to survive the long voyage to London. He did not press his own ideas, however, but decided to act behind the scenes with James, in order to retain Mitchell as his close associate in London.[60]

Mitchell was vexed by Edward Blyth's response to his request for support. Blyth demanded that Thompson should take his own animals to London, where Mitchell could purchase them for the Zoological Society or otherwise find reliable clients. Given that Blyth worked for a pittance as the curator of the Asiatic Society's Museum, his commercial motivation is understandable.[61] To supplement his low salary, Blyth had occasionally shipped animals to London for sale, but had enjoyed little success because he had no reliable brokers. In his reply to Mitchell, Blyth complained that his London agent had once sold a mongoose for £10 to Edward Cross, proprietor of the Surrey Zoo, who sold it on to the Zoological Society for £20. Since Blyth could not control the trade from Calcutta, selling animals under Mitchell's supervision seemed to guarantee reasonable profits.[62] In Calcutta, Thompson recognised Blyth's need for money and was warned by Mitchell that 'I have no doubt that whatever success you have will be without any aid from him.'[63] But Blyth's self-interested attitude did not damage the project. Half of the specimens taken on board were presented by Mullick, who had allowed Thompson to select 110 specimens of over thirty species from his Marble Palace Zoo. The other half consisted of birds delivered from the hill stations by the East India Company. To the whole collection Thompson added a limited number of animals that he had discovered in a Calcutta bazaar and at the Barrackpore Menagerie. He left for London with 230 birds and animals in March 1857.[64]

Correspondence on the acclimatisation project suggests that it opened up a mixed cultural space where the individuals involved could communicate their ideas and anxieties (see Figure 24). As indicated by Blyth's negotiation with Mitchell to sell his own animals in London, their communications were varied and sometimes included information irrelevant to the project, but valuable in revealing how the project was perceived by those participants who had their own interests, perhaps in wealth or honour. The monal pheasant was also given a variety of meanings. The desire for a monal – whether springing from a desire for ornament, the establishment of a new

59 *Reports of the council and auditors* (1834), 13.
60 Hodgson to Mitchell, 11 Feb. 1857, ZSL, Hodgson papers.
61 Brandon-Jones, 'Edward Blyth', 156.
62 Blyth to Mitchell, 4 May 1857, ZSL, Blyth papers.
63 Mitchell to Thompson, 10 Mar. 1857, ibid. Thompson papers.
64 Mitchell to Phipps, 4 May 1857, ibid. BADP, Charles Phipps papers.

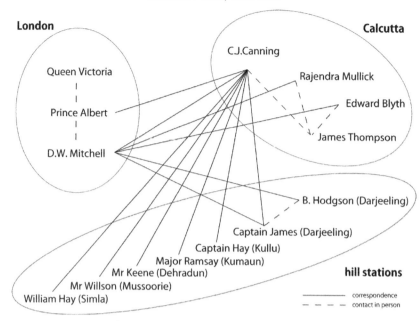

Figure 24. Correspondence networks of the acclimatisation campaigners, 1856–7, ZSL, BAD, nineteenth-century letters to the secretary.

scientific discipline that it would symbolise, or some other material benefits that the project would effect – directly or indirectly connected people of different ranks and from different regions who would otherwise have had no reason to know one another.

Ambivalent commitment to science

Although the collecting campaign was carried out on an unprecedentedly large scale, there was no guarantee that the outcome would be good: of 230 specimens shipped with Thompson from Calcutta to London, only a quarter survived. Mitchell had wanted between twelve and fifteen pairs of monals to make a good breeding stock, but only one male survived the voyage. 'It is with the greatest possible regret that I have to inform you of my almost total failure with the Pheas[an]ts', reported Thompson to Mitchell upon his arrival at London.[65]

There were three main reasons for the disaster. In the first place, it turned out to be far more complicated to keep birds in captivity than to shoot them down. Captain James reported to Mitchell that his assistants gathered a large

---

[65] Thompson to Mitchell, 13 July 1857, ibid. Thompson papers.

Table 5
Results of the East India Company's campaign, 1856–7

Gathering station	person in charge	number of birds			
		captured alive	sent to Calcutta	arriving at Calcutta	shipped to London
Darjeeling	Captain James	N/A	94	89	111
Simla	Lord William Hay		102	82	
Kullu	Captain Hay	200	N/A	69	
Kumaun	Major Ramsay	200	65		150
Mussoorie	Mr Wilson	411	166	206	
Dehradun	Mr Keene	N/A	29		
Total		>1036	>525	446	261

Source: Talbot to Mitchell, 3 Mar. 1857, ZSL, BAD, Talbot papers.

number of monals, but all of them were dying from injuries that they had received in the traps. Several specimens of the snow partridge were captured, but they died from the lack of proper food.[66] This happened in all the six hill stations (see Table 5). In total, over 1,000 specimens were collected, but less than half survived to reach Calcutta. Even those that did reach the city were in such poor condition that Thompson was shocked at their suffering and poor health. Predicting difficulties during shipping, James tried to accustom all his birds to the sort of food that they would have on the journey. That, together with the easier distance to Calcutta, might explain the very limited losses from the Darjeeling specimens. On the whole, however, it was not enough to help the birds survive the subsequent voyage.

The second reason for the fiasco was that the time required to gather the specimens together in Calcutta was miscalculated. The homeward voyage was initially scheduled for February 1857 so that the birds would arrive in time for the May breeding season.[67] It was vital that all the birds be delivered from the hill stations promptly and that the stay in Calcutta be as short as possible, because its tropical climate was impossible for them, even though the heat on the plains was less severe during this season. Yet only the birds sent from Simla and Darjeeling reached Calcutta in time for Thompson's already postponed departure for London in March 1857.[68] Birds delivered

---

[66] James to Mitchell, 3 Feb. 1857, ibid. James papers.

[67] It was observed that the breeding season of birds in the Himalayas was chiefly March, April and May: G. F. L. Marshall, *Bird's nesting in India: a calendar of the breeding seasons and a popular guide to the habits and haunts of birds*, Calcutta 1877, 7.

[68] The collections from Simla and Darjeeling arrived at Calcutta on 11 and 15 February respectively. They stayed in Calcutta for a month before embarkation on 11 March. This delay seriously damaged the health of the captured birds.

from the other hill stations had to remain in Calcutta until Canning could arrange for another vessel to ship them to London. Writing to Prince Albert, Canning regretted the lack of flexibility in Mitchell's plan: 'He [Thompson] seemed to be an intelligent man & earnest in his task, but he has been hampered by the arrangements made at home.'[69]

The miscalculation of the timescale was compounded by Mitchell's underestimation of the practical difficulty of acclimatisation. He was trying to complete a series of tasks, from capture to shipment, within a few months, but in practice much more time should have been taken to prepare the birds for their long voyage, during which they had to cross the equator twice. Then, when the ship entered cooler waters, nearly all of the birds suffered from inflammation and constipation because of 'cold draught'. Thompson's efforts to save the sick birds were in vain: 'I have no doubt', he wrote to Mitchell, 'when all is properly explained, it will be seen how little chance there was of succeeding or in fact that success under the circumstances was, simply, impossible.'[70] Mitchell could have considered Canning's suggestion of a longer timetable so that each stage of the project could be better managed, but he stuck to the original scheme, and now had to explain the outcome.

With a massive death toll and a handful of pitiful survivors, it was obvious to every collaborator and sponsor that the project had failed, but Mitchell was not discouraged by adversity and turned every circumstance to good account. In fact, the project introduced to the Regent's Park Zoo at least some pheasant species, and raised expectations for the next enterprise. It also created closer relationships with the officers and officials of the East India Company and with Mullick at Calcutta. To commemorate their patronage, the Zoological Society awarded silver medals to Canning, Hodgson, Mullick and the authorities of the six hill stations (but not to Blyth).[71] Canning and Prince Albert were in no way discouraged. While Canning decided on a new project, to propagate Himalayan birds at the hill stations, Albert recommended another subscription scheme to Mitchell.[72] At the general meeting of the Zoological Society in May 1857, Mitchell reported the results of the project and presented his next plan, which was warmly approved, two of those in attendance approaching him to promise their subscription.[73] But for the Indian Mutiny it might have been carried out.

It is hard to evaluate the long-term results of the acclimatisation project. Initially Mitchell had envisaged that the society would mobilise animal resources on an unprecedentedly large scale. When he was expecting the

[69] Talbot to Mitchell, 23 Mar. 1857, ZSL, Talbot papers; Canning to Phipps, 20 Mar. 1857, Phipps papers.

[70] Thompson to Mitchell, 13 July 1857, ibid. Thompson papers.

[71] ZSL, MC, xiii, fo. 152.

[72] ZSL, MC, xiii, fos 336–7.

[73] Mitchell to Phipps, 4 May 1857, ibid. Phipps papers.

Table 6
Results of the acclimatisation experiments, 1858–60

Year	Species	Number of hens	Eggs laid	Hatched	Reared	Success (%)
1858	Black-backed Kalij	5		63	61	
	White-crested Kalij	1		6	5	
	Purple Kalij	1	184	19	17	N/A
	Cheer pheasant	2		26	25	
	Impeyan pheasant	2		12	8	
	Total	11	184	126	116	63.0
1859	Black-backed Kalij	3	59	18	16	27.1
	White-crested Kalij	2	33	12	9	27.3
	Purple Kalij	1	22	8	7	31.8
	Cheer pheasant	2	44	19	15	34.1
	Impeyan pheasant	2	10	5	3	30.0
	Total	10	168	62	50	29.8
1860	Black-backed Kalij	3	47	27	14	29.8
	White-crested Kalij	2	24	20	12	50.0
	Purple Kalij	1	17	11	8	47.1
	Cheer pheasant	1	20	13	7	35.0
	Impeyan pheasant	3	33	11	4	12.1
	Total	10	141	82	45	31.9

Source: Scherren, *Zoological Society*, 118.

arrival of the birds from Calcutta, he wrote to an unknown recipient in Paris: 'I am confident that the acclimatation of exotic animals in Europe may be carried out to a much greater extent than has yet been supposed possible.'[74] He believed that he would be able to establish a science of acclimatisation, but his hopes were not realised. Yet the acclimatisation project marked a watershed. In April 1858 four pheasant species were successfully introduced to the London Zoo and over a hundred specimens were reared.[75] As for the monal, the Zoological Society borrowed two pairs from its members and eight specimens were bred in the zoo.[76] Table 6 shows the results for the three years 1858–60. In the long haul, the acclimatisation project established the basis for a steady supply of home-bred Himalayan game birds. The monal pheasant can be found in the list of the zoo animals published respectively in 1862 and 1865, although the zoo seemed to require regular breeding stock

[74] Mitchell to unknown recipient, 29 Apr. 1857, ibid. Mitchell papers.

[75] D. W. Mitchell, 'On the Indian pheasants bred in the menagerie', *Proceedings of the Zoological Society of London* xxvi (1858), 544–5.

[76] ZSL, MC, xiii, fo. 238.

for use in producing the next generations.[77] Ten years after their initial introduction to the London Zoo, the Zoological Society could take pride in its sustained efforts, as the 1870 edition of the official guide remarked:[78]

> The Game-Birds of the Himalayas and other parts of Eastern Asia include so many fine species which are capable of living in Europe, that their introduction to this country has, from the first, been a cherished object of the Zoological Society.... Some have succeeded well, and bred regularly in the Society's Gardens. Others have done well for the first year or so after their acquisition, but have subsequently fallen off, and will require fresh introduction.

By the time that this guide was published, Mitchell had already left the Zoological Society. In May 1859 he decided to take up a new appointment as director of the *Jardin zoologique d'acclimatation* and shortly afterwards he died in Paris. Acclimatisation had lost its most enthusiastic proponent.[79]

In 1860 the Acclimatisation Society of the United Kingdom was founded, but its short-lived activities demonstrate that its aims were not those of Mitchell; it reverted to ornamental and practical zoology. Unlike the *Société zoologique d'acclimatation*, this London-based society did not posses its own facilities but consigned acclimatisation experiments to the London Zoo and to the private menageries of its members. The main function of the society was to offer a forum for discussion, where aristocratic breeders and zoologists gathered to exchange breeding specimens and practical information. The public image of the society was a sumptuous dinner club, where the members dined not only on exotic partridges, pheasants and geese but also on roast eland, kangaroo hams, trepang (sea-slug, a luxury in Chinese and Japanese cuisine) and seaweed jelly.[80] Although they had the excuse of seeking to find sources of cheaper meat to distribute among the working classes, it is unlikely that the public took this seriously. The acclimatisation movement found many more enthusiastic supporters in Australia, New Zealand and North America and introduced many European species there where they transformed the natural landscape.[81]

In 1863 Alfred Wallace, who had just returned from the Malay archipelago where he had been investigating species distribution as part of his

---

[77] P. L. Sclater, A *list of vertebrated animals living in the Gardens of the Zoological Society of London*, London 1862, 68, and A *list of vertebrated animals living in the Gardens of the Zoological Society of London*, London 1865, 98.

[78] Idem, *Guide to the gardens of the Zoological Society of London*, London 1870, 19–20; also cited in N. T. Rothfels, 'Bring 'em back alive: Carl Hagenbeck and the exotic animal and people trades in Germany, 1848–1914', unpubl. PhD diss. Harvard 1994, 10.

[79] Osborne, *Nature, the exotic and the science of French colonisation*, 105. Mitchell died suddenly shortly afterwards: see chapter 4 n. 85 above.

[80] Lever, *They dined on eland*, 44–7.

[81] T. R. Dunlap, 'Remaking the land: the acclimatization movement and Anglo ideas of nature', *Journal of World History* viii (1997), 303–19.

own theory of evolution, formed an acclimatisation committee at the British Association for the Advancement of Science. The committee was joined by Philip Lutley Sclater, who specialised in the geographical distribution of birds and had succeeded David Mitchell as secretary of the Zoological Society.[82] The involvement of these zoogeographers could have promoted acclimatisation as an object of scientific investigation, but John Edward Gray, who was another member of the committee, castigated the optimism of acclimatisers at the annual meeting of the BAAS in 1864: 'Some of the schemes of the would-be acclimatisers are incapable of being carried out, and would never have been suggested if their promoters had been better acquainted with the habits and manners of the animals on which the experiments are proposed to be made.'[83] This criticism could not be taken at face value. The subtext was a warning against the pro-breeding interests of the Zoological Society, which he considered led to a neglect of museum-based study.

The philanthropist Charles Buxton MP was among those gentlemen breeders who were not persuaded by Gray's address. When another meeting of the British Association for the Advancement of Science took place at Norwich in 1868, Buxton invited its members to Northrepps Hall in Norfolk, one of his family's properties, and entertained them generously. The main reason for his invitation was to demonstrate to his guests over twenty tropical birds, which had been originally obtained from Africa, South America, the Philippines and India and had been acclimatised to the English climate. The guests were amazed to see these tropical birds flying freely in the garden, and then listened to Buxton's paper, which explained that he had experienced some initial failures during a severe winter, but finally succeeded in acclimatising the tropical birds currently living in the woods around his house throughout all the four seasons, some of them even being capable of surviving when the temperature fell to six degrees centigrade below zero.[84] The way in which Buxton told the story, moving from failure to success, plus the rural conviviality of the occasion, suggested that acclimatisation was still practised as a private activity by gentleman breeders who would refuse to be controlled by bureaucratic organisations.

Acclimatisation was without any strong theoretical basis or powerful advocate. Alfred Wallace's article on acclimatisation in the ninth edition of the *Encyclopedia Britannica* is most revealing. Although he explored the phenomenon as 'the process of adaptation by which animals and plants are gradually rendered capable of surviving and flourishing in countries remote

---

[82] J. E. Gray, 'Some notes on acclimatised animals', *Annals and Magazine of Natural History* 3rd ser. xii (1863), 76. For Sclater's contributions to the development of biogeography see P. Vincent, *The biogeography of the British Isles: an introduction*, London 1990, 4.

[83] *Report of 34th Meeting of the British Association for the Advancement of Science: notes and abstracts*, London 1864, 80; Lever, *They dined on eland*, 98.

[84] [C. Buxton], 'Acclimatisation of parrots at Northrepps Hall, Norfolk', *Annals and Magazine of Natural History* 4th ser. ii (1868), 381–6.

from their original habitats, or under meteorological conditions different from whose which they have usually to endure, and which are at first injurious to them', he had to concede that 'the subject of acclimatisation is very little understood, and some writers have denied that it can ever take place'.[85] The publication in the same year of Rose Hubbard's manual on the acclimatisation of waterfowl, which followed Sclater's advice on species identification and claimed to be the first practical handbook to the subject also testified to the ambivalent status of acclimatisation. Hubbard was confident that gentlemen breeders possessed 'sufficient capital and sufficient knowledge', but she regarded them as 'amateurs' and recommended acclimatisation as 'a delightful and instructive recreation and a remunerative business'.[86] Because of its 'amateurism' and independence of institutional control, acclimatisation continued to attract an extensive circle of gentlemanly breeders gathered around the Zoological Society and still maintaining associations with specialist zoologists. However, throughout the late nineteenth century acclimatisation refused easy categorisation into one or other of the separate scientific disciplines.

Acclimatisation had sprung from the 'ornamental and practical zoology', which the Zoological Society had conducted at both the Kingston Farm and the London Zoo. The earl of Derby, who took most advantage of the zoo's resources, was its enthusiastic patron during the 1830s and the 1840s. In 1856–7 acclimatisation was given a new momentum by David Mitchell, who sought to establish it as a science of manipulating species distribution by empowering the Zoological Society to take advantage of the infrastructure and manpower of the British Empire. Mitchell believed that the society would pioneer this new field of science in collaboration with royal and aristocratic patrons as well as with animal collectors and zoologists in the colonial field. The illusion of 'zoological empire' was so attractive that a wide range of collaborators had their own reasons for participating and formed an intensive network of communications through which their desires and anxieties were exchanged and identified. Nevertheless, the failure of the collecting campaign made it impossible to reformulate acclimatisation as the basis of zoological empire. Acclimatisation thus remained the spontaneous and leisurely practice of the gentleman breeder. There was little likelihood that it would evolve into a disciplinary science. Accordingly, when institutional developments in biology began to widen the gaps between specialists and the public, the zoo was marginalised but continued to offer a meeting place for acclimatisers and zoologists, especially zoogeographers such as

[85] A. Wallace, 'Acclimatisation', in Encyclopaedia Britannica, 9th edn, Edinburgh 1878, i. 84.
[86] R. Hubbard, Ornamental waterfowl: a practical manual on the acclimatization of the swimming birds, London 1888, 1.

Wallace and Sclater. The zoo and science remained neither too close nor too distant from each other: the zoo revealed moments of science to those who were intent upon them.

Reverting to the concept of 'imperial zoo', an analysis of experiments with acclimatisation suggests that empire-building and scientific enterprise were not always mutually supportive. Recent literature on Christian missionary activity in colonial Asia has refuted the thesis that the expansion of British territory and the growth of the missionary project were complementary and reciprocal processes. Instead, it has argued that relations between State and Church in the colonial field were fluid and occasionally undermined each other.[87] This was also the case for science and empire. As the East India Company and the Zoological Society operated in very different ways, their collaboration hardly went beyond the spontaneous activities of individual agents. These individuals were so differently qualified and motivated that they failed to act collectively as liaison between colonial governance and scientific enterprise. The presidency of Prince Albert together with the secretaryship of David Mitchell at the Zoological Society was an exceptional instance when two institutions could co-operate systematically in pursuit of the same goal. It was none the less a coincidence of timing and did not develop to create a symbiotic relationship between science and empire.

An analysis of the acclimatisaiton project therefore raises further questions. The referential frame of empire is helpful for understanding scientific enterprise operating in the colonial field, but its use ignores essential questions concerning the history and present *raison d'être* of zoos. Should a human desire to collect exotic animals always be called 'imperial' or 'imperialistic'? What was the opposite concept to 'imperial zoo', and was any zoo so categorised? Are all zoos essentially 'imperial' in that they stem from a human desire to manipulate the animal world (though this sounds tautological)? But, if so, how are the activities of modern zoos to promote species conservation to be labelled? Although these questions cannot be answered through one case study, of the London Zoo, this book has demonstrated that 'empire' is not the only contextual element for the zoo, but just one factor with which it engaged. Otherwise, the London Zoo would have perished with the British Empire.

---

[87] A. Porter, *Religion versus empire? British Protestant missionaries and overseas expansion, 1700–1914*, Manchester 2004; B. Stanley, *The Bible and the flag: Protestant missions and British imperialism in the nineteenth and twentieth centuries*, Leicester 1990. For the argument against this revisionist stance see I. Copland, 'Christianity as an arm of empire: the ambiguous case of India under the Company, *c.* 1813–1858', *HJ* xlix (2006), 1025–54.

Conclusion: The Darwinian Moment

Charles Darwin loved to visit the London Zoo.[1] He wrote to his sister Caroline in April 1831 that 'what I liked most in all London is the Zoolog[ical] Gardens: on a hot day when the beasts look happy and the people gay it is most delightful'.[2] In March 1838, after returning from his voyage on the *Beagle*, Darwin visited the zoo again. He was fortunate enough to see the rhinoceros emerging from her house and galloping in the enclosure 'surprisingly quickly, like a huge cow'. The elephant in the next yard responded to his neighbour and began 'trotting himself' and 'squealing & braying like a half dozen broken trumpets'. The most exciting attraction of the year was, however, Jenny, the first orangutan exhibited to the public at the London Zoo. Darwin observed her intelligence and emotional expression and compared her to a human child:[3]

> I saw also the Ourang-outang in great perfection: the keeper showed her an apple, but did not give it her, whereupon she threw herself on her back, kicked & cried, precisely like a naughty child. – She then looked very sulky & after two or three fits of passion, the keeper said, 'Jenny if you will stop bawling & be a good girl, I will give you the apple' – She certainly understood every word of this, & though like a child, she had great work to stop whining, she at last succeeded, & then got the apple, with which she jumped into an armchair & began eating it, with the most contented countenance imaginable.

The London Zoo was part of Darwin's mental world, not only as a site for him to visit, but also in providing a scholarly community in the form of the Zoological Society. Although he abhorred the indecorous style of discussion in the society and distanced himself from its internal bickering, Darwin remained a member and donated his collection of eighty mammals and 450 birds to the society in January 1837.[4] Moreover, the London Zoo assisted Darwin with various breeding experiments and provided him with valuable information, which he analysed in his *On the origin of species* (1859) and *The variation of animals and plants under domestication* (1868).[5] In 1860 Darwin

---

[1] Darwin's visits to the London Zoo are also discussed in Åkerberg, *Knowledge and pleasures*, 170, and A. Desmond and J. Moore, *Darwin: the life of a tormented evolutionist*, New York 1991, 65, 93, 199, 202.

[2] Charles Darwin to Caroline Darwin, 28 Apr. 1831, CCD i. 121–2.

[3] C. Darwin to Susan Darwin, 1 Apr. 1838, CCD ii. 80–1.

[4] Desmond and Moore, *Darwin*, 208–9, 231, 235, 240.

[5] C. Darwin, *On the origin of the species by means of natural selection: or, the preservation*

sent a copy of *On the origin of the species* to the superintendent of the zoo and asked him to examine a hybrid between a donkey and a wild ass – a subject that had aroused much interest at the Kingston Farm a few decades earlier. Darwin expected him to confirm that stripes appearing on the shoulders and legs of the foal would indicate a reversion to a primitive character.[6]

For Darwin, therefore, the zoo was not merely a place to spend one's leisure time. It also helped him to develop his evolutionary theories and led him further to pioneer the study of animal intelligence and emotions. By locating Darwin at the zoo, the three themes of the book – cultural politics, public science and animal history – may be revisited.

Cultural politics

As Darwin and his contemporaries saw, the London Zoo attracted people from different intellectual and social backgrounds. Various factors contributed to its appeal. The momentum arose initially when those interested in taxonomy and breeding came together to establish the Zoological Society of London in 1826. These two interests were essentially at odds, but they shared a goal: they wished to establish a large open-air menagerie in the urban space. The siting of the proposed zoo was of great importance: the society's plans came to fruition only after prolonged negotiations with government officials, neighbours and the public, all of whom had different plans for the proposed site. Although these negotiations were difficult and often held back development, they confirmed the Zoological Society's determination to consolidate its institutional identity as well as to justify the zoo's public role. Consequently, at the dawn of the Victorian era, the Regent's Park Zoo was one of the largest cultural institutions in Britain, rivalling the British Museum and the National Gallery. In the course of the nineteenth century, aristocratic patrons featured less at the zoo, which they had used as a place for social gathering, and 'respectable' middle-class families gradually came to constitute its main clientele, although people from the lower social ranges were not completely excluded. Irregular access was common: admission tickets, including forgeries, were distributed. 'Illegitimate' visitors presumably had their own means of entry and shared their methods by word-of-mouth. Over time the society lost control of the admission system in the face of increasing demand for public access: in 1847 it was opened to the general public.

Why was the zoo so popular? This book has considered the attraction of a reputedly ideal form of animal exhibition. As Gore's metaphor of 'the

---

of favoured races in the struggle for life, London 1859, and *The variation of animals and plants under domestication*, London 1868. For Darwin's interest in breeding see J. A. Secord, 'Nature's fancy: Charles Darwin and the breeding of pigeons', *Isis* lxxii (1981), 163–86.

6 C. Darwin to A. D. Bartlett, 24 Aug. 1860, *CCD*, xiii. 431–2.

Eden of Northern Marylebone' suggests, the location of the zoo, with its relevance to the changing metropolitan topography, was a key element. The zoo employed the surrounding landscape of Regent's Park to present a new environment in which animals were seen, smelled, touched and fed by spectators. Although London had hosted various types of animal display from the Tower Menageries to the Bartholomew Fair, the London Zoo was unique: it intended to demonstrate that the zoo's animals, although in captivity, lived a healthy, happy life. It was an enchanting reality, Darwin's favourite place in London. Darwin was only one of many who were enthusiastic about its opening. Such enthusiasm, part of the celebration of a range of the metropolitan improvements, was visualised in George Scharf's *Six views of the Zoological Gardens* (1835). Scharf's lithographs presented a view of the animals enjoying their spacious enclosures, sufficient food and fresh air – the view that was disseminated by periodical articles and popular guides. This euphoric vision disguised the true realities of animal life in the zoo: the names of sick and dead animals were registered almost every day in the zoo's journal. Frail monkeys were left to die in the winter cold and healthy replacements bought in the spring. But this 'mortal economy' was rarely known to the public. Uncertainties about keeping animals in captivity were sometimes expressed, but they were not necessarily brought into the remit of the early animal welfare movements, which aimed initially at the prohibition of baiting and cruelty to domestic animals and disagreed over antivivisection in the 1870s. The human-animal interactions offered by the zoo remained a socially and morally acceptable form of entertainment. It was a long time before the London Zoo was criticised as 'the Bastille of the beasts' at the beginning of the twentieth century.[7]

The other aspect of zoo that Scharf's lithographs concealed was the heterogeneous nature of its clientele, probably because it was virtually impossible for an artist to compose an agreeable scene that was populated by different social groups. An example of a literary description of the zoo, which unlike a painting could describe changes over time, hinted that different groups visited the zoo at different times:[8]

> [I]t is no small part of the pleasure afforded to a benevolent mind, by a visit to these Gardens [the London Zoo], to see the fashionable and gay for once so well amused; and, as the higher order of triflers drop off at the close of their morning, to notice those of the lower grades, the artisan and the mechanic, with their families, drinking at once health, pleasure, and useful knowledge in a ramble through these Gardens, after the toil of the day.

This comment suggests an ideal vision of how the zoo's space might be

7 R. W. Burkhardt, Jr. 'Constructing the zoo: science, society, and animal nature at the Paris menagerie, 1794–1838', in Henninger-Voss, *Animals in human histories*, 249.

8 J. Ryley, 'Zoological Society's gardens', *Eclectic Review* (Aug. 1831), 179.

shared. Spatial segregation was at its most evident on Sundays, when only subscribers and their companions were allowed into the zoo. As a passage from one of Catharine Gore's novels suggests, Sunday visits to the zoo might seem to be their exclusive privilege, but the many complaints from weekday visitors, especially at what they discerned as the hypocrisy of the privileged, testified that the success was only partial. This book has shown that the question of accessibility was not merely about the inclusion or exclusion of particular social categories, but was also a matter of cultural transmission: how culture should be controlled in the new public domain, how it should be conveyed to the public and, above all, how this public could be represented.

Evidence of the social mix of the zoo's audience counters the view that modern zoos were predominantly a site of social expression for the urban middle classes – a view derived from such as Scharf's *Six views of the Zoological Gardens*. The idealisation of a harmonious audience was part of social reality. The zoo was in fact a contested space that was not monopolised by any single social class; its clientele needed careful handling so as to create a balance of social integration and segregation. The zoo's audience demonstrated both imagined unity and actual heterogeneity, and the increasing gaps between the two led to discussions on admission policy in newspapers and parliamentary committees, and also linked it to the reform of art galleries and scientific institutions. Cultural politics had already emerged onto the national agenda long before the state implemented enormous projects such as the Great Exhibition and the South Kensington Museum. In the light of this long-term change in cultural politics, the zoo refuted the theory of virtual representation and demonstrated that the public was a legitimate recipient of culture.

Public science

Darwin's contribution to making the zoo a site of cultural transmission can be illustrated by a putative exchange between Thomas Huxley and Samuel Wilberforce, the bishop of Oxford. In *On the origin of species*, Darwin certainly did not state specifically that monkeys were possibly the ancestors of man, but the reading public was quick to explore this implication. In May 1861 *Punch* published an illustration of a gorilla inquiring 'Am I a Man and a Brother?'[9] As the question suggests, it is no surprise that the London Zoo encouraged popular adaptations of Darwin's theory of evolution, which acknowledged a kinship between humans and monkeys.[10] Many visitors to the zoo were familiar, in general terms, with evolutionary ideas, but, as a

---

9   J. Browne, 'Darwin in caricature: a study in the popularisation and dissemination of evolution', *Proceedings of American Philosophical Society* cxlv (2001), 500.
10   Secord, *Victorian sensation*, 443–4.

High Churchman, Wilberforce was alarmed and prepared to speak against Darwin at a meeting of the British Association for the Advancement of Science in 1860. It is said that Huxley was asked offensively by Wilberforce whether his ancestors were related to apes. Huxley angrily replied that he would not be ashamed to have a monkey for his ancestor, but that he would be ashamed to be related to a man who ridiculed scientific truth. It has been claimed that this sort of verbal warfare illustrates the intellectual reception of Darwin's theory of evolution. However, research has shown that much was invented after the fact by Darwin's supporters, including that particular reported dialogue. What Wilberforce really said to Huxley was more likely to have been that 'he [Wilberforce] would not look at the monkeys in the Zoological [Gardens] as connected with his ancestors'.[11] Reference to the zoo implies a link between evolutionary theories and changing perceptions of animals, and highlights the zoo's presence on the intellectual landscape of Victorian society.

This book has examined how the zoo mediated between the scientific community and the non-specialist public and has noted the methodological pitfalls involved in asserting a dichotomy model between two entities – science and public – as prior conditions for analysis. The Zoological Society was not a scientific institution in the modern sense of the phrase. Although the society was chartered on the grounds that it aimed to advance the study of zoological science, most of its members were aristocratic patrons, gentlemen breeders and wealthy promenaders. The society none the less continued to be regarded as a scientific institution, chiefly because of its role in managing the zoo for the purpose of providing the public with scientific knowledge. Heavy reliance on the zoo, especially for financial resources, influenced not only the membership but also the content of the science practised within the society. While museum-based study such as taxonomy, malacology and conchology declined, gentlemen menagerists continued to promote experiments in breeding. There was even a time when breeding enthusiasts were taken with the prospect of acclimatisation – an allegedly new science which manipulated animal distribution. In retrospect acclimatisation is generally regarded not as a matter of scientific research, but as a subject of social or philosophical interest. Yet various attempts and experiments in acclimatisation testified to the zoo's claim that it was a science.

The public was also affected by the social and spatial experience of the zoo. An analysis of the private responses of visitors to the zoo suggests that they gave meanings to their experience by sharing it with their friends and families. As noted in a letter from an anonymous elderly lady – whose memoir was published by her niece in the early twentieth century – a visit

---

[11] R. G. Wilberforce, *Life of Bishop Wilberforce*, London 1881, ii. 450–1. See also J. R. Lucas, 'Wilberforce and Huxley: a legendary encounter', *HJ* xxii (1979), 313–30, and I. Hesketh, *Of apes and ancestors: evolution, Christianity, and the Oxford debate*, Toronto 2009.

to the zoo was part of family history. She did not like to go to church on Sundays in her childhood:[12]

> But there was one joy which Sunday brought round, after a breakfast reading of Robinson Crusoe ... and an after dinner visit to the Zoological Gardens and home by the Botanic Society's Pleasance in the Regent's Park where we used to see Mr. Rogers the poet of 'Italy'. My father was one of the original members of both Societies.

Articles in periodicals on the zoo and its animals encouraged such memories to be shared with the anonymous reading public. *Punch* was the best example, showing how literary devices integrated the experience of a visit to the zoo into everyday life and increased its appeal. As it sometimes anthropomorphised animals such as monkeys and exaggerated the physical enjoyment of the zoo experience, the stimulation of the popular imagination was central to the zoo's management policy. David Mitchell recognised this well and mastered ways of indulging the visitors' appetite for zoological amusement. He regularly arranged exhibitions of new animals, catered for the differing needs of different groups and actively invested in advertisement. Compared with other institutions such as museums and galleries, the physical activity involved, together with the degree of freedom allowed to spectators, certainly attracted families with young children.

The provision of 'zoological entertainment', however, enhanced tensions between science and commerce in the management of the zoo. How such tensions led to the categorisation of different scientific practices has been another focal point of this book. The introduction of commercial elements was initially discussed when the Surrey Zoo profited from hosting special shows and events in the early 1830s. The London Zoo followed its example but did not completely transform itself into a scientific amusement park because of the strong opposition of pro-museum members. Under David Mitchell's secretaryship in the 1850s, however, there was more commercial entertainment which came to undermine the society's claim to be a scientific body, which had allowed it to benefit from the Exemption Act of 1843. The Zoological Society eventually fell outside the scope of the legislation, but the zoo's *raison d'être* was officially commended: one judge remarked that the zoo achieved its object of 'bringing people together for rational amusement and recreation'.[13] Litigation on exemption defined the two scientific spheres – the one that was exclusively scientific and the other that was adapted for the public good – and placed the zoo in the domain of popular science. The zoo's association with specialised science none the less remained, as in the acclimatisation project and much later in the emergence of ethology. On

---

12 S. S. Beale (ed.), *Recollections of a spinster aunt*, London 1908, 57–8.
13 See p. 136 above.

the whole, however, the zoo was more comfortable as an arm of popular science.[14]

The key contribution of this book to the understanding of the historical categorisation of specialised and popular science is that it sees the question from the point of view of those who 'consumed' science in their own social and intellectual milieux. The processes of professionalisation and popularisation have usually been examined chiefly through the eyes of men of science, including Darwinians, artisan collectors, missionary naturalists and authorities of *quasi-science* such as phrenology. This book has approached the subject from a structural perspective and has suggested that the state, the public, the judiciary, the scientific institution and local authorities, all played their part in the promotion and categorisation of science. It was not exclusively men of science who tried to define their roles and status: their attempts could produce unexpected reactions. The dynamism of the interactions can be better understood by analogy with the 'mixed economy of welfare'.[15] In nineteenth-century Britain, the state, the market and voluntary societies shared in financing and promoting science.[16] The management of the London Zoo crystallised the essence of a 'mixed economy' of knowledge and exemplified the hybridity of science in the zoo. It was in the 1930s that the Zoological Society was finally registered as a charity, and this was in a very different climate.[17] The institutional transformation of the London Zoo can be contrasted with the different trajectories of the Paris *Muséum national d'histoire naturelle* (state-funded), the Schönbrunn in Vienna (originally monarchical) and the Tierpark Hagenbeck (private, commercial). Comparing them can help to develop the genealogy and typology of modern zoos.

Animal history

The hybridity of science in the London Zoo partly explains how Charles Darwin has come to be regarded as the scientist who acknowledged kinship between humans and animals. Animal rights literature emphasises Darwin's view that their difference was 'a matter of degree and not of kind' – the claim upon which the theory of animal rights is principally grounded.[18] The

[14] G. Mitman, 'When nature is the zoo: vision and power in the art of science of natural history', *Osiris* 2nd ser. xi (1996), 117–43.

[15] M. Daunton, 'Introduction', to Daunton, *The organisation of knowledge*, 18.

[16] The balance of responsibility is a subject that divides historians: Mandler, 'Art in a cool climate', 101–20; H. Hoock, 'The British state and the Anglo-French wars over antiquities, 1798–1858', *H J* 1 (2007), 1–40.

[17] Zuckerman, 'Zoological Society of London', 10–11.

[18] G. L. Francione and R. Garner, *The animal rights debate: abolition or regulation?* New York 2010, 14.

effect of Darwin's theory of evolution on the Victorians' view of human-animal relationships needs to be investigated thoroughly; in such an enquiry the London Zoo would play a significant part.[19] A notable example of the connection between the zoo and evolutionary theory was Darwin's comparative study of the mental development of his first son, William, and orangutans in the zoo. His experiments included placing a mirror in a cage of orangutans and observing changes in their expressions as signs of intelligence and emotions.[20] The biographer of William Darwin speculated that this study influenced the polemical passage in On the origins of species: 'Light will be thrown on the origin of man and his history.'[21] Wilberforce's refusal to perceive traces of human evolution in the appearance of monkeys and Punch's anthropomorphisation of the gorilla demonstrate that the imagined display of evolution at the zoo provoked mixed reactions that defy simple generalisation.

The London Zoo had a unique capacity both to evoke and receive different and sometimes competing ideas. The richness of the zoo's intellectual resources can be contrasted with the poverty of the concept of 'imperial zoo', which interprets the zoo as a manifestation of the synthesis of science and empire, often mediated by Christian ideology. This concept hinders rather than helps to explain the cultural implications of the zoo. A historical perspective must instead reach beyond the referential frame of empire. To this end the 1836 giraffe exhibition has been analysed to offer an objective view of the contingent and transitory nature of the animal-collecting networks. The Zoological Society used the infrastructure of the British Empire, but recognised the limits of its geographical reach. Mehmed Ali took power in Egypt by taking advantage of the balance of international competition and compromise of the British, French and Ottoman empires. Thibault the French merchant, who mediated between the Zoological Society and Ali's Egypt, further added to the complexity of the animal-collecting networks. Examination of these networks suggests that they can be better understood as a sequence of fluctuating and amorphous forms of communication that stretched beyond the reach of the British Empire.

An analysis of the acclimatisation project comes to the same conclusion. The project offered an ideal opportunity for colonial governance and zoological enterprise to work together to create an empire/science symbiosis. Its foundering thus counters the view that empire building and scientific enterprise were essentially integrated. In the long run, the animal-collecting networks served, pragmatically rather than ideologically, the interests of

[19] R. Preece, 'Darwinism, Christianity and the great vivisection debate', Journal of the History of Ideas lxiv (2003), 399–419.

[20] C. Darwin, The expression of the emotions in man and animals, London 1872, 141–2; P. H. Barrett and others (eds), Charles Darwin's notebooks, Cambridge 1987, 264, 551.

[21] R. Keynes, 'Darwin, William Erasmus', ODNB [http://www.oxforddnb.com/view/article/94741, accessed 18 June 2012].

Figure 25. A souvenir of a family visit to the zoo. Wellcome Library, London, no. 42424i.

Rajendro Mullick, who continued to be an important supplier of Asian animals to European and Australian institutions. In 1863 he was elected a corresponding member of the Zoological Society of London and honorary member of the Acclimatisation Society of Victoria. Later he contributed to the foundation of the Alipur Zoological Gardens (opened in 1876), by donating many animals from his own collection.[22] The establishment of this Calcutta Zoo involved many other Indians and enabled them to develop the systematic study of Indian zoology.[23]

The notion of imperial zoo also fails to give a comprehensive account of the zoo as a site of human-animal interactions. As the giraffe exhibition suggested, the physical space of animal display in the zoo, and the mental space of animal display that occupied the spectators' imagination, worked to expand the range of possible interpretations. Religious, aesthetic, emotional and scientific motifs could be found at the zoo. But none dominated because each spectator had his own blend. The diversity of popular perceptions thus counters assumptions that spectators were systematically encouraged to perceive exotic animals in the context of empire. In fact, the style of exhibition, which associated animals primarily with their habitats was invented quite unintentionally, the result of Hagenbeck's 'panorama', and was pursued scientifically with the rise of ethology and the wildlife park in the early twentieth century.[24]

By contrast, the nineteenth-century mode of display was more domestic. This is highlighted by an illustration of the zoo and its animals, which was produced, presumably as a souvenir for children, in the late nineteenth century (see Figure 25). While animals appear in the foreground with their names written down to add to the educational value of the picture, the bear pit is also illustrated with a father trying to feed the animal, his son and wife looking on. Unlike topographical prints, this picture created an imaginary space by putting together different scenes and animals in the zoo. Judging by the way in which it was done, it can be interpreted as highlighting not only the zoo's role in family life, but also the domesticity of the site in which human-animal interactions took place.

Overall, it cannot be denied that some aspects of the British Empire contributed to the development of the London Zoo. But this does not mean that the imperial moments were metaphrased into the domain of animal display and determinately affected popular perceptions of animals. A much more flexible frame of explanation emerges from the sources: different interpretations coexisted. In this sense the London Zoo can be compared to Charles Darwin. There are so many different aspects to Darwin as a subject of

---

[22] Chatterjee, *Rajah Rajendro Mullick Bahadur*, 32–3.

[23] D. K. Mittra, 'Ram Bramha Sanyal and the establishment of the Calcutta Zoological Gardens', in Hoage and Deiss, *New worlds, new animals*, 86–93.

[24] Rothfels, *Savages and beasts*, 161–88.

scholarly research, from his evolutionary theories to the history of emotions, that he cannot be placed within a single frame of analysis. Any historical study must present multiple interpretations of his life and ideas.[25] This is also the case with the London Zoo. As the meeting point for various ideas and practices about cultural politics, public science and human-animal interactions, the zoo engaged with the important motifs in nineteenth-century society. It had the versatility to survive despite changing social conditions. Its dynamism has moved its history forwards beyond the age of empire to the present day.

[25] J. Smith, 'Darwin and the evolution of Victorian studies', VS li (2009), 215–21; P. White, 'Darwin's emotions: the scientific self and the sentiment of objectivity', Isis c (2009), 811–26; M. Ruse, 'The Darwin industry: a guide', VS xxxix (1996), 217–35.

Receipts and Expenditure of the Zoological Society in Relation to Attendance at the London Zoo

Financial details of the Zoological Society of London are contained in the *Reports of the council and auditors*, published annually from 1829. The fiscal year began on 1 January, and the *Report* for the previous year was printed by the council in the following late April or early May, to be presented at the annual meeting of the society. The *Report* also showed attendance figures at the London Zoo over the previous year. The original source for attendance figures was the daily record kept at the zoo gate. Monthly attendance is calculated from this record. The exact annual attendance figures from 1828 to 1900 are also summarised in Scherren, *The Zoological Society*, and Åkerberg, *Knowledge and pleasures*.

It should be noted, however, that attendance figures do not indicate how many individuals visited the zoo, because some were likely to attend more than once a year. There might also be a considerable number of 'illegitimate' visitors whose entries were not registered in the daily record, especially during the period between 1828 and 1847/8, when the society maintained its exclusive admissions policy. Nevertheless, the statistics can be read, with some reservation, as a barometer of the zoo's popularity. In comparison with the British Museum and the National Gallery, the London Zoo was the most popular institution during the first few years after its opening, but gradually declined in the late 1830s and the 1840s. Clearly, the trend in attendance affected the financial situation of the Zoological Society. In 1836 substantial spending on the giraffe exhibition created a deficit, and for the next ten years the society's budget continued to shrink. It was only after the opening of the zoo to the general public in 1847–8 that the financial condition of the society began to improve. In the 1850s, with income from gate receipts at more than 60 per cent of total revenue, admission fees became the society's largest source of income.

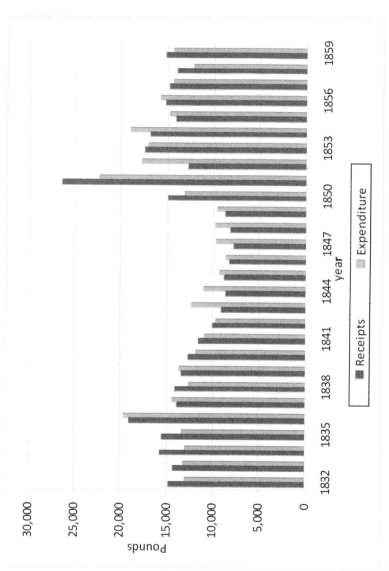

Figure 26. Receipts and expenditure of the Zoological Society of London, 1832–59

Source: Reports of the council and auditors (1829–)

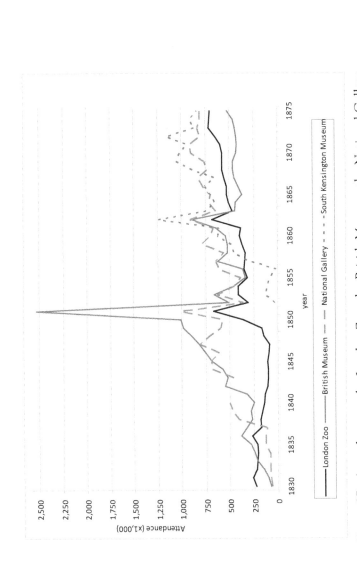

Figure 27. Attendance at the London Zoo, the British Museum, the National Gallery and the South Kensington Museum, 1830–75

Note: Annual attendance figures at the British Museum, the National Gallery and the South Kensington Museum (later Victoria & Albert Museum) were reported to parliament and were printed in PP (e.g. *Account of the income and expenditure of the British Museum* and *Annual report of the Director of the National Gallery*). The records for the National Gallery from 1841 to 1842 could not be found. The annual attendance at the London Zoo was summarised in the *Reports of the council and auditors* (1829–)

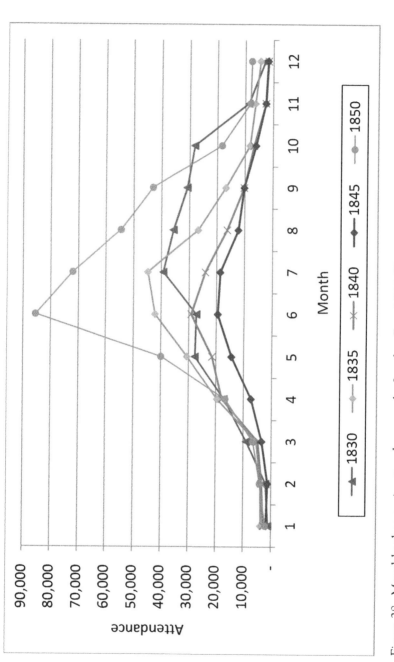

Figure 28. Monthly changes in attendance at the London Zoo, 1830–50

Source: ZSL, QAA, OG

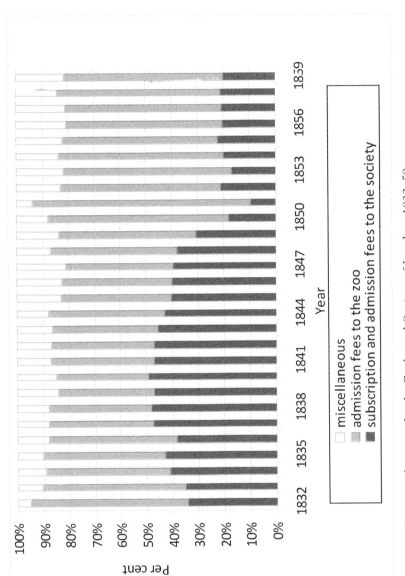

Figure 29. Sources of income for the Zoological Society of London, 1832–59

Source: Reports of the council and auditors (1829–)

Bibliography

Unpublished primary sources

Aylesbury, Buckinghamshire Record Office
D/FR   Fremantle papers

Durham, University of Durham Archive
GRE/B76/6   Earl Grey papers: letters from George Eden, 1st earl of Auckland

Hereford, Herefordshire Record Office
G2/IV/J   Biddulph collection: diaries of John Biddulph of Ledbury

Kew, The National Archives
CRES 25   Minutes, Office of Woods, Forests and Land Revenues
HO 44   Home Office papers
MPE 1/900, 1/906/1–5   Plans for the proposed Zoological Gardens
RAIL 989/33   Robert Durham papers
WORK 16/399, 16/722–30   Zoological Gardens papers, 1826–1912
WORK 32/64–5   Plans for the proposed Zoological Gardens

London, British Library
MS Add. 29717   John Edward Gray papers
MS Add. 37185   Charles Babbage papers
MS Add. 37949   Francis Place papers
MS Add. 39554   Southgate papers
MS Add. 47294A, 47296, 47309   Prince Christoph Heinrich von Lieven papers
MS Add. 50849   Miscellaneous letters
MS Egerton 2348   George Robert Gray papers

London, London Metropolitan Archives
ACC/2042/002/1   Journal of Sophy Shirley Codd, 1835–6
MR/S/LR   Middlesex Sessions Records, Literary and Scientific Societies and
            Libraries: exemption from rates, 1843–85
Main Print Collection

London, National Portrait Gallery Archive
NPG7/3/7/2 Sir George Johann Scharf: journals, correspondence and
            personalia

London, Natural History Museum
OC25   Richard Owen collection: notebooks
OC62   Richard Owen collection: correspondence

London, Royal Institution
F1   Michael Faraday papers: correspondence
HD26/D   Humphry Davy papers: miscellaneous correspondence
Pep/B   William Hazledine Pepys papers: correspondence

London, Wellcome Library
Iconographic collections

London, Westminster City Archives,
TI/84a   St Marylebone parish, vestry minutes, 2nd ser. lxxiv, 2 Mar.–7 Oct.
            1854

London, Zoological Society of London Archives
GB 0814 BABA   Returns, memoranda, 1828–1903
        BAD   Nineteenth-century letters to the secretary (alphabetically
                ordered)
        BADA   Allan, Deffell & Co. papers
        BADB   W. Batty papers
                Edward Blyth papers
        BADC   Charles John Canning, 1st Earl Canning, papers
                Hugh Cuming papers
        BADG   John Gould papers
                John Edward Gray papers
                Edward Greenaway papers
                John Gritton papers
        BADH   I. P. Hearsey papers
                Brian H. Hodgson papers
        BADJ   H. C. James papers
        BADM   D. W. Mitchell papers
        BADO   Office of Woods and Forests
                Richard Owen papers
        BADP   Charles Phipps papers
        BADR   Rajendra Mullick papers
        BADT   Gerald Chetwynd Talbot papers
                James Thompson papers
        EAA   Minutes of meetings (MM)
        FAA   Minutes of council (MC)
        GAAW   Reports of the Receipts and Expenditure Committee
        GACP   Newspaper cuttings
        GAGB   Staff salaries
        QAA   Occurrences at the garden (OG)
        UAA   Visitor book

Matlock, Derbyshire Record Office
D239/M   FitzHerbert papers

Oxford, Bodleian Library
John Johnson Collection
  Animals on Show
  London Play Places

Published primary sources

Barrett, P. H. and others (eds), *Charles Darwin's notebooks*, Cambridge 1987

Beale, S. S. (ed.), *Recollections of a spinster aunt*, London 1908

Blackie, A. W. (ed.), *Letter and journals of Anne Chalmers*, London 1923

Burkhardt, F. and others (eds), *Correspondence of Charles Darwin*, Cambridge 1985–2012

Curwen, E. C. (ed.), *The journal of Gideon Mantell: surgeon and geologist covering the years 1818–52*, London 1940

Hansen, L. (ed.), *Impressions of London from the late summer of 1840: the thoughts and experiences of a Swedish gentleman*, London 2001

James, F. A. J. L. (ed.), *The correspondence of Michael Faraday*, London 1996

Metcalf, E. M. (ed.), *Journal of a visit to London and the continent by Herman Melville, 1849–50*, Cambridge, MA 1948

Pollen, J. H. (ed.), *A journal kept by Richard Doyle in the year 1840*, London 1885

Sauer, G. C. (ed.), *John Gould, the bird man: correspondence*, London 1998–2001

Spevack, M. (ed.), *A Victorian chronicle: the diary of Henrietta Halliwell-Phillips*, Hildesheim 1999

Wise, D. (ed.), *Diary of William Tayler, footman, 1837*, London 1962

Official publications (in chronological order)

Report from the select committee on the British Museum, PP vii (1835)

Annual report of the Poor Law Commissioners, i–xiv (1835–48)

Report from the select committee on the British Museum, PP x (1836)

Minutes of the Trustees of the British Museum, PP xxxix (1837)

Poor Law Board, *Official circulars of public documents and information*, i–x (1840–53)

Report from the select committee on National Monuments and Works of Arts, PP vi (1841 sess. 1)

'An act to exempt from county, borough, parochial, and other local rates, land and buildings occupied by scientific and literary societies', in *A collection of the public general statutes passed in the sixth and seventh year of the reign of her majesty Queen Victoria*, London 1843, 318–20

Returns of all applications to the certifying barristers, under the act [6 & 7 Vict. c. 36], for certificates of exemption from parochial rates by literary and scientific institutions stating the name and locality of each society, and whether the certificates were granted or refused, and specifying the grounds of refusal in each, PP xlii (1844); xlv (1849)

Return from the Trustees of the British Museum and the National Gallery, PP xxv (1846)

Hansard's parliamentary debates, 3rd series

Newspapers and periodicals

Annals and Magazine of Natural History
Athenaeum
Le Belle Assemblée
Bell's Weekly Messenger
Bentley's Miscellany
Eclectic Review
Ellis and Blackburn's Report of the Judges of the Court of Queen's Bench
Gentleman's Magazine
Household Words
Illustrated London News
John Bull
Journal of the Society of Arts and of the Institutions of Union
Justice of the Peace, and County, Borough, Poor Law Union, and Parish Law Recorder
Lancet
Legal Examiner
Literary Gazette
Magazine of Natural History
Magazine of Popular Science and Journal of the Useful Arts
Malta Government Gazette
Medical Times
Mirror
Morning Chronicle
New Monthly Magazine
North American Review
Observer
Penny Magazine
Punch
Quarterly Review
Saturday Magazine
Spectator
The Times
Weekly Times

Contemporary books and articles

Allen, T., A guide to the Zoological Gardens and Museum: with a brief account of the rise and progress of the Zoological Society, London 1829

Anon., A companion to the Royal Surrey Zoological Gardens, London 1835

Anon., The omnibus men of London: their occupation, lives and deaths, London 1851

Anon., The picturesque companion to the Regent's Park, Zoological Gardens, Colosseum, and Diorama, London 1832

Anon., A picturesque guide to the Regent's Park with accurate descriptions of the Colosseum, the Diorama, and the Zoological Gardens, London 1829

Anon., A popular description and history of the giraffe, or cameleopard, now exhib-

iting in the Zoological Gardens, Regent's Park: with an account of their Nubian attendants and the adventures of M. Thibaut, who at a great risk and expenses procured them in Africa, London 1836

Anon., *A summer ramble in the Himalayas with sporting adventures in the Vale of Cashmere*, London 1860

Anon., *Walks in London, or extracts from the journal of Mr. Joseph Wilkins*, London [?1840]

Archer, E. C., *Tours in upper India and in parts of the Himalayan mountains with accounts of the courts of the native princes*, London 1833

Babbage, C., *Reflections on the decline of science in England and on some of its causes*, London 1830

Belli-Gontard, M., *Lebens-Erinnerungen*, Frankfurt-am-Main 1872

Bennett, E. T., *Tower Menagerie*, London 1829

[——], *The gardens and menagerie of the Zoological Society, delineated: published, with the sanction of the council, under the superintendence of the secretary and vice-secretary of the society*, London 1830–1

Bewick, T., *A general history of quadrupeds*, Newcastle-upon-Tyne 1790

Blomfield, A. (ed.), *Memoir of Charles James Blomfield, bishop of London: with selections from his correspondence*, London 1863

Blomfield, C., *A letter on the present neglect of the Lord's Day*, London 1830

Booth, A., *The stranger's intellectual guide to London for 1839–40*, London 1839

Bostock, J. and H. T. Riley (eds), *The natural history of Pliny*, London 1855

Boulton, W. B., *The amusements of old London*, London 1901

Broderip, W. J., *Hints for collecting animals and their products*, London 1832

[——] 'The Zoological Gardens, Regent's Park', *Quarterly Review* (July 1836), 309–32

—— *Zoological recreations*, London 1847

—— *Leaves from a notebook of a naturalist*, London 1852

Buckland, E. T., *Curiosities of natural history*, London 1858

Buckland, W., *Geology and mineralogy considered with reference to natural theology*, London 1836

Burchell, W. J., *Travels in the interior of South Africa*, London 1822–4

Burkhardt, J. L., *Travels in Nubia*, London 1819

[Buxton, C.], 'Acclimatisation of parrots at Northrepps Hall, Norfolk', *Annals and Magazine of Natural History* 4th ser. ii (1868), 381–6

Carpenter, W., *Scripture natural history*, London 1828

Coghlan, F., *A visit to London: or stranger's guide to every object worthy of attention in the metropolis*, London 1833

Crisp, E., 'On the causes of death of the animals in the Society's Gardens from 1850 to the present time', *Proceedings of the Zoological Society of London* xxxiii (1860), 175–83, 190–3

Darwin, C., *On the origin of the species by means of natural selection: or, the preservation of favoured races in the struggle for life*, London 1859

—— *The variation of animals and plants under domestication*, London 1868

—— *The expression of the emotions in man and animals*, London 1872

Doyle, R. *The foreign tour of Messrs. Brown, Jones, and Robinson: being the history of what they saw and did in Belgium, Germany, Switzerland and Italy*, London 1854

Eden, E., *Letters from India*, London 1872

[Ellis, H.], *The British Museum: Elgin and Phigaleian marbles*, London 1833

Elmes, J., *Metropolitan improvements: or, London in the nineteenth century*, London 1827

Elwick, G., *Bankrupt dictionary: from December 1820 to April 1843*, London 1843

[Foggo, G.], *Report of the proceedings at a public meeting, held at the Freemasons Hall, on the 29th of May, 1837, to promote the admission of the public, without charge, to Westminster Abbey, St Paul's Cathedral, and all depositories of works of art, of natural history, and objects of historical and literary interest in public edifices*, London 1837

Frost, T., *Circus life and circus celebrities*, London 1881

Gibbon, E., *The history of the decline and fall of the Roman Empire* (Milman's edn), London 1838

[Gore, C. G. F.], *The diary of a désennuyée*, London 1836

Gosse, P. H., *Romance of natural history*, London 1860

Gray, G. R., *The genera of birds: comprising their generic characters, a notice of the habits of each genus, and an extensive list of species referred to their several genera*, London 1844–9

Gray, J. E., 'Some notes on acclimatised animals', *Annals and Magazine of Natural History* 3rd ser. xii (1863), 76–7

Hakewill, J. *Ten views of the Zoological Gardens*, London 1831

Hooker, J. D., *Rhododendrons of the Sikkim-Himalaya*, London 1849–51

—— *Himalayan journals, or notes of a naturalist in Bengal, the Sikkim and Nepal Himalayas, the Khasia Mountains, &c*, London 1854

Hubbard, R., *Ornamental waterfowl: a practical manual on the acclimatization of the swimming birds*, London 1888

Hulme, W. H., *Views in the Gardens of the Zoological Society of London*, London 1848

Hume, A. and C. H. T. Marshall, *The game birds of India, Burmah, and Ceylon*, Calcutta 1879

Hunt, J. H. L., 'A visit to the Zoological Gardens', *New Monthly Magazine* (Aug. 1836), 479–91

Kayat, A. Y., *Journal of a residence in England: and of a journal from and to Syria, of their royal highness Reeza Loolee Meerza, Najaf Koolee Meerza, and Taymoor Meerza of Persia*, London 1839

Kirby, W. and W. Spencer, *An introduction to entomology: or elements of the natural history of insects*, London 1822–3

Knight, C., *The menageries*, London 1829–40

—— *London*, London 1841–6

—— *Passages of a working life*, London 1864

Le Vaillant, F., *Travels from the Cape of Good Hope into the interior parts of Africa*, London 1790

Lovett, W., *The life and struggles of William Lovett*, London 1876

Lumley, W. G., *The Literary and Scientific Institutions Act, 1854 [17&18 Vict. c. 112] and the Act [6&7 Vict. c. 36] which exempts such institutions from rateability with notes and index and an introduction, containing a commentary upon both acts, and all the decisions of the courts of law in the construction of the Exempting Act*, London 1855

[Lyell, C.], 'Scientific institutions', *Quarterly Review* (June 1826), 153–79

Marshall, G. F. L., *Bird's nesting in India: a calendar of the breeding seasons and a popular guide to the habits and haunts of birds*, Calcutta 1877

Mathias, H. V., *Five week's sport in the interior of the Himalayas: together with a description of the game found there*, London 1865

Maude, T., *Observations on a subject in natural history*, London 1792

Mitchell, D. W., *A popular guide to the gardens of the Zoological Society of London*, London 1852

—— 'On the Indian pheasants bred in the menagerie', *Proceedings of the Zoological Society of London* xxvi (1858), 544–5

Nowrojee, J. and H. Merwanjee, *Journal of a residence of two years and a half in Great Britain*, London 1841

[Owen, R.], 'Broderip's Zoological recreations', *Quarterly Review* (Dec.1847), 119–42

[——] 'Poisonous serpents', *Household Words*, 6 Nov. 1852, 186–8

Pallme, I., *Travels in Kordofan*, London 1844

Parley, P., *Tales of animals: comprising quadrupeds, birds, reptiles and insects*, London 1833

Paterson, W., *A narrative of four journeys into the country of the Hottentots and Caffraria in the years 1777, 1778, 1779*, London 1789

Raffles S., *Memoir of the life and public services of Sir Thomas Stamford Raffles*, new edn, London 1835

Reeve, L., *Conchologia iconica*, London 1843–78

—— *Letter to the right honourable the earl of Derby, K.G., D.C.L., on the management, character, and progress of the Zoological Society of London*, London 1846

Reports of the council and auditors of the Zoological Society of London, 1829–

Report of 34th meeting of the British Association for the Advancement of Science: notes and abstracts, London 1864

Royle, J. F., *Illustrations of botany and other branches of the natural history of the Himalayan mountains*, London 1839

Rüppell, E., *Reisen in Nubien, Kordofan und den peträischen Arabien*, Frankfurt-am-Main 1829

Ryland, A., 'To the council of the Society of Arts', *Journal of the Society of Arts and of the Institutions of Union* i (1852–3)

Ryley, J., 'Zoological Society's gardens', *Eclectic Review* (Aug. 1831), 179–82

Saint Mars, L., *The hippopotamus polka as a pianoforte duet*, London 1850

Scharf, G., *Six views of the Zoological Gardens*, London 1835

Sclater, P. L., *A list of vertebrated animals living in the gardens of the Zoological Society of London*, London 1862

—— *A list of vertebrated animals living in the gardens of the Zoological Society of London*, London 1865

—— *Guide to the gardens of the Zoological Society of London*, London 1870

Sopwith, T., *Reminiscences of first visits to Scotland, London, and the south west of England in the years 1828, 1830, and 1833*, privately published 1847

[Southey, R.], 'Fables and other pieces in verse by Marry Maria Colling', *Quarterly Review* (Mar. 1832), 80–102

Stevens. J. C., *Catalogue of the menagerie and aviary at Knowsley formed by the late earl of Derby, K.G.*, Liverpool 1851

Swainson, W., *A preliminary discourse on the study of natural history*, London 1834

Sweny, H. W. and A. Lee, *Walking in the zoo*, London 1869

Sykes, J., (ed.), *Biographical notices of Colonel William Henry Sykes, F.R.S., M.P.* London 1857

Taylor, J., *A month in London: or, some of its modern wonders described*, London 1832

Vigors, N. A. and W. J. Broderip, *Guide to the Gardens of the Zoological Society*, London 1829

Wallace, A., 'Acclimatisation', in *Encyclopaedia Britannica*, 9th edn, Edinburgh 1878, i. 84–90

Warwick, J. E., *Description and history with anecdotes of the giraffes*, London 1836

Wilberforce, R. G., *Life of Bishop Wilberforce*, London 1881

Wright, T., *Some habits and customs of the working classes*, London 1867

[Wynter, A.], 'The Zoological Gardens', *Quarterly Review* (Dec. 1855), 220–48

Zoological Society of London, *List of animals in the Gardens of the Zoological Society of London*, London 1834

—— *List of the members of the Zoological Society of London*, London 1837

Secondary sources

Adams, B., *London illustrated, 1604–1851: a survey and index of topographical books and their plates*, London 1983

Åkerberg, S., *Knowledge and pleasure at Regent's Park: the gardens of the Zoological Society of London during the nineteenth century*, Umeå 2001

Alberti, S. J. M. M., 'Objects and the museum', *Isis* xcvi (2005), 559–71

Alison, A., *Silver fork society: fashionable life and literature from 1814 to 1840*, London 1983

Allen, D. E., *The naturalist in Britain: a social history*, London 1976

Allin, M., *Zaraf: a giraffe's true story, from deep in Africa to the heart of Paris*, London 1998

Altick, R. D., *The shows of London*, Cambridge, MA 1978

—— *English common reader: a social history of the mass reading public, 1800–1900*, 2nd edn, Columbus 1998

Anderson, K., 'Culture and nature at the Adelaide Zoo: at the frontiers of "human" geography', *Transactions of the Institute of British Geography* xx (1995), 275–94

Anderson, W., 'Climates of opinion: acclimatization in nineteenth-century France and England', *VS* xxxv (1992), 134–57

Andrew, D., '"Adultery à la mode": privilege, the law and attitudes to adultery, 1770–1809', *History* lxxxii (1997), 5–23

Arnold, Dana, 'Decimus Burton and the urban picturesque', in D. Arnold (ed.), *The picturesque in late Georgian England*, London 1995, 51–6

—— 'A family affair: Decimus Burton's designs for the Regent's Park villas', in Dana Arnold (ed.), *The Georgian villa*, Stroud 1996, 105–17

Arnold, David, 'India's place in the tropical world', *Journal of Imperial and Commonwealth History* xxvi (1998), 1–21

—— *Science, technology and medicine in colonial India*, Cambridge 2000

Arscott, C., 'The representation of the city in the visual arts', in Daunton, *Cambridge urban history*, iii. 811–32

Assael, B., *Circus and Victorian society*, Charlottesville 2005

Atkins, P. J. (ed.), *Animal cities: beastly urban histories*, Aldershot 2012

Auerbach, J. A. and P. H. Hoffenburg (eds), *Britain, the empire and the world at the Great Exhibition of 1851*, Aldershot 2008

Bailey, P., *Leisure and class in Victorian England: rational recreation and the contest for control*, London 1978

Baratay, E., and E. Hardouin-Fugier, *Zoo: a history of zoological gardens in the West*, London 2002

Barker, T. C. and M. Robbins, *A history of London transport: passenger travel and the development of the metropolis*, London 1963

Barlow, P., and C. Trodd (eds), *Governing cultures: art institutions in Victorian London*, Aldershot 2000

Bastin, J., 'The first prospectus of the Zoological Society of London: new light on the society's origin', *JSBNH* v (1970), 369–88

—— 'A further note on the origin of the Zoological Society of London', *JSBNH* xi (1973), 236–41.

—— 'Sir Stamford Raffles and the study of natural history in Penang, Singapore and Indonesia', *Journal of the Malaysian Branch of the Royal Asiatic Society* lxiii (1991), 1–25

Bayly, C. A., 'The second British empire', in Winks, *Oxford history of British Empire*, v. 54–72

Bebbington, D. W., *Evangelicalism in modern Britain*, London 1989

Beinart, W., *The rise of conservation in South Africa: settlers, livestock, and the environment, 1770–1950*, Oxford 2003

Bergdoll, B., *European architecture, 1750–1890*, Oxford 2000

Blanchard, P. and others (eds), *Human zoos: science and spectacle in the age of colonial empires*, Liverpool 2008

Blunt, W., *The ark in the park: the zoo in the nineteenth century*, London 1976

Bonython, E. and A. Burton, *The great exhibitor: the life and works of Henry Cole*, London 2003

Bostock, S., *Zoos and animal rights: ethics of keeping animals*, London 1993

Brandon-Jones, C., 'Long gone and forgotten: reassessing the life and career of Edward Blyth, zoologist', *Archives of Natural History* xxii (1995), 91–5

—— 'Edward Blyth, Charles Darwin, and the animal trade in nineteenth-century India and Britain', *Journal of the History of Biology* xxx (1997), 145–78

Brewer, J., *Party ideology and popular politics at the accession of George III*, Cambridge 1976

Brown, M., 'From foetid air to filth: the cultural transformation of British epidemiological thought, ca. 1780–1848', *Bulletin of the History of Medicine* lxxxii (2008), 515–44

Browne, J., 'Darwin in caricature: a study in the popularisation and dissemination of evolution', *Proceedings of American Philosophical Society* cxlv (2001), 496–509

Burke, P., *Popular culture in early modern Europe*, rev. repr., Aldershot 1994

Burkhardt, Jr, R. W., 'Constructing the zoo: science, society, and animal nature at the Paris menagerie, 1794–1838', in Henninger-Voss, *Animals in human histories*, 231–57

Burney, I. A., 'Medicine in the age of reform', in Burns and Innes, *Rethinking the age of reform*, 163–81

Burns, R. A., 'English "church reform" revisited, 1780–1840', in Burns and Innes, *Rethinking the age of reform*, 136–62

—— and J. Innes (eds), *Rethinking the age of reform: Britain, 1780–1850*, Cambridge 2003

Burt, J., 'Violent health and the moving image: the London Zoo and monkey hill', in Henninger-Voss, *Animals in human histories*, 258–92

Calhoun, C. (ed.), *Habermas and the public sphere*, Cambridge, MA 1992

Cannadine, E., *Class in Britain*, New Haven 1998

Cannan, E., *The history of local rates in England: in relation to the proper distribution of the burden of taxation*, London 1912

Cantor, G. and S. Shuttleworth (eds), *Science serialised: representation of sciences in nineteenth-century periodicals*, Cambridge, MA 2004

Cash, D., *Access to museum culture: the British Museum from 1753 to 1836* (The British Museum Occasional Paper cxxxiii, 2002)

[Cecil, A. N.], *London parks and gardens*, London 1907

Chancellor, E. B., *The pleasure haunts of London*, London 1925

Charmley, J., *The princess and the politicians: sex, intrigue and diplomacy, 1812–40*, London 2005

Chartier, R., *Cultural history: between practices and representations*, Ithaca 1988

—— *The order of books: readers, authors, and libraries in Europe between the fourteenth and eighteenth century*, Cambridge 1994

Chatterjee, D., *A short sketch of Rajah Rajendro Mullick Bahadur and his family*, Calcutta 1917

Clark, P. (ed.), *The Cambridge urban history of Britain*, II: *1540–1840*, Cambridge 2000.

—— and R. A. Houston, 'Culture and leisure, 1700–1840', in Clark, *Cambridge urban history*, 575–613

Classen, C., D. Howes and A. Synnott, *Aroma: the cultural history of smell*, London 1994

Cocker, M. and C. Inskipp, *A Himalayan ornithologist: the life and work of Brian Houghton Hodgson*, Oxford 1988

Colley, L., *Britons: forging the nation, 1707–1837*, New Haven 1992

Conlin, J., *The nation's mantelpiece: a history of the National Gallery*, London 2006, 57–66

—— 'Vauxhall revisited: the afterlife of a London pleasure garden, 1770–1859', *Journal of British Studies* lxv (2006), 718–43.

Cooter, R. and S. Pumfrey, 'Separate spheres and public places: reflections of the history of science popularization and science in popular culture', *BJHS* xxxii (1994), 237–67

Copeland, E., 'Crossing Oxford Street: silverfork geopolitics, *Eighteenth-Century Life* xxv (2001), 116–34

Copland, I., 'Christianity as an arm of empire: the ambiguous case of India under the Company, c. 1813–1858', *HJ* xlix (2006), 1025–54

Corbey, R., 'Ethnographic showcases, 1870–1930', *Cultural Anthropology* viii (1993), 338–69

Corbin, A., *The foul and the fragrant: odour and the French social imagination*, Leamington Spa 1986

Corfield, P. J., 'English "church reform" revisited, 1780–1840', in Burns and Innes, *Rethinking the age of reform*, 136–62

—— 'Introduction: history and language', in Corfield, *Language, history and class*, 1–29

—— *Power and the professions in Britain, 1700–1850*, London 1995

—— *Vauxhall and the invention of the urban pleasure gardens*, London 2008

—— (ed.), *Language, history and class*, Oxford 1991

Cromwell, J. L., *Dorothea Lieven: a Russian princess in London and Paris, 1785–1857*, London 2006

Crook, J. M., 'Metropolitan improvements: John Nash and the picturesque', in Fox, *London*, 77–96

Crossick, G., 'From gentlemen to the residuum: language of social description in Victorian Britain', in Corfield, *Language, history and class*, 150–78

Cunningham, H., *Leisure in the Industrial Revolution, c.1780–1880*, London 1980

—— 'Leisure and culture', in F. M. L. Thompson (ed.), *The Cambridge social history of Britain*, III: *1750–1950*, Cambridge 1990, 279–339

Dagg, A. I. and J. B. Foster, *The giraffe: its biology, behaviour and ecology*, New York 1976

Dance, S. P., 'Hugh Cuming (1791–1865): prince of collectors', *JSBNH* v (1970), 369–88

—— *A history of shell collecting*, Leiden 1986

Daston, L. (ed.), *Biographies of scientific objects*, Chicago 2000

—— and P. Galison, *Objectivity*, Cambridge, MA 2007

Daunton, M., *Trusting Leviathan: the politics of taxation in Britain, 1799–1914*, Cambridge 2001

—— *The organisation of knowledge in Victorian Britain*, Oxford 2006

—— 'Introduction', to Daunton, *The organisation of knowledge*, 1–27

—— (ed.), *The Cambridge urban history of Britain*, III: *1840–1950*, Cambridge 2000

Davidoff, L., and C. Hall, *Family fortunes: men and women of the English middle class, 1780–1850*, London 1987

Davis, T., *John Nash: the Prince Regent's architect*, Newton Abbot 1973

Dennis, R., 'Modern London', in Daunton, *Cambridge urban history*, iii. 95–131

Desmond, A., 'The making of institutional zoology in London, 1822–36', *HS* xxiii (1985), 133–85

—— 'Artisan resistance and evolution in Britain, 1819–48', *Osiris* 2nd ser. iii (1987), 77–110

—— *The politics of evolution: morphology, medicine, and reform in radical London*, Chicago 1989

—— *Huxley: from devil's disciple to evolution's high priest*, London 1997

—— and J. Moore, *Darwin: the life of a tormented evolutionist*, New York 1991

Donald, D., '"Beastly sights": the treatment of animals as a moral theme in representations of London, c. 1820–50', *Art History* xxii (1999), 514–44

—— *Picturing animals in Britain*, New Haven 2007

Drayton, R., 'Science, medicine, and the British Empire', in Winks, *Oxford history of British Empire*, v. 264–76

—— 'Science and the European empire', *Journal of Imperial and Commonwealth History* xxiii (1995), 503–10

—— *Nature's government: science, imperial Britain, and the 'improvement' of the world*, New Haven 2000

Driver, F., *Geography militant: cultures of exploration and empire*, Oxford 2001

—— '"The struggle for luxuriance': William Burchell collects tropical nature', in F. Driver and I. Martin (eds), *Tropical vision in the age of empire*, Chicago 2009, 59–74

—— and D. Gilbert (eds), *Imperial cities: landscape, display and identity*, Manchester 1999

Duffy, M., 'World-wide war and British expansion, 1793–1815', in P. J. Marshall (ed.), *The Oxford history of the British Empire*, II: *The eighteenth century*, Oxford 1998, 184–207

Duncan, C., 'From the princely gallery to the public art museum: the Louvre Museum and the National Gallery, London', in C. Duncan (ed.), *Civilising rituals: inside public art museums*, London 1995, 21–47

Dunlap, T. R., 'Remaking the land: the acclimatization movement and Anglo ideas of nature', *Journal of World History* viii (1997), 303–19

Edelstein, T. J., 'Vauxhall Gardens', in B. Ford (ed.), *The Cambridge guide to the arts in Britain*, V: *The Augustan age*, Cambridge 1991, 202–15

Edwards, M. A., 'The library and scientific publications of the Zoological Society of London: part II', in Zuckerman, *Zoological Society of London*, 235–67

Enderby, J., *Imperial nature: Joseph Hooker and the practices of Victorian science*, Chicago 2008

—— 'Sympathetic science: Charles Darwin, Joseph Hooker and the passions of Victorian naturalists', *VS* li (2009), 299–320

Fahmy, K., *All the Pasha's men: Mehmed Ali, his army and the making of modern Egypt*, Cairo 1997

—— 'The era of Muhammad Ali Pasha, 1805–1848', in M. W. Daly (ed.), *The Cambridge history of Egypt*, II: *Modern Egypt from 1517 to the end of the twentieth century*, Cambridge 1998, 139–70

Fisher, M. H., 'East Indian travel guides to Britain', in T. Youngs (ed.), *Travel writing in the nineteenth century: filling the blank spaces*, London 2006, 87–106

Fletcher, H. R., *The story of the Royal Horticultural Society, 1804–1968*, London 1969

Forbes, T. R., 'William Yarrell, British naturalist', *Proceedings of American Philosophical Society* cvi (1962), 505–15

Forgan, S., 'The architecture of display: museums, universities and objects in nineteenth-century Britain', *BJHS* xxxii (1994), 139–62

—— '"But indifferently lodged …": perception and place in buildings for science in Victorian Britain', in Smith and Agar, *Making space for science*, 195–215

Fox, C. (ed.), *London: world city, 1800–40*, New Haven 1992

Francione, G. L. and R. Garner, *The animal rights debate: abolition or regulation?* New York 2010

Fudge, E., *Perceiving animals: humans and beast in early modern English culture*, Urbana 2002

Fyfe, A. *Science and salvation: Evangelicals and popular science publishing*, Chicago 2004

—— and B. Lightman, 'Science in the marketplace: an introduction', in Fyfe and Lightman, *Science in the marketplace*, 1–19

—— and B. Lightman (eds), *Science in the marketplace: nineteenth-century sites and experiences*, Chicago 2007

Gallagher, J. A. and R. E. Robinson, 'The imperialism of free trade', *EcHR* vi (1953), 1–15

Glaisyer, N., 'Networking: trade and exchange in the eighteenth-century British Empire', *HJ* xlvii (2004), 451–76

Goldgar, A., 'British Museum and the virtual representation of culture', *Albion* xxxii (2000), 195–231

Golinski, J., *Science as public culture: chemistry and Enlightenment in Britain, 1760–1820*, Cambridge 1992

Green, D. R., *From artisans to paupers: economic change and poverty in London, 1790–1870*, Aldershot 1995

Griffin, E., 'Popular culture in industrialising England', *HJ* xlv (2002), 619–35

—— *England's revelry: a history of popular sports and pastimes, 1660–1830*, Oxford 2005

Guillery, P., *The buildings of London Zoo*, London 1993

Gunn, M. and L. E. Codd, *Botanical exploration of South Africa*, Cape Town 1981

Hahn, D., *The Tower Menagerie: being the amazing true story of the royal collection of wild and ferocious beasts*, London 2003

Hall, C., *Civilising subjects: metropole and colony in the English imagination, 1830–67*, London 2002

—— and S. O. Rose (eds), *At home with the empire*, Cambridge 2006

Hallett, R. (ed.), *Records of the African Association, 1788–1831*, London 1964

Hall-Witt, J. L., 'Reforming the aristocracy: opera and elite culture, 1780–1860', in Burns and Innes, *Rethinking the age of reform*, 221–37

Hamlin, C., *Public health and social justice in the age of Chadwick: Britain, 1800–1954*, Cambridge 1998

Hanson, E., *Animal attractions: nature on display in American zoos*, Princeton 2002

Harrison, B., 'Religion and recreation in nineteenth-century England', *P&P* xxxviii (1967), 98–125

—— 'Animals and the state in nineteenth-century England', *EHR* lxxxviii (1973), 786–820

Harrison, M., 'Science and the British empire', *Isis* xcvi (2005), 56–63

Hellmuth, E. (ed.), *The transformation of political culture: England and Germany in the late eighteenth century*, London 1990

Henninger-Voss, M. (ed.), *Animals in human histories*, Rochester 2002

Henson, L. and others (eds), *Culture and science in the nineteenth-century media*, Aldershot 2004

Hesketh, I., *Of apes and ancestors: evolution, Christianity, and the Oxford debate*, Toronto 2009

Hillard, L., *A giraffe for France*, Sydney 1998

Hilton, B., *The age of atonement: the impact of Evangelicalism on social and economic thought, 1795–1865*, Oxford 1988

Hoage, R. J. and W. A. Deiss (eds), *New worlds, new animals: from menagerie to zoological park in the nineteenth century*, Baltimore 1996

Hoffenberg, P., *An empire on display: English, Indian, and Australian exhibitions from the Crystal Palace to the Great War*, Berkeley 2001

Hoher, D., 'The composition of music hall audiences, 1850–1900', in P. Bailey (ed.), *Music hall: the business of pleasure*, Milton Keynes 1986, 73–92

Hoock, *The king's artists: the Royal Academy of Arts and the politics of British culture, 1760–1840*, Oxford 2003

—— 'Reforming culture: national art institutions in the age of reform', in Burns and Innes, *Rethinking the age of reform*, 254–70

—— 'The British state and the Anglo-French wars over antiquities, 1798–1858', *HJ* 1 (2007), 1–40

Hughes, W., 'Silver fork writers and readers: social contexts of a best seller', *Novel: A Forum on Fiction* xxv (1992), 328–47

Huigen, S., *Knowledge and colonialism: eighteenth-century travellers in South Africa*, Leiden 2009

Hunt, J. D., *Vauxhall and London's garden theatres*, Cambridge 1985

Hunter, W. W., *Life of Brian Houghton Hodgson: British resident at the court of Nepal*, London 1896

Hyde, R. and V. Cumming, 'The prints of Benjamin Read, tailor and print-maker', *Print Quarterly* xlii (2000), 262–84

Hyde, R. N., 'The act to regulate parochial assessments (1836) and its contribution to the mapping of London', *Guildhall Studies in London History* ii (1976), 54–68

Ito, T., 'Between ideals, realities, and popular perceptions: an analysis of the multifaceted nature of London Zoo, 1828–48', *Society and Animals* xiv (2006), 159–78

Jackson, P., *George Scharf's London: sketches and watercolours of a changing city, 1820–50*, London 1987

Jahn, I., 'Zoologische Gärten in Stadtkultur und Wissenschaft im 19 Jahrhundert', *Berichte zur Wissenschaftsgeschichte* xv (1992), 213–25

Jamieson, D., 'Against zoos', in P. Singer (ed.), *In defense of animals*, Oxford 1985, 108–17

Jardine, N. and E. C. Spary, 'The natures of cultural history', in Jardine, Secord and Spary, *Cultures of natural history*, 1–37

Jardine, N., J. A. Secord and E. C. Spary (eds), *Cultures of natural history*, Cambridge 1996

Jasanoff, M., *Edge of empire: lives, culture and conquest in the East, 1750–1850*, New York 2005

Jenner, M. S. R., 'Civilization and deodorization? Smell in early modern English culture', in P. Burke, B. Harrison and P. Slack (eds), *Civil histories: essays presented to Sir Keith Thomas*, Oxford 2000, 127–44

Johnson, M., *Bustling intermeddler? The life and work of Charles James Blomfield*, Leominster 2001

Jones, R. W., '"The sight of creatures strange to our climate": London Zoo and the consumption of the exotic', *Journal of Victorian Culture* ii (1997), 1–26

Kalof, L. and B. Resl (eds), *A cultural history of animals*, Oxford 2007

Kean, H., *Animal rights: political and social change in Britain since 1800*, London 1998, 39–69

Kelly, T., *George Birkbeck: pioneer of adult education*, Liverpool 1957

Kendra, A., 'Gendering the silver fork: Catherine Gore and the society novel', *Women's Writing* xi (2004), 25–38

Kennedy, D., *The magic mountains: hill stations and the British raj*, Delhi 1996

Kenny, J. T., 'Climate, race, and imperial authority: the symbolic landscape of the British hill station in India', *Annals of the Association of American Geographers* lxxxv (1995), 694–714

Keynes, R., 'Darwin, William Erasmus', *ODNB* [http://www.oxforddnb.com/view/article/94741, accessed 18 June 2012]

Kift, D., *The Victorian music hall: culture, class and conflict*, Cambridge 1996

Kisling, Jr, V. N., 'Colonial menageries and the exchange of exotic faunas', *Archives of Natural History* xxi (1994), 312–14

—— 'The origin and development of American zoological parks to 1899', in Hoage and Deiss, *New worlds, new animals*, 109–25

—— (ed.), *Zoo and aquarium history: ancient animal collections to zoological gardens*, Boca Raton 2001

Kocka, J. and A. Mitchell (eds), *Bourgeois society in nineteenth-century Europe*, Oxford 1993

Kubrick, R., 'British expansion, empire, and technological change', in A. Porter (ed.), *The Oxford history of the British Empire*, III: *The nineteenth century*, Oxford 1999, 247–69

Kusamitsu, T., 'Great Exhibitions before 1851', *HWJ* ix (1981), 70–89

Kwint, M., 'The circus and nature in late Georgian England', in R. Koshar (ed.), *Histories of leisure*, Oxford 2002, 45–60

—— 'The legitimization of the circus in late Georgian England', *P&P* clxxiv (2002), 72–115

Lambert, A. D., 'The British naval strategic revolution, 1815–54', in G. Jackson and D. M. Williams (eds), *Shipping, technology and imperialism*, Aldershot 1996, 145–61

Lambert, D. and A. Lester (eds), *Colonial lives across the British Empire: imperial careering in the long nineteenth century*, Cambridge 2006

Langford, P., 'Property and "virtual representation" in eighteenth-century England', *HJ* xxxi (1988), 83–111

Laufer, B., *The giraffe in history and art*, Chicago 1928

Lawrence, H. W., 'The greening of the squares of London: transformation of urban landscape and ideals', *Annals of the Association of American Geographers* lxxxiii (1993), 90–118

Lester, A., *Imperial networks: creating identities in nineteenth-century South Africa and Britain*, London 2001

Lever, C., *They dined on eland: the story of the acclimatisation societies*, London 1992

Livingston, D. N., *Putting science in its place: geographies of scientific knowledge*, Chicago 2003

Lohrili, A., *Household Words: a weekly journal, 1850–9, conducted by Charles Dickens*, Toronto 1973

Lucas, J. R., 'Wilberforce and Huxley: a legendary encounter', *HJ* xxii (1979), 313–30

Lutfi al-Sayyid Marsot, A., *Egypt in the reign of Muhammad Ali*, Cambridge 1984

Lydekker, R., 'On old pictures of giraffes and zebras', *Proceedings of the General Meetings of the Zoological Society of London* ii (1904), 339–42

McDougall, E. (ed.), *John Cladius Loudon and the early nineteenth century in England*, Washington, DC 1980

MacDougall, P., 'The formative years: Malta dockyard, 1800–15', *MM* lxxvi (1990), 205–14

MacFarland, S. E. and R. Hediger (eds), *Animals and agency: interdisciplinary exploration*, Leiden 2009

Mackay, D., 'Agents of empire: the Banksian collectors and evaluation of new land', in D. P. Miller (ed.), *Visions of empire: voyages, botany and representations of nature*, Cambridge 1996, 38–57

McKeller, E., 'Peripheral visions: alternative aspect and rural presences in mid-eighteenth century London', Art History xxii 1999, 495–513

MacKenzie, J. M., The empire of nature: hunting, conservation and British imperialism, Manchester 1988

—— (ed.), Imperialism and popular culture, Manchester 1986

McLeod, H., Religion and the working class in nineteenth-century Britain, London 1984

MacLeod, R. M., 'Whigs and savants: reflections on the reform movement in the Royal Society, 1830–48', in I. Inkster and J. Morrell (eds.), Metropolis and province: science in British culture, 1780–1850, London 1983, 55 90

—— Public science and public policy in Victorian England, Aldershot 1996

—— (ed.), Nature and empire: science and the colonial enterprise, Osiris 2nd ser. xv (2000)

—— and P. Collins (eds), The parliament of science: the British Association for the Advancement of Science, 1831–1981, Nothwood 1981

McQuat, G. R., 'Species, rules and meaning: the politics of language and the ends of definitions in nineteenth-century natural history', Studies in History and Philosophy of Science xxvii (1996), 473–519

Magee, G. B. and A. S. Thompson, Empire and globalisation: networks of people, goods and capital in the British world, c. 1850–1914, Cambridge 2010

Mah, H., 'Phantasies of the public sphere: rethinking of the Habermas of historians', Journal of Modern History lxxii (2000), 153–82

Major, A., 'Shillibeer and his London omnibus', Transport History x (1979), 67–9

Malcomson, R. W., Popular recreations in English society, 1700–1850, Cambridge 1973

Mandler, P., Aristocratic government in the age of reform: Whigs and Liberals, 1830–52, Oxford 1990

—— 'The problem with cultural history', Cultural and Social History i (2004), 94–117

—— 'Art in a cool climate: the cultural policy of the British state in European context, 1780–1850', in T. G. W. Blanning and Hagen Schulze (eds), Unity and diversity in European culture, c. 1800, London 2006, 101–20

—— Liberty and authority in Victorian Britain, Oxford 2006

Marshall, P. J., 'The first British empire', in Winks, Oxford history of British Empire, v. 43–53

Mehos, D. C., Science and culture for members only: the Amsterdam Zoo artists in the nineteenth century, Amsterdam 2006

Melvill, J. C., 'Lovell Reeve: a brief sketch of his life and career', Journal of Conchology ix (1898–1900), 344–57

Meynell, G., 'The Royal Botanic Society's garden, Regent's Park', London Journal xi (1980), 135–46

Miller, D. P., 'Between hostile camps: Sir Humphry Davy's presidency of the Royal Society of London, 1820–7', BJHS xvi (1983), 1–47

Mitchell, C., Zoological Society of London: centenary history, London 1829

Mitman, G., 'When nature is the zoo: vision and power in the art of science of natural history', Osiris 2nd ser. xi (1996), 117–43

Mittra, D. K., 'Ram Bramha Sanyal and the establishment of the Calcutta Zoological Gardens', in Hoage and Deiss, New worlds, new animals, 86–93

Morrell, J. and A. Thackray, *Gentlemen of science: early years of the British Association for the Advancement of Science*, Oxford 1981

Morse, D. D. and M. A. Danahay, *Victorian animal dreams*, Aldershot 2007

Morus, I., S. Schaffer and J. Secord, 'Scientific London', in Fox, *London*, 77–96

Mullan, B. and G. Marvin, *Zoo culture*, London 1987

Neave, S. A., *The history of the Entomological Society of London, 1833–1933*, London 1933

Neil, T., 'White wings and six-legged muttons: the freakish animal', in M. Tromp (ed.), *Victorian freaks: the social context of freakery in Britain*, Columbus 2008, 60 75

Norman, E. R., *Church and society in England, 1770–1970*, Oxford 1976

Norton, B. G. and others (eds), *Ethics on the ark: zoos, animal welfare, and wildlife conservation*, Washington, DC 1995

Osborn, M., *Nature, the exotic and the science of French colonisation*, Bloomington 1994

—— 'Acclimatizing the world: a history of the paradigmatic colonial science', *Osiris* 2nd ser. xv (2000), 135–51

Outram, D., 'New spaces in natural history', in Jardine, Secord and Spary, *Cultures of natural history*, 249–65

Owen, R., *The life of Richard Owen*, London 1894

Pandian, M. S. S., 'Gendered negotiations: hunting and colonialism in the late nineteenth-century Nilgiris', in P. Uberoi (ed.), *Social reform, sexuality and the state*, New Delhi 1996, 239–64

Peltz, L., 'Aesthecizing the ancestral city: antiquarianism, topography and the representation of London in the long eighteenth century', *Art History* xxii (1999), 472–94

Petijean, P., C. Jami and A. M. Moulin, *Science and empires: historical studies about scientific development and European expansion*, Dordrecht 1992

Philo, C., 'Animals, geography and the city: notes on inclusions and exclusions', in J. Wolch and J. Emel (eds), *Animal geographies: place, politics, and identity in the nature-culture boundaries*, London 1998, 51–71

Pickering, J., 'Willam J. Burchell's South African Mammal Collection, 1810–15', *Archives of Natural History* xxiv (1997), 311–26

Pickstone, J., 'Science in nineteenth-century England: plural configurations and singular politics', in Daunton, *The organisation of knowledge*, 29–60

Plumb, C., 'In fact, one cannot see it without laughing': the spectacle of the kangaroo in London, 1770–1830', *Museum History Journal* iii (2010), 7–32

—— 'Strange and wonderful': encountering the elephant in Britain, 1675–1830', *JECS* xxxiii (2010), 525–43

Porter, A., *Religion versus empire? British Protestant missionaries and overseas expansion, 1700–1914*, Manchester 2004

Porter, R., *London: a social history*, London 1994

—— *The greatest benefit to mankind: a medical history of humanity*, New York 1998

Potter, S. J. (ed.), *Imperial communication: Australia, Britain and the British Empire c. 1830–50*, London 2005

Potts, A., 'Picturing the modern metropolis: images of London in the nineteenth century', *HWJ* xxvi (1998), 28–56

Powell, C., 'Topography, imagination and travel: Tuner's relationship with James Hakewill', *Art History* v (1982), 408–25

Pradhan, Q., 'Empire in the hills: the making of hill stations in colonial India', *Studies in History* xxiii (2007), 33–91

Pratt, M. L., *Imperial eyes: travel writing and transculturation*, London 1992

Preece, R., 'Darwinism, Christianity and the great vivisection debate', *Journal of the History of Ideas* lxiv (2003), 399–419

Qureshi, S., *Peoples on parade: exhibitions, empire and anthropology in nineteenth-century Britain*, Chicago 2011

Raj, K., *Relocating modern science: circulation and the construction of knowledge in South Asia and Europe, 1650–1900*, Basingstoke 2007

Rappaport, E., 'Art, commerce, or empire? The rebuilding of Regent Street, 1880–1927', *HWJ* viii (2002), 94–117

Reid, D. A., 'The decline of saint Monday, 1766–1876', *P&P* lxi (1976), 76–101

——'Weddings, weekdays, work and leisure in urban England, 1791–1911: the decline of saint Monday revisited', *P&P* cliii (1996), 135–163

Richards, T., *The commodity culture of Victorian England: advertising and spectacle, 1851–1914*, London 1991

Richardson, B. W. (ed.), *Thomas Sopwith*, London 1891

Ridley, G. (ed.), *Animals in the eighteenth century*, JECS xxxiii/4 (2010), 427–683

Ritvo, H., *The animal estate: the English and other creatures in the Victorian age*, Cambridge, MA 1987

—— 'Zoological nomenclature and the empire of Victorian science', in B. Lightman (ed.), *Victorian science in context*, Chicago 1997, 334–53

—— 'The order of nature: constructing the collection of Victorian zoos', in Hoage and Deiss, *New worlds, new animals*, 43–50

Roberts, M. J. D., *Making English morals: voluntary association and moral reform in England, 1787–1886*, Cambridge 2004

Rootmaaker, L. C., *The zoological exploration of South Africa, 1650–1790*, Rotterdam 1989

Roselle, D., *Samuel Griswold Goodrich, creator of Peter Parley: a study of his life and work*, New York 1968

Rothfels, N., *Savages and beasts: the birth of the modern zoo*, Baltimore 2002

—— 'How the caged bird sings: animals and entertainment', in K. Kate (ed.), *A cultural history of animals, V: In the age of empire*, Oxford 2007, 95–112

Ruse, M., 'The Darwin industry: a guide', *VS* xxxix (1996), 217–35

Sadiah, Q., 'Displaying Sara Baartman: the "Hottentot Venus"', *BJHS* lxii (2004), 237–57

Sakurai, A., *Science and societies in Frankfurt am Main*, London 2013

Samuel, E. C., *The villas in Regent's Park and their residents*, London 1959

Sangwan, S., 'From gentlemen amateurs to professionals: reassessing the natural science tradition in colonial India, 1780–1840', in R. H. Grove, V. Damodran and S. Sangwan (eds), *Nature and the orient: the environmental history of South and Southeast Asia*, Delhi 1998, 210–36

Schaffer, S. and S. Shapin, *Leviathan and the air pump: Hobbes, Boyle and the experimental life*, Princeton 1985

Scherren, H., *The Zoological Society of London: a sketch of its foundation and development and the story of its farm, museum, gardens, menageries and library*, London 1905

Schneer, J., *London 1900: the imperial metropolis*, New Haven 1999

Schwarz, L. 'London, 1700–1840', in Clark, *Cambridge urban history*, 641–71

Schwarzbach, F. S., 'George Scharf and early Victorian London', in I. B. Nadel and F. S. Schwarzbach (eds), *Victorian artists and the city: a collection of critical essays*, New York 1980, 93–105

Secord, A., 'Corresponding interests: artisans and gentlemen in nineteenth–century natural history', *BJHS* xxvii (1994), 383–408

—'Science in the pub: artisan botanists in early nineteenth-century Lancashire', *BJHS* xxxii (1994), 269–315

—— 'Botany on a plate: pleasure and the power of pictures in promoting early nineteenth-century scientific knowledge', *Isis* xciii (2002), 28–57

Secord, J. A., 'Nature's fancy: Charles Darwin and the breeding of pigeons', *Isis* lxxii (1981), 163–86

—— 'Natural history in depth', *Social Studies of Science* xv (1985), 181–200

—— *Victorian sensation: the extraordinary publication, reception and secret authorship of 'Vestiges of the natural history of creation'*, Chicago 2000

—— 'How scientific conversation became shop talk', in Fyfe and Lightman, *Science in the markplace*, 23–59

Shapin, S., 'Science and its public', in R. C. Olby and others (eds), *Companion to the history of modern science*, London 1990, 990–1007

Sheets-Pyenson, S., 'War and peace in natural history publishing: the *Naturalist's Library*, 1833–43', *Isis* lxxii (1981), 50–72

Showers, F. W., 'Anomalies and inequalities in local rating', *Public Administration* xxi (1943), 145–57

Simmons, J., *The Victorian railway*, New York 1991

Simo, M., *Loudon and the landscape: from country seat to metropolis, 1783–1843*, New Haven, 1988

Sivasundaram, S., *Nature and the godly empire: science and Evangelical mission in the Pacific, 1795–1850*, Cambridge 2005

—— 'Trading knowledge: the East India Company's elephants in India and Britain', *HJ* xlviii (2005), 27–63

Smith, C. and J. Agar (eds), *Making space for science: territorial themes in the shaping of knowledge*, Manchester 1998

Smith, J., 'Darwin and the evolution of Victorian studies', *VS* li (2009), 215–21

Sprigge, S. S., *The life and times of Thomas Wakley*, London 1899

Sramek, J., "Face him like a Briton": tiger hunting, imperialism and British masculinity in colonial India, 1800–1875', *VS* xlviii (2006), 659–80

Stack, D., 'William Lovett and the National Association for the Political and Social Improvement of the People', *HJ* xlii (1999), 127–50

Stanley, B., *The Bible and the flag: Protestant missions and British imperialism in the nineteenth and twentieth centuries*, Leicester 1990

Stewart, L., *The rise of public science: rhetoric, technology and natural philosophy in Newtonian Britain, 1660–1750*, Cambridge 1992

Storey, W. K., 'Big cats and imperialism: lion and tiger hunting in Kenya and Northern India, 1898–1930', *Journal of World History* ii (1991), 135–73

Summerson, J., *John Nash: architect to King George IV*, London 1935

Tanner, A., 'The casual poor and the City of London Poor Law Union, 1837–69', *HJ* xlii (1999), 183–206

Tayler, G., *The law as to the exemption of scientific and literary societies from the parish and other local rates*, London 1851

Taylor, M., 'Queen Victoria and India, 1837–61', *VS* lxvi (2004), 264–74

Thorne, R. G., (ed.), *The history of parliament: the House of Commons, 1790–1820*, London 1986

Topham, J. R., 'Rethinking the history of science: popularisation/popular science', in F. Papanelopoulou, A. Nieto-Galan and E. Perdiguero (eds), *Popularising science and technology in the European periphery, 1800–2000*, Aldershot 1988, 1–20

—— 'Science and popular education in the 1830s: the role of the *Bridgewater Treatises*', *BJHS* xxv (1992), 397–430

—— 'Beyond the "common context": the production and reading of the *Bridgewater Treatises*', *Isis* lxxxix (1998), 233–62

Tree, I., *The bird man: the extraordinary story of John Gould*, London 1991

Turner, F. M., 'Public science in Britain, 1880–1919', *Isis* lxxi (1980), 589–608

Turner, J., *Reckoning with the beast: animals, pain and humanity in the Victorian mind*, Baltimore 1980

Twyman, M., *Lithography, 1800–50: the techniques of drawing on stone in England and France and their application in works of topography*, London 1970

Vevers, G., *London's zoo: an anthology to celebrate 150 years of the Zoological Society of London*, London 1976

Vincent, D., *Bread, knowledge and freedom: a study of nineteenth-century working class autobiography*, London 1981

Vincent, P., *The biogeography of the British Isles: an introduction*, London 1990

Walters, A. N., 'Conversation piece: science and politeness in eighteenth-century England', *BJHS* xxxv (1997), 121–54

Waterhouse, D. (ed.), *The origin of Himalayan studies: Brian Houghton Hodgson in Nepal and Darjeeling, 1820–1858*, London 2004

Wheeler, A. C., 'Zoological collections in the early British Museum: the Zoological Society's museum', *Archives of Natural History* xxiv (1997), 89–126

White, P., 'Darwin's emotions: the scientific self and the sentiment of objectivity', *Isis* c (2009), 811–26

Whitehead, C., *The public art museum in nineteenth-century Britain: the development of the National Gallery*, Aldershot 2005

Wigley, J., *The rise and fall of the Victorian Sunday*, Manchester 1980

Williams, L. P., 'The Royal Society and the foundation of the British Association for the Advancement of Science', *Notes and Records of the Royal Society of London* xvi (1961), 221–33

Wilson, A. N., *The Victorians*, London 2002

Wilson, D. M., *The British Museum: a history*, London 2002

Winks, R. W. (ed.), *The Oxford history of British Empire*, V: *Historiography*, Oxford 1999

Woodward, H. B., *The history of the Geological Society of London*, London 1907

Woolfall, S. J., 'History of the 13th earl of Derby's menagerie and aviary at Knowsley Hall, Liverpool (1806–1851)', *Archives of Natural History* xvii (1990), 1–47

Wroth, W. W. and A. E. Wroth, *The London pleasure gardens of the eighteenth century*, London 1896

Yeo, R., *Defining science: William Whewell, natural knowledge and public debate in early Victorian Britain*, Cambridge 1993

Zuckerman, S., 'The Zoological Society of London: evolution of a constitution', in Zuckerman and others, *Zoological Society of London*, 1–16
—— and others (eds), *The Zoological Society of London, 1826–1976 and beyond*, London 1976

Unpublished theses

Anderson, J., 'Marylebone Park and the New Street: a study of the development of Regent's Park and the buildings of Regent Street, London, in the first quarter of the nineteenth century', PhD, London 1998
Nakamura, T., 'Rulers of the sea: naval commemoration and British political culture, c.1780–1815', PhD, Osaka 2007
Rothfels, N. T., 'Bring 'em back alive: Carl Hagenbeck and the exotic animal and people trades in Germany, 1848–1914', PhD, Harvard 1994

Index

203

Printed and bound by CPI Group (UK) Ltd, Croydon, CR0 4YY

09/06/2025

14685719-0001